LAW OF CHILD CARE

ABOUT THE AUTHOR

Jim Nestor is a lecturer in law at the Institute of Technology, Sligo. He previously practised as a solicitor. He is the author of a textbook entitled *An Introduction to Irish Family Law*, Gill and MacMillan, 2004.

LAW OF CHILD CARE

JIM NESTOR

BLACKHALL
Publishing

This book was typeset by Gilbert Gough Typesetting for
Blackhall Publishing
27 Carysfort Avenue
Blackrock
Co. Dublin
Ireland
e-mail: info@blackhallpublishing.com
www.blackhallpublishing.com

ISBN: 1 842180 75 4

Printed in Ireland by
ColourBooks Ltd

To Maud and our children

PREFACE

The present strict application of the *in camera* rule in family law and child welfare matters means that there is very limited reporting of cases in these areas. The restrictions on reporting were designed mainly to protect the identity of parents and children involved in such cases. However, when carried to the extreme, the rule meant that the decisions of judges, particularly in the District and Circuit Courts, were not open to public scrutiny. The Civil Liability and Courts Bill 2004 provides for the relaxation of the *in camera* rule, so as to provide more transparency in the operation of the family law courts. Arrangements for the reporting of such proceedings will be put in place. However, in order to protect their privacy, the parties or any child to whom the proceedings relate cannot be identified in such reports. The Bill will enable legislators, the legal profession and the general public to get a knowledge of how family law provisions operate, something which is seriously hindered by the *in camera* rule as it currently stands.

The restrictions on reporting family law cases place obstacles in the way of research. With the exception of a number of Circuit Court judgments referred to in the text, the cases cited are decisions of the High Court and Supreme Court. Of course, there is a vast amount of reported material available on the interpretation of the provisions of the Children Act 1989 in England and Wales. As the provisions of that Act are largely similar to the Child Care Act 1991, particularly in areas such as care and supervision orders, and access to children in care, I have relied on English decisions throughout. However, I am at all times mindful of the crucial distinction between the effects of a care order in both jurisdictions. In England and Wales the local authority in whose favour a care order is made acquires ultimate responsibility for the welfare of the child. In Ireland, however, the District Court retains ultimate responsibility for the child, and the court cannot pass or delegate that responsibility to a health board (*Eastern Health Board v McDonnell* 2000).

There are many people to whom I must express my gratitude. This undertaking would not have been possible without the encouragement and help of my wife Maud, our daughters Kathy, Sandra and Olivia, our son Brendan and his wife Jackie. Sandra's expertise in information technology was at my disposal at all times. My dear friend and colleague Grainne Callanan at Waterford Institute of Technology supplied me with a lot of material that I did not have at my disposal. Dr Margaret Gilmore, a colleague here at the Institute in Sligo, gave me unfailing help and encouragement. She read many of the chapters at draft stage and made suggestions which I adopted without hesitation. Deirdre Scott also made valuable suggestions which I took on board. My roommates, Dana Vasiloaica, Margaret Feeney, Una L'Estrange, Brenda Boyle and Dianne O'Brien, were very helpful at all times, as were the staff of the library at the Institute. Special thanks also to Ailbhe O'Reilly and Ruth Garvey of Blackhall Publishing for their help and support at all stages of the publication process.

Jim Nestor
Institute of Technology, Sligo

CONTENTS

PART ONE: INTRODUCTORY MATTERS

PART TWO: PROMOTING THE WELFARE OF CHILDREN

PART THREE: STATE INTERVENTION TO PROTECT CHILDREN

PART FOUR: CHILDREN IN THE CARE OF HEALTH BOARDS

PART FIVE: REFORM

            Glossary of Terms 197

            References and Further Reading 201

            Index 203

TABLE OF CASES

TABLE OF STATUTES

TABLE OF STATUTORY INSTRUMENTS

TABLE OF ARTICLES OF THE CONSTITUTION

TABLE OF INTERNATIONAL CONVENTIONS

Part One

INTRODUCTORY MATTERS

CHAPTER 1

INTRODUCTION

The Role of the Family in the Social Order

There are unique advantages for children in experiencing "normal" family life in their birth family, and every effort should be made to preserve the child's home and family links. Indeed, most of the problems confronting the child care professional can be attributed to some crisis in family life. Most people's notion of what might constitute a "normal" family is husband and wife and the children of their marriage. This family unit is generally regarded as providing the ideal environment in which to bring up children, and is given special protection under Article 41 of the Constitution as the "fundamental unit group of society". In *North Western Health Board v H.W. and C.W.* 2001, Keane CJ spoke of "the exclusive and privileged role of the family in the social order". He said that the family "is endowed with an authority which the Constitution recognises as being superior even to the authority of the State itself", and that "the Constitution firmly outlaws any attempt by the State to usurp the exclusive and privileged role of the family in the social order".

In *L. v L.* 1992, the Supreme Court held that Article 41 does not grant to any individual member of the family rights against other members of the family, but rather protects the family from external sources. This emphasis on the family as a unit very often acts to the detriment of individuals, as it prevents intervention by the State where this is necessary to protect them. Hence, there was a marked reluctance in the past to intervene in the affairs of the family for the protection of vulnerable and at risk children. While it is desirable that the family should retain a certain authority and autonomy, this should not be so as to prevent the State from intervening "where the protection of the individual rights of one member of the family requires this" (see the Report of the Constitution Review Group 1996). Of course, the members of the family, including children, have personal rights under Article 40 as well as the family rights protected by Articles 41 and 42 of the Constitution. In *North Western Health Board v H.W. and C.W* 2001, Keane CJ did acknowledge that the family as a concept is meaningless if "divorced from the individuals of which it is composed". He went on to endorse the "compelling reasons" test for intervention by the State in the life of the family to vindicate the personal rights of a child, as laid down by the Supreme Court in *K.C. and A.C. v An Bord Uchtala* 1985. Under Article 42.5 of the Constitution, where parents for physical or moral reasons fail in their duty to their children, the State, as guardian of the common good, can interfere in the life of the family to supply the place of parents.

The Legislative Framework

The Child Care Act 1991, as amended by the Children Acts of 1997 and 2001, provides the legislative framework for promoting the welfare of children who are in need of care and protection. It was enacted by the Oireachtas with the purpose of replacing and updating the provisions of the Children Act 1908, which was described by O'Flaherty J in *M.F. v Ballymun Garda Station* 1990 as having been "an enlightened piece of legislation" when enacted "but now showing its age". The 1991 Act finally reached the statute book following many years of discussion, consultation and pressure by persons and bodies interested in child care issues. Although enacted in 1991 and brought into force piecemeal, the Act did not become finally operative until December 1996. In *Western Health Board v K.M.* 2001, McGuinness J in the Supreme Court described the 1991 Act as "a remedial social statute" intended to protect children, which should be construed "as widely as can fairly be done".

The 1991 Act can be viewed as the State's response to the obligation imposed on it by Article 42.5 of the Constitution to vindicate the rights and provide for the needs of children who require care and protection. In the words of McCracken J, in *North Western Health Board v H.W. and C.W.* 2000, when the case was before the High Court, the 1991 Act "simply provides a mechanism whereby the State undertakes its obligations under Article 42.5". The underlying philosophy of the Act is that children should be supported in their own homes where possible and the necessary supports should be put in place to enable this to happen. In extreme cases, the Act provides for State intervention in the life of a child through the medium of a health board and the removal of the child from the home for his protection. Where a child is taken into care, the Act gives a health board the powers of a parent in respect of that child. Of course, State intervention should be seen only as a matter of last resort in cases where the welfare of the child cannot be otherwise protected. It is for this reason that the Act provides that a health board, in promoting the welfare of children, should have regard to the rights and duties of parents under the Constitution and enacted law, and the principle that it is generally in the best interests of a child to be brought up in his own family.

Prior to the implementation of the 1991 Act, the power to take children into care on a non-voluntary basis was regulated by the Children Act 1908, which was regarded by many professionals working in the area of child care as discouraging the initiation of child protection proceedings. Finlay CJ highlighted the shortcomings of the 1908 Act in *M.F. v Ballymun Garda Station* 1990 where he said, "the necessity for a modern Children Act making a more efficient and simpler procedure for the protection of children available to the courts remains one of urgency". The 1991 Act streamlines the operation of an effective child protection system by providing in Part III for the protection of children in emergencies, in effect replacing sections 20–24 of the 1908 Act. Part IV of the 1991 Act provides for the making of care orders, thereby replacing section 58 of the 1908 Act. Part IV also provides for the making of a new type of protection order, known as a supervision order, which does not require the removal of the child from the family, but enables the child to be supervised in the home by a social worker. Both in emergency situations and for the purposes of making long-term protection orders, provision is made for the court to direct "the medical or psychiatric examination, treatment or assessment of the child", even where parental consent is not forthcoming.

Frequent reference is made throughout the 1991 Act to rules or regulations (statutory instruments) to be made by the Minister. The purpose of these rules and regulations is to deal with detailed supplementary issues, mention of which in the Act itself would only serve to confuse the reader. It is important to bear in mind that the various rules and regulations have the full force of law and should be regarded in much the same way as the provisions of the Act themselves. The District Court (Child Care) Regulations 1995 regulate legal procedures under the Act and contain appropriate application forms for use in care proceedings. The Child Care Regulations 1995 impose detailed obligations on health boards in relation to the placement of children in foster care, with relatives and in residential care. The standards that are to be observed in children's residential centres are set out in the Child Care (Standards in Children's Residential Centres) 1996. The operation of pre-school services is regulated by the Child Care (Pre-school Services) Regulations 1996.

Whereas regulations made under the 1991 Act regulate the exercise by health boards of their powers under the Act, they do not in any way restrict the court in exercising its powers under the Act. In the exercise of its own powers, the court should have regard to the considerations of public policy which underlie and are evidenced by the regulations. However, the court's overriding duty, as prescribed in section 24 of the Act, is to regard the welfare of the child as the first and paramount consideration. In considering the role of the court under the corresponding provisions of the English Children Act 1989 in *Re R.-J. (Minors)* 1998, Chadwick LJ said that, where the court is satisfied in a particular case that a decision which would give effect to an element of public policy evidenced by the regulations would be contrary to the welfare of the child with whom it is concerned, it has a duty to treat that element of public policy as subordinate to its duty to give paramount consideration to the child's welfare.

Policy Developments

In addition to putting in place the legislative framework for the care and protection of children, the Government has issued the following guidance

and strategy documents to explain the relevant provisions of the legislation
and outline major policy developments.

*Children First: National Guidelines for the Protection and Welfare of
Children*

Many findings and recommendations of the Report of the Kilkenny Incest
Investigation 1993, referred to below, and the reports of other inquiries into
cases of serious child abuse, have informed and shaped current child protection
policy and procedures. These are now enshrined in *Children First: National
Guidelines for the Protection and Welfare of Children* 1999. This major
guidance document, referred to throughout the text as *Children First*, is
designed to give an indication of what central government expects from health
boards and other statutory agencies working with children in terms of practical
implementation of child care legislation. The guidelines set out are intended
to provide a framework for inter-agency and multi-professional work practices.
The aim of *Children First* is to assist people in identifying and reporting child
abuse and, in particular, "to clarify and promote mutual understanding among
statutory and voluntary organisations about the contributions of different
disciplines and professionals to child protection (Paragraph 1.2.1).

The guidelines contained in *Children First* are designed to bring to
managers and practitioners an understanding of the principles of the 1991
Act, as amended, and associated regulations. Although they do not have the
force of law, the guidelines are likely to be quoted or used in court proceedings.
The precise legal standing of the guidelines is unclear. In the case of health
boards, they have a legislative background, having been issued in the context
of the 1991 Act (Paragraph 1.3.6). Accordingly, in the absence of a court
order, health boards have to comply with the procedures set out in the
guidelines to ensure a close working relationship between the various agencies
involved in the protection of children from abuse. Commenting on the
corresponding procedures for co-operation between the various agencies
contained in *Working Together* (the English equivalent of *Children First*), in
X. v Bedfordshire County Council 1995, Brown-Wilkinson LJ said: "The
procedure by way of joint action takes place, not merely because it is good
practice, but because it is required by guidance having statutory force binding
on the local authority." *Children First* is considered further in various chapters
throughout this text.

Our Duty to Care

Children First recognises the need to support community and voluntary groups
to develop best practice in their dealings with children. *Our Duty to Care*,
which should be read in conjunction with *Children First*, is a guidance
document published in 2002 aimed at community and voluntary organisations

of any kind or size that provide services for children. *Our Duty to Care* offers guidance on the promotion of child welfare and the development of safe practices in work with children. It also gives information on how to recognise signs of child abuse and the correct steps to take within organisations if it is suspected, witnessed or disclosed. The process of reporting suspected or actual child abuse to the health board is described step by step, and guidance is given on how to handle sensitive areas. For the purpose of protecting and promoting children's rights, it is advised that all organisations providing services for children should have a designated person to act as a liaison with outside agencies. The designated officer should be responsible for reporting allegations or suspicions of child abuse to the health boards or An Garda Síochána.

The National Children's Strategy

One of the recommendations of the Committee on the Rights of the Child in its final report on Ireland's compliance with the terms of the United Nations Convention on the Rights of the Child was that Ireland should adopt a comprehensive national strategy for children "incorporating the principles and provisions of the Convention in a systematic manner in the designing of all its policies and programmes" (see Chapter 4). In response, the Government launched the National Children's Strategy in November 2000. It is a major Government initiative intended to improve the quality of children's lives in Ireland. It follows a public consultation process with both adults and children. A total of 2,488 children and young people participated in the consultation process. There are three national goals guiding the Strategy, namely children should have a voice in matters affecting them, their lives should be understood and they should receive the supports they need. Each of these goals has objectives, designed to secure the desired outcomes. A number of operational principles inform the operation of the Strategy as a whole, and an infrastructure has been identified to progress the Strategy. This infrastructure includes:

(a) An independent Office of Ombudsman for Children, to consult children and advise the Government on issues of importance to children. The establishment of the office by the Ombudsman for Children Act 2002 is a very significant development in ensuring that the views and concerns of children are taken into account in matters concerning their welfare. In this regard, the Ombudsman shall promote the welfare and rights of children generally, and be the voice for every child, putting forward positive policies and pointing the way for Government. He shall have regard to the best interests of the child and shall, in so far as is practicable, have regard to the wishes of the child, taking into account his age and level of understanding.

The Ombudsman shall set up structures to consult with children, ensuring that their views are taken into account when policies and legislation affecting them are being considered. He will investigate complaints made by children, parents and members of the public against any public body, school or voluntary hospital. The action complained of must be one which is taken in the performance of an administrative function. The Ombudsman shall not investigate actions in relation to which civil legal proceedings are pending on behalf of the child affected and actions in respect of which the child has a right of appeal, reference or review to a court or person or body, other than the body being investigated. Where the Ombudsman decides not to investigate a complaint, he shall give reasons for his decision in writing to the child or person who made the complaint on behalf of the child.

Where an investigation is carried out, the Ombudsman shall send a statement in writing of the result to the public body, school or voluntary body concerned and any other person to whom he considers it appropriate to send a statement. Where it appears to the Ombudsman following an investigation that the action complained of adversely affected the child, he may recommend to the public body, school or voluntary hospital that certain measures are taken to remedy, mitigate or alter the adverse effect of the action, or that the body in question gives reasons for taking the action. If the Ombudsman thinks fit to do so, he may request the body in question to notify him within a specified time of its response to the recommendation. The child who made the complaint, or the person who made it on his behalf, must be notified of the result of the investigation, the recommendation and the response of the body the subject of the complaint.

The decision of the Ombudsman will not be legally binding, although it will have huge moral authority. Any attempt to make the decision of the Ombudsman legally binding could raise constitutional difficulties and interfere with judicial procedure. Where the Ombudsman considers that the measures taken by a public body, school or voluntary hospital in response to a recommendation are not satisfactory, he shall include this fact in his annual report to both houses of the Oireachtas. However, the Ombudsman may not make a finding or criticism adverse to a person or body without first affording that person or body an opportunity to consider the finding or criticism and to make representations to him in relation to it. The Ombudsman shall cause a report on the performance of his functions to be laid before each house of the Oireachtas annually, and the contents of same shall be absolutely privileged.

(b) A National Children's Advisory Council, to advise the Minister on all aspects of children's lives and on the better co-ordination and delivery of services to children. The Council was launched by the Minister for Children in May 2001. It will contribute to monitoring and evaluating the implementation of the National Children's Strategy, and will advise on research, training and the development of mechanisms to consult with children. Children's organisations, parents and children themselves are represented on the Council.

(c) A National Children's Office, established on an administrative basis to ensure inter-governmental co-operation and support the role of the Minister for Children. The role of the Office is to lead and oversee implementation of the National Children's Strategy. The Minister will report to a Cabinet Sub-Committee established to oversee the implementation of the Strategy. There are two important aspects to the work of the National Children's Office. Individual departments retain responsibility for implementing the Strategy and the Office co-ordinates and monitors progress in this regard. The Office also progresses actions under the three national goals of the Strategy in regard to certain key policy issues identified by the Cabinet Sub-Committee as priorities, and which require cross-departmental action.

(d) The creation of Dáil na nÓg, whose aim is to give children and young people an opportunity to express their views and have them heard by Government, as well as the public, private and voluntary sectors in a way never done before. The objectives of Dáil na nÓg are to:

• provide a place where children who are representatives of the average Irish child can raise and debate issues of concern to them,

• act as a tool for children's concerns to be fed into the development of public policy making,

• provide a model for children's participation which can be developed at local level with links to the national Dáil, and

• support civic, social and personal development in children.

Social Services Inspectorate

The Department of Health and Children established the Inspectorate in 1999 as an independent body to inspect the social services functions of the health boards. The main aim of the Inspectorate is to work with health boards, the Department and other relevant organisations to ensure that child care, social work and social care services are responsive to the needs of the population and allow the public have confidence in them. As part of the remit of the Inspectorate, inspectors visit children's centres and carry out an inspection. Following each inspection, which involves meeting staff within a centre and talking to children and parents, inspectors report their findings to the Minister. See further Chapter 18.

Report of the Working Group on Foster Care 2001

The Report, entitled *Foster Care: A Child-Centred Partnership*, highlighted a number of problems in the existing foster care services and made a wide range of recommendations to strengthen and further develop the services. The key recommendation of the Report is that the standards of practice applied in looking after children in care and in supervising and supporting foster carers should be of the highest level. The Report is considered in more detail in Chapter 18.

About this Book

At present, there are approximately 4,000 children in the care of health boards in Ireland. Children come into care for a variety of reasons. The aim of the text is to provide a general understanding of the law relating to children in care which will be of use primarily to social workers, social care professionals and students pursuing courses in those disciplines. However, the text should also prove useful to legal practitioners and law students generally. Because the language of the law tends to be very technical, a conscious effort has been made to present the various legal principles in a reasonably straightforward way. Mindful of the fact that this may not always be possible, a glossary of legal terms has been included, which endeavours to explain the technical words and phrases most commonly referred to in the text.

Part 1 of the text is designed to introduce the reader to the working of the courts system. The jurisdiction and procedures of the courts dealing with child care matters are explained. The special measures designed to facilitate children giving evidence, in order to make a child's day in court as stress free as possible, are discussed. The very important part played by international law in shaping and influencing Irish social policy is dealt with in some detail. Of course, no book dealing with children in need of care and protection would be complete without reference to the controversial and topical issue of child sexual abuse.

The important role played by the State in fulfilling its constitutional duty to promote the welfare of children who may be in need of care and protection is covered in Part 2. The statutory function of a health board under section 3 of the 1991 Act is examined, in the light of recent decisions of both the High Court and Supreme Court. In carrying out its statutory function, a health board has the delicate task of balancing the rights and duties of parents and the corresponding rights of the child under the Constitution.

Part 3 deals with the different ways in which children come into care. Many parents, unable to cope with their children due to illness, poverty or substance addiction, place the children in the voluntary care of a health board. Before a court can make an order that a child be removed from the custody of his parents and placed in the care of a health board, certain threshold criteria must be met. The alternatives to removing the child from his family are examined. The child can be made the subject of a supervision order and visited by a social worker in the home. Alternatively, a health board can support the child by means of the various family supports, thereby eliminating the need for a court order. In emergency situations, there are fairly drastic measures available to the Garda Síochána, which enable a member of the force to remove a child from the home and hand him over to a health board, so that the board can apply for an emergency care order.

The options available to a health board once a child is taken into care are examined in Part 4. The child may be placed in an alternative family with foster parents. Where the child needs residential care, the legislation lays down standards which must be met to ensure the welfare of the child. The inspection process operated by the Social Services Inspectorate is examined. Finally, this part of the text emphasises the importance of access by children in care to their parents. Access is regarded as an automatic right of the child, rather than a parental right, only to be denied in exceptional circumstances, where the welfare of the child so requires.

For the sake of standardisation, the masculine gender is used to include the feminine gender throughout the text.

CHAPTER 2

JURISDICTION OF THE COURTS

Introduction

Jurisdiction is concerned with the power or authority of a particular court to deal with matters of a legal nature. The 1991 Act has put in place a number of legal procedures under which applications can be made to "the court" for various orders. The District Court is the court vested with jurisdiction under the Act. The various provisions of the Act dealing with jurisdiction are reasonably straightforward. In keeping with the general scheme of the legislation, the detailed rules are contained in regulations made by the Minister, as set out in the District Court (Child Care) Rules 1995. The main thrust of the legislation is to ensure that proceedings in child care matters shall be conducted, in so far as possible, in keeping with the requirements of fair procedures, in a child-friendly fashion with the minimum of formality and in private.

The District Court

The District Court has original jurisdiction in proceedings under the 1991 Act (section 28). Proceedings are dealt with by the justice for the time being assigned to the district where the child resides or is for the time being. In *A. and B. v Eastern Health Board* 1998, the High Court reviewed the role of the District Court in care proceedings. The District Court is a court established by the Constitution. In relation to every matter that a district judge decides, he must always be conscious of the Constitution and the rights thereunder. However, the District Court does not have jurisdiction to question the constitutional validity of any statute. Proceedings under the 1991 Act are in the nature of an inquiry rather than adversarial. At the same time, a district judge hearing proceedings under the Act must ensure that the various parties are afforded fair procedures.

Proceedings involving the care and welfare of a child shall be held otherwise than in public, and they must be as informal as possible, without wigs or gowns being worn by judges or barristers. The District Court, and the Circuit Court on appeal, must sit at a different place, or at different times, or on different days from those at or which ordinary sittings of the court are held (section 29). The publication or broadcast of any matter that would be likely to identify the child who is the subject of care proceedings is prohibited by section 31. However, where the court is satisfied that it would be appropriate to do so in the interests of the child, it may dispense with the prohibition on publication or broadcast to such extent as may be specified. The penalty for a contravention of section 31 is a fine of up to £1,000 and/or a term of imprisonment for up to twelve months on summary conviction.

In any proceedings under the 1991 Act, the court has power to presume or declare the age of a child after making due inquiry as to his age (section 32). It is an offence, punishable by a fine of £500 and/or imprisonment of up to six months, for any person having custody of a child to fail or refuse to deliver up the child on foot of an order of the court to do so. A copy of the order must have been shown to the person in question (section 34). The court may issue a warrant for the purpose of enforcing an interim care order or a care order. The warrant authorises a member of An Garda Síochána, accompanied by other members of the force or other persons as may be necessary, to enter (if need be by force) any premises where the child is, or where there are reasonable grounds to believe that the child is, and to deliver the child into the custody of the health board (section 35).

In *DPP (Murphy) v P.T.* 1998, the High Court held that there should be a clear division between criminal proceedings, deciding the guilt or innocence of an accused and child care proceedings which provided for the welfare and future care and custody of a child. The case involved a fifteen-year-old boy in the care of the Eastern Health Board who was before the District Court on charges of larceny and receiving stolen property. As the primary issue before the District Court was the guilt or innocence of the accused and his right to a reasonably expeditious trial in due course of law, the district judge should confine himself to deciding whether the accused was fit to plead and stand trial. In a criminal trial, where there is a clash between the "general welfare" rights and the rights specifically delineated by the Constitution relevant to the trial of offences, "this latter category of rights should, in general, have priority and prevail". In *J. (a minor) v Judge Miriam Malone* 2003, the High Court reiterated the distinction between criminal charges and child care cases. In the course of his judgment, Murphy J said that the "primacy of the welfare of the child" with relation to the custody, guardianship or upbringing of a child "cannot be carried over to apply to criminal proceedings".

The Circuit Court

The Circuit Court hears appeals from the District Court. A judge considering an application for a care or supervision order has to be satisfied that one of the threshold conditions set out in section 18(1) of the 1991 Act exists. There will be a marked conflict of evidence and a conflict of approach towards the needs of the child who is the subject of the application. The judge will accept some evidence and reject other evidence in arriving at a decision. Provided the judge exercises his discretion in accordance with accepted guidelines, and that there is no error of principle in the way in which he approached the case, an appeal court is not in a position to interfere with the judge's findings unless he was plainly wrong or he took into account what he should not have taken into account, or failed to take into account what he should have taken into account. In *D. v D.* 2003, the Supreme Court held that, although an appeal court may interfere with the discretion of the trial judge if it is felt that it has been wrongly exercised, "great weight would also be given to the discretion of the trial judge". In refusing to interfere with the decision of the trial judge to transmit a judicial separation case from the High Court to the Circuit Court, McGuinness J said that she would be reluctant to interfere "without very strong reasons" with the discretion exercised by the High Court judge (see also *Hay v O'Grady* 1992).

In general, fresh evidence, other than evidence as to matters which have occurred after the date of the trial or hearing, shall only be admitted on appeal on special grounds. The appeal court should be slow to admit fresh evidence where such evidence could reasonably have been obtained before the court at first instance. Before fresh evidence is admitted it must be evidence which is of considerable importance and be capable of so affecting the case that it may result in a different conclusion to that reached by the judge.

Whereas the right to appeal the decision of the trial judge is beyond question, it should be borne in mind that where a decision in a child's case is appealed, the potential for inflicting further damage on the child is considerable. The delay in a case reaching the appeal court will have the effect of putting off for the time being the health board's plans for the child, possibly to the detriment of the child. The ordeal of another court appearance for the child and his family will add greatly to the trauma already experienced at the trial. An appeal against an interim care order, a care order or supervision order will not automatically stay the operation of the order. However, section 21 of the 1991 Act enables the court that made such an order to stay its operation on such terms, if any, as may be imposed by the court making the determination. Where the court stays the operation of a care order or supervision order, the question of protecting the child pending the hearing of the appeal arises. In this regard, it is likely that the child will already be the subject of an interim care order and under the control of the health board. The court could secure the interim protection of the child by making it a term of its decision to stay the operation of an order pending appeal that the interim care order already in force should continue to have effect.

The High Court

The High Court exercises its consultative jurisdiction by hearing a case stated from the District Court on an important point of law. In the course of proceedings before the District Court, or on the conclusion of the proceedings, either party can request a district judge to state a case requesting the High Court to interpret a particular statutory provision. A district judge may also state a case of his own motion. In the submission of a case to the High Court, the district judge states the nature of the proceedings and gives a summary of the evidence adduced and legal arguments advanced by both sides. The High Court conducts a hearing at which both sides are entitled to make legal submissions. Having decided the point of law, the matter is referred back to the district judge, who must make a finding in accordance with the law as interpreted by the High Court. *DPP v (Murphy) v P.T.*, above, involved a case stated to the High Court as to whether a district judge had power to make child care orders in the course of criminal proceedings.

The High Court deals with applications for the writ of *habeas corpus*. This ancient remedy, which enables a person to question the lawfulness of his detention, is now enshrined in Article 40.4.2 of the Constitution. Upon complaint being made to it by, or on behalf of, a person that he is being unlawfully detained, the High Court must inquire into the matter, as a result of which it may order the person or body who is detaining the complainant to produce him in court and satisfy the court that the detention is lawful. Unless the detention can be justified, the court must order the immediate release of the complainant. The procedure may be used to question the detention of a child in a children's residential centre or in a special care unit. In *Eastern Health Board v E., A. and A.* 1999, the High Court conducted an inquiry into the detention of a baby who, shortly after being born, had been given into the custody of the owners of a pregnancy counselling agency, who were to arrange a private placement for adoption. The court held that the custody of the child by the owners of the agency had at all times been unlawful, as being in direct contravention of section 7 of the Adoption Act 1998.

The supervisory jurisdiction of the High Court in child care matters extends to the exercise by a health board of its executive function and the exercise by the District Court of its judicial function under the 1991 Act. In the exercise of that jurisdiction, the High Court can make orders of *certiorari, mandamus* or *prohibition*. *Certiorari* has the effect of quashing a decision of a public body or inferior court made in excess of jurisdiction. *Mandamus* compels compliance with the terms of a statute or statutory instrument. *Prohibition* has the effect of prohibiting a public body or inferior court acting in excess of jurisdiction. The various orders are considered further in Chapter 11.

The Role of the Court

In general, the 1991 Act sets out the duties and powers of both the health boards and the courts in child care matters. The Act achieves a delicate balance between the role of the judge and the role of the health board, and defines the fundamental boundary between the functions and responsibilities of the court and the health board. The making of a care order is a judicial function of the

State, while its implementation is an executive function. This suggests that there is a clear line of demarcation between the respective functions of court and health board. However, there must be certain interaction between the court and the health board. Any such interaction must be as far as appropriate collaborative, and with no other objective than to promote the welfare of the child and to ensure for the child and the other parties to the proceedings their rights both under the Constitution and the European Convention on Human Rights. The inevitable tension which is created between the jurisdiction of the court and the power of a health board following the making of a care order was highlighted in *Eastern Health Board v McDonnell* 2000 (see also Chapters 14 and 18).

The powers of the court in any proceedings under the 1991 Act are discretionary in nature. When exercising its discretion, the court must comply with section 24 of the Act, which provides that in any proceedings relating to the care and protection of a child, the welfare of the child is the first and paramount consideration. However, in considering the child's best interests, the court must have regard to the rights and duties of parents, whether under the Constitution or otherwise, and the wishes of the child, having regard to his age and understanding. This requires the court to carry out a delicate balancing act. Since a health board is subject to the same obligations in carrying out its function under section 3 of the 1991 Act, the principles set out in Chapter 7 are equally applicable to the court's deliberations.

On occasion, in fulfilling its statutory obligation under section 24, the court will be faced with the task of balancing public policy against the welfare of the child. This can occur when a health board is required by regulations made under the 1991 Act to exercise its statutory function in a particular way, which might prove detrimental to the child's best interests. In such a situation, public policy, as expressed in the regulations, should not be treated as supreme. The regulations could not fetter or set aside the clear policy of the Act to place the welfare of the child as paramount. The court is bound to give first and paramount consideration to the welfare of the child (see decision of Court of Appeal in *Re R.-J. (Minors)* 1998).

Conclusion

Proceedings in a children's court involving the welfare of a child are dealt with in a more informal way than in an adult court. It should be borne in mind that nobody is on trial in care proceedings. The function of the court is to conduct an inquiry as to whether one of the protection orders should be made. A general discussion takes place between the district judge and all the parties as to what is the best way to help the child and his family out of their difficulties. The main thrust of the statutory provisions is to protect the child. To a considerable extent, this is achieved by providing that proceedings will be as informal as possible, and prohibiting any publicity that might cause further stress and anxiety for the child. Where the proceedings involve allegations of child abuse or neglect, the person or persons against whom such allegations have been made must be afforded due process and fair procedures, in so far as that is possible in providing for the welfare of the child.

CHAPTER 3

EVIDENCE OF CHILDREN

Introduction

The fundamental right of a child to be heard in legal proceedings affecting his welfare is now beyond doubt. The corresponding obligation on the State to provide appropriate facilities to enable a child to give evidence in a child-friendly setting is now firmly enshrined in the United Nations Convention on the Rights of the Child, which Ireland ratified in 1992. Article 12 of the Convention provides that the child who is capable of forming his own views shall be provided with the opportunity to be heard in any judicial or administrative proceedings affecting the child, either directly or through a representative or an appropriate body, in a manner consistent with the procedural rules of national law. While not specifically referring to children, the right to a fair hearing under Article 6 of the European Convention on Human Rights would afford a child the right to be heard in proceedings affecting him.

It is important to emphasise that the obligation imposed on the State by Article 12 of the United Nations Convention on the Rights of the Child is to provide the child with "the opportunity to be heard". This proviso would allow facilities to be put in place, such as a live television link, to avoid the necessity of a very young child having to give evidence in open court in the presence of an accused who has abused or maltreated the child. In *Southern Health Board v C.H.* 1996, Costello P acknowledged in the High Court that "a court room is in general, an unsuitable environment for [a] child of such tender years as this child". The adverse impact that a court appearance might have on a child of tender years is clear from the judgment of Hamilton CJ in *Donnelly v Ireland* 1998, where he remarked that "it is generally accepted that young persons under the age of seventeen are likely to be traumatised by the experience of giving evidence in court and that its purpose is to minimise such trauma".

Pre-trial Interviews with Children

The interviewing of children by social workers and the police, with a view to establishing whether there has been child abuse, is an essential aspect of pre-trial investigations in child protection matters. There is little point in putting children through the harrowing experience of giving evidence in court, unless the evidence adduced from pre-trial interviews is likely to stand up to court scrutiny. Any such interviews should be investigative in nature (for the purpose of obtaining facts), rather than therapeutic (designed to help a child to unburden his worries). An interview conducted for separate therapeutic purposes, where the restrictions on prompting do not apply to the same extent that they do in an investigative interview, is generally unsuitable for use as part of any evidence given in court. *Children First* contains guidelines for the conduct of a meeting between a health board worker and a child in the initial stages of a child protection inquiry. As the purpose of this meeting is therapeutic in nature, the guidelines emphasise that the child should not be interviewed in detail about sexual or serious physical abuse. This may be more appropriately done at a later stage by specialist personnel or by An Garda Síochána, or both (Paragraph 8.12).

It is generally accepted that the interviewing of children for the purpose of gathering evidence can be problematic. The questioning of children can be a difficult and skilled art. Some children will require help in the questioning process. While it is generally accepted that some children have to be helped in giving an account of what has taken place, it is important to bear in mind that the greater the help given in facilitating the answers, the less reliable the answers will be. Any help given should be as far as possible in a non-leading form, so as not to indicate to the child the possible answer. Wherever possible, interviews with a child who may have been the victim of sexual abuse should be recorded on videotape. Recording early interviews with a child who has been abused preserves an accurate record of his account while the event is still fresh in his mind. It enables the viewer to hear the child recount his experience in his own words while observing the child's non-verbal behaviour. In the absence of a video recording, an interview with a child will carry less weight in subsequent court proceedings, because the court will not be able to assess the child's allegation for itself. The existence of a video recording of the interview with the child will also remove the need for repeated interviews with other professionals, which can add to the stress already experienced by the child.

Where a video recording exists, it is a form of hearsay, and the key issue for the court is whether videotapes can be admitted as evidence in exception to the hearsay rule and without sacrificing the rights of the alleged abuser. In considering the weight and credibility to be given to evidence obtained at pre-trial interview, the judge should have regard for the fact that the evidence from the child may have been elicited in response to leading questions and under some pressure. Spontaneous information provided by a child is more valuable than information fed to the child by leading questions and prompting. The more often the child is asked questions about the same subject matter, the less one can trust the answers given. Where a video recording is not possible, an audio recording should take place. It is significant that in *Re M.K., S.K. and W.K.* 1999, Barrington J referred to the "disturbing insight" into the child's attitude at the interviews which emerged from the tape recordings. However, despite the social worker's "well-intentioned coaxing", the child declined to repeat to the social worker what he was reported to have said to the speech therapist.

On a number of occasions, the Supreme Court has acknowledged the importance of videotapes to support claims of sexual abuse made by a child to a social worker, doctor or other health professional. In the *State (D.) v Groarke* 1990, Finlay CJ held that in order to determine whether the conclusion reached by the doctor who had interviewed the child was sound, the court should have had the basic evidence from which such conclusion was reached, which was the videotapes. In *Southern Health Board v C.H.*, above, O'Flaherty J held that the court should have access to the videotapes of an interview conducted by a social worker with the child, as these were the basic material from which the social worker's conclusions that the child had been sexually abused were reached. In *Re M.K., S.K. and W.K.*, Barr J said that a video recording, once established to be authentic, "may be the best evidence of the happening of a particular event". Such a recording can give the court "the exact words which the person whose speech is recorded used and also the demeanour of that person at the time he used them".

If a video recording, or for that matter an audio recording, is to be used as evidence, the rights of the alleged abuser must be considered. By its very nature, an allegation of sexual abuse of a child is a serious matter. In *Re M.K., S.K. and W.K.*, the Supreme Court held that the nature of the allegation, the age of the child and, in the instant case, the issue of disability place a heavy burden on the courts to achieve justice. A balance must be struck between the welfare of the child, while at the same time affording fair procedures to the alleged abuser. However, in achieving the necessary balance in proceedings regarding the welfare of a child, the Supreme Court held in *Southern Health Board v C.H.* that the child's welfare must always be of far graver concern to the court. In that case, the rights of the accused were respected, in that he and his solicitor were furnished with copies of the tape in advance, to enable them meet the allegations fairly and squarely. On the other hand, in *Re M.K., S.K. and W.K.*, the Supreme Court held that the process whereby hearsay evidence was admitted in the case was not in accordance with fair procedures to the mother, the father or the children. This was so as the trial judge had failed to carry out a separate inquiry as to whether it was necessary to adduce hearsay evidence and, if so, in what circumstances.

Criminal Trials

The adversarial nature of the Irish legal system requires that, subject to limited exceptions, all evidence shall be given on oath in open court, and that the veracity of such evidence is subject to adversarial examination. The perceived right of an accused in a criminal trial to confront by cross-examination any witness giving evidence against him has contributed in no small measure to the difficulties posed in the prosecution of child abuse cases, particularly in the case of sexual abuse. The experience of going to court can be very stressful for child witnesses. The main fear of all child witnesses is seeing the accused in court and the fact that the accused in turn can see the child. While it is not possible in criminal trials to eliminate the need for a court appearance by a child victim of abuse, every effort should be made to make the child's appearance as stress free as possible. It is very much a case of balancing the right of an accused to due process and the best interests of the child. In this regard, it should be borne in mind that in *Donnelly v Ireland,* above, the Supreme Court held that the right of an accused person to a fair trial is a fundamental constitutional right and that in so far as it is possible or desirable to construct a hierarchy of constitutional rights, it is a superior right.

The Criminal Evidence Act 1992 represents an attempt by the legislature to facilitate children giving evidence otherwise than in open court, while at the same time ensuring that the constitutional rights of the accused are vindicated. In cases involving sexual offences or violence, or an attempt to commit such offences, section 13 of the 1992 Act enables a person under seventeen years of age, other than the accused, or any other person with leave of the court, to give evidence, whether from within or outside the State, through a live television link, unless the court sees good reason to the contrary. Evidence given in this way shall be video recorded. In a further effort to normalise proceedings, where a child is giving evidence through a live television link, except through an intermediary, neither the judge, nor the barrister or solicitor concerned in the examination of the child shall wear a wig or gown.

For the purpose of giving evidence by means of a live television link, the witness is located in a special witness room set up for the purpose away from the courtroom. The system, as far as is technically possible, allows the court proceedings to be conducted as if the witness were giving evidence in the courtroom, while at the same time protecting the witness. The special witness room has a waiting room attached, which has been carefully furnished in a child-friendly fashion. A special court usher attends the witness prior to and during the trial. The usher familiarises the witness and others, such as parents who have been allowed to accompany the witness, with the operation of the television and video equipment. Where the necessary technical facilities for enabling evidence to be given through a television link or by means of video recording are not available in any Circuit or District Court district, section 17 of the 1992 Act provides that the proceedings may be transferred to a Circuit or District Court district which has the necessary technical facilities.

Before the commencement of the trial, the usher returns to the courtroom and when the time comes to activate the video link, the judge informs the jury of the role of the usher and cautions him. The usher is cautioned that he must be present in the remote witness room with the child throughout the time the child is required to be there, and that no person other than one approved by the court is entitled to be there. No attempt to interrupt, intervene or intimidate the child during that time should be allowed. The usher must not himself intervene or interrupt during the giving of evidence via the television link, unless to inform the court of some irregularity. The usher must not prompt the child or offer him any explanation, interpretation or guidance. The usher must remain with the child at all times, and on no account should he speak to the child. While the usher must at all times maintain a neutral role, he may in a sympathetic manner comfort and reassure the child, and help him to give evidence clearly and with the minimum of stress. When the caution has been completed, the usher returns to the special witness room and ensures that the directions of the judge are carried out.

In *White v Ireland* 1995, Kinlen J went to great lengths to explain the working of the system and the inbuilt safeguards to ensure that the rights of the accused and the interests of the child witness are fully protected. There is a control panel in front of the judge, which he can operate by pressing various buttons. The judge is in complete control of what can be seen by the witness, jury and barristers. Before the trial commenced in this case, the trial judge conducted an experiment to show how the system worked. Everybody in court can see and hear the witness simultaneously. The witness can only see whoever is addressing him at the time. The button in front of the judge controls this. However, when counsel is addressing the witness, the camera can be arranged so that only counsel can be seen by the witness, and the accused can be excluded.

In *Donnelly v Ireland*, above, the accused, who had been convicted of the sexual assault of a fourteen-year-old girl, sought an order of *certiorari* quashing his conviction, and a declaration that sections 12, 13 and 18 of the 1992 Act were repugnant to the Constitution, specifically Articles 38 (right to due process) and 40 (personal rights). The main thrust of the accused's challenge was that the giving of evidence through a live television link constituted an infringement of his right through counsel to cross-examine and/or confront the complainant and his accusers in the presence of the jury, and discriminated unjustly and invidiously against him in the conduct of his defence. The Supreme Court held that there is no constitutional right to confrontation as would require in all circumstances that the evidence of a witness be given in the physical presence of the accused. The requirements of fair procedures are adequately fulfilled by requiring that the witness give evidence on oath and be subjected to cross-examination, during which the judge and jury may observe the demeanour of the witness and have ample opportunity to assess the reliability of such testimony.

Where a person under seventeen years of age is giving evidence through a live television link, the court may appoint an intermediary to convey questions to the witness, if satisfied that such is required, having regard to the age or mental condition of the witness and the interests of justice. The intermediary may convey the question in a way that is appropriate to the age or mental condition of the witness. The intermediary shall be appointed by the court and must be a person who, in the opinion of the court, is competent to act as such (section 14 of the 1992 Act). A person under fourteen years of age, or over that age where he is intellectually disabled, may give evidence, otherwise than under oath or affirmation, if the court is satisfied that he is capable of giving an intelligible account of events that are relevant to the proceedings. A child giving unsworn evidence who deliberately gives false evidence shall be guilty of an offence carrying the same sanction as that applicable to perjury (section 27 of the 1992 Act). There is no longer any need for corroboration of the unsworn evidence of a child (section 28 of the 1992 Act).

Civil Proceedings

Part III of the Children Act 1997 makes the reception of children's evidence in civil cases easier, in much the same circumstances as the Criminal Evidence Act 1992 facilitates the reception of evidence from witnesses under the age of seventeen. However, the 1997 Act differs in one important respect from the 1992 Act, in that hearsay evidence is admissible in civil proceedings in certain conditions. The main provisions of Part III of the 1997 Act, other than for the reception of hearsay evidence, are:

(a) A child may give evidence by live television link in the same circumstances as in a criminal trial (section 21),

(b) A child giving evidence through a live television link may do so through an intermediary (section 22),

(c) The court may transfer proceedings to a Circuit or District Court district which has the necessary technical facilities for enabling evidence to be given through a television link or by means of video recording (section 27),

(d) In any civil proceedings, the court may receive the evidence of children under the age of fourteen years, or, in the case of a person with a mental disability who has reached the age of fourteen years, otherwise than on oath or affirmation in the same circumstances as in a criminal trial (section 28).

Hearsay Evidence

The rule against hearsay provides that a statement, other than one made while giving oral evidence, is inadmissible as evidence of any fact stated. In *Re M.K., S.K. and S.K.,* above, Barrington J described hearsay evidence as "evidence given in court of something the witness heard a third party say out of court", and pointed out that "it is generally not admissible as a method of proving what the third party did though it may be admissible as proof of what the third party said". Such evidence is generally excluded in our law, according to Keane J in the same case, "because the person is not present in court to give evidence on oath or affirmation and to be cross-examined and the court is thus deprived of the normal methods of testing the credibility of the witness".

Both the courts and the legislature have permitted a number of exceptions to the rule against hearsay, on the basis that an unyielding adherence to the rule would be unjust and inconvenient. The general principle underlying the exceptions to the rule is that hearsay evidence may become admissible where the court is satisfied that there are sufficient grounds for not requiring the witness to give oral evidence. Where the court allows hearsay evidence to be admitted, it should consider what weight should be given to the evidence, having regard to the fact that the person who made the statement had not been produced and to any other relevant circumstances which arose in the particular case.

Wardship Proceedings

Prior to the coming into force of the Children Act 1997, the courts were prepared to admit hearsay evidence in wardship proceedings in certain circumstances. In *Re M.K., S.K. and W.K.*, above, the hearsay consisted of an abused child reporting the abuse to a speech therapist. The Supreme Court described the judge presiding over wardship proceedings as being placed in the position of a good parent who must decide prudently on issues relating to the welfare of the child. The special nature of the jurisdiction of the President of the High Court in wardship proceedings and the special duty to protect the child's welfare are important factors. Therefore, it is entirely consistent that a judge exercising wardship jurisdiction has a discretion as to the use of hearsay evidence. He may admit such evidence in certain circumstances. The judge must inquire as to whether the child is competent to give evidence. The inquiry should take the form of an interview with the child in court or in chambers. If, following such an inquiry, the judge is satisfied that the child is too young to give evidence or that the giving of such evidence would be traumatic for the child and that it would be unjust to exclude the child's hearsay evidence for the purpose of deciding his welfare, the judge may admit such hearsay evidence.

Hearsay evidence, unless uncontroversial, should be regarded with extreme caution. Where hearsay evidence is admitted, the reliability and weight to be afforded to such evidence will depend on the circumstances of each case. These will include issues such as the child's age, ability, intelligence, comprehension of the circumstances, skill in communication and coherence. The previous behaviour of the child, his opportunity to have knowledge from other sources and the absence of any reason to expect fabrication should also be taken into account. The circumstances in which the hearsay evidence is obtained is relevant. The content of the hearsay evidence and its consistency to other relevant evidence will also be relevant. However, the fact that hearsay evidence is admitted does not exclude the exercise of due process and the protection of constitutional rights. Any person affected by the hearsay evidence must be afforded the opportunity to address the issues involved.

The Children Act 1997

Section 23 of the 1997 Act confers a discretion on the court to admit hearsay evidence in civil cases where the child is too young to give evidence in court, or where the giving of oral evidence by a child would be contrary to the welfare of the child. However, the court may refuse to admit such evidence or part of it having regard to all the circumstances, including any risk that admission will result in unfairness to any of the parties to the proceedings. Any party proposing to adduce hearsay evidence must give to the other party or parties to the proceedings such notice, if any, of that fact and, on request, such particulars of or relating to the evidence as is reasonable and practicable in the circumstances, to enable such party or parties to deal with any matter arising from the fact that the evidence is hearsay. The giving of notice in the circumstances just described shall not be necessary where the parties reach agreement beforehand to that effect.

Just in the same way as the courts exercised caution as to the weight to be attached to hearsay evidence where it is admitted, the 1997 Act sets out strict guidelines for assessing the weight of such evidence. Section 24 requires the court to have regard to all the circumstances from which inferences can reasonably be drawn as to the accuracy or otherwise of the hearsay. Regard must be had, in particular, as to whether:

(a) The original statement was made contemporaneously with the occurrence or existence of the matters stated,

(b) The evidence involves multiple hearsay,

(c) Any person involved has any motive to conceal or misrepresent matters,

(d) The original statement was an edited account or was made in collaboration with another for a particular purpose, and

(e) The circumstances in which the evidence is adduced as hearsay are such as to suggest an attempt to prevent proper evaluation of its weight.

Because of the serious implications for persons who might be adversely affected by the admission of the hearsay evidence of a child, the court should be in a position to test the credibility of that evidence. Evidence that would be admissible to test the credibility of the child had he been allowed to give direct evidence can be considered by the court. Where any matter could have been put to the child in cross-examination as to his credibility had he been called as a witness, the court may allow evidence of that matter to be adduced by the cross-examining party. The court may also admit evidence that tends to prove that the child is inconsistent in what he says, in that he is contradicting a statement previously made by him (section 25 of the 1997 Act).

Conclusion

There can be little doubt that a court appearance by children who are either the victims of a crime or witnesses to a crime can be a stressful occasion for them. In many cases, they will be upset and worried about what will happen to them in court. They may even feel that they have done something wrong. That is why children need the support of parents or carers to see them through their ordeal. The State also has responsibility for the welfare of children, and must put in place the necessary procedures and facilities to make a court appearance as stress free as possible. The legislative framework provides that a child under 14 years of age who is capable of giving an intelligible account of events may give evidence otherwise than under oath. In cases involving a sexual offence or an offence involving violence, a child under the age of seventeen can give evidence via a closed circuit television system called video link. In civil trials involving children and in child protection proceedings in the nature of an inquiry, hearsay evidence may be admitted where the court is satisfied that the child is too young to give evidence in court or that a court appearance might be too traumatic for the child. While it is desirable to try to make a court appearance by a child as stress free as possible, it is important to ensure that persons who are accused of child abuse or crimes of violence against children are afforded fair procedures, in order to vindicate the constitutional rights of both the accused and children.

CHAPTER 4

THE INTERNATIONAL DIMENSION OF CHILD CARE

Introduction

Increasingly, the influence of international conventions is being felt in the framing of legislation on family law and child welfare. The development of international children's rights since the adoption of the United Nations Convention on the Rights of the Child has been quite significant. The other international instrument that has had a major impact on children's rights is the European Convention on Human Rights. Implicit in both conventions is the need for international co-operation at all levels in protecting children's rights across frontiers. Ireland's membership of the European Union commits the State to the EU Charter of Fundamental Rights. The Charter confers specific rights on children. The overall theme of all three international instruments requires states to show respect for children as individual people and to treat them no less favourably than adults.

The United Nations Convention on the Rights of the Child

The Convention was ratified by Ireland without any reservations or declarations in September 1992. It is, in essence, a 'bill of rights' for all children, and sets the standards and should be the yardstick by which the Government, voluntary agencies and individuals measure their actions and efforts in protecting the welfare of children. Ratification places an obligation on ratifying states to uphold and enforce all the stipulated rights. As a result, domestic legislation relating to children must comply with the minimum threshold standards for children's rights embodied in the Convention. The Convention identifies and asserts the civil, political, social, cultural and economic rights of all persons under the age of eighteen. Ratifying states shall ensure that each child enjoys full rights without discrimination (Article 2), that the best interests of the child shall be a primary consideration (Article 3), that every child has an inherent right to life (Article 6), that children have the right to be heard (Article 12) and that children shall have the right to be protected from all forms of abuse while in the care of parents, guardians and other persons charged with the care of children (Article 19). The Convention sets out a detailed list of children's rights, including the right of all children to an adequate standard of living, to education, to the best available health care, to protection from all forms of abuse, neglect and exploitation, and to freedom of thought, conscience and religion. These rights can be categorised as welfare rights (the right to a happy childhood, encompassing health, education and recreation), protection rights (the right to freedom from abuse and neglect) and social justice rights (rights which adults have and which should be extended to children).

Unlike the European Convention on Human Rights, the United Nations Convention on the Rights of the Child does not have an inbuilt enforcement mechanism. There is provision in Articles 44 and 45 of the Convention on the Rights of the Child for the establishment of a Committee on the Rights of the Child, whose role it is to examine and monitor the progress made by ratifying states in complying with their obligations under the Convention. The Committee shall consist of ten experts in the field of children's rights to be elected by the ratifying states. Each ratifying state must submit a report to the Committee on the Rights of the Child within two years of ratification of the Convention and thereafter every five years. The report must detail the manner in which implementation of the Convention has been achieved. The first Irish report was submitted in May 1996. In January 1998 a formal hearing took place before the Committee at which the Irish delegation was questioned on the report. As a result of its deliberations following this hearing, the Committee in its concluding observations (CRC/C/15/Add.85, 23 January 1998) expressed certain concerns regarding the State's commitment to implement the provisions of the Convention. One of the principal concerns of the Committee was that action on behalf of children was fragmented. The need for a comprehensive national policy on children was stressed, as was a children's rights approach to welfare policies and practices. The Convention is considered further at various stages throughout the text.

The European Convention on Human Rights

The European Convention on Human Rights is a regional human rights instrument drawn up by the member states of the Council of Europe in 1950. The Convention is a charter of basic civil rights, and its provisions echo many of the fundamental and personal rights contained in the Constitution. The general purpose of the Convention is to protect human rights and fundamental freedoms, and to maintain and promote the ideals and values of a democratic society. Human rights are expressed in general terms, and the interpretation of those rights will change as society changes. For this reason, the Convention should be read as a living instrument, and the rights set out should be given a broad interpretation rather than a strict legalistic one.

The rights to be protected by the Convention are set out in Articles 2–18. A striking feature of the Convention is that children barely feature in it at all. It is by application and renovation of the principles it sets out that children have come to be accorded at least some of the protections accorded to adults.

In dealing with cases where children's rights are involved, the European Court of Human Rights has referred to the United Nations Convention on the Rights of the Child, and reports submitted thereunder by ratifying states and reviewed by the Committee on the Rights of the Child. The Articles most frequently litigated before the Court of Human Rights in family and child care matters are: Article 2 – the right to life; Article 3 – freedom from torture, inhuman or degrading treatment; Article 5 – the right not to be unlawfully detained; Article 6 – the right to a fair hearing; Article 8 – the right to respect for private and family life, for home and correspondence; Article 10 – freedom of expression and freedom to receive information without interference; and Article 13 – the right to an effective remedy before a national authority where there has been a violation of a Convention right. The scope of the protection afforded by these Articles of the Convention to children who are in need of care and protection is considered throughout the text.

The Convention was ratified by Ireland and entered into force for Ireland in 1953. On ratification, the Convention became binding on the State as part of its obligations under international law. However, it did not form part of domestic law, and, as such, could not be pleaded in any proceedings before an Irish court. Any person wishing to vindicate a right under the Convention had to bring a case before the Court of Human Rights in Strasbourg. Before doing so, the applicant had to exhaust all possible remedies available under national law. In effect, the Supreme Court on appeal must have refused the applicant a remedy under domestic law before the case could proceed to Strasbourg. A finding by the Court of Human Rights that a state has violated the Convention requires the state in question to take steps to remove the offending statutory provision or rule of law. For example, the finding of the Court of Human Rights in *Keegan v Ireland* 1994 that Ireland was in breach of Articles 6 and 8 of the Convention, in not affording Keegan a say in the adoption of his non-marital child, necessitated the passing of the Adoption Act 1998. The Act requires that the father of a non-marital child be consulted in the adoption process to afford him the opportunity to apply to the Circuit Court to be appointed guardian. A failure by a State to comply with the judgment of the Court of Human Rights could result in its expulsion from the Council of Europe.

The European Convention on Human Rights Act 2003, while not incorporating the Convention directly into Irish law, gives effect to it at sub-constitutional level. Cases may now be taken and remedies may be obtained before national courts in respect of violations of the Convention. In interpreting the provisions of the Convention, Irish courts may take the Court of Human Rights interpretations into account (section 4). Direct incorporation was not possible because of the constitutional requirement that the judiciary interpret the law in accordance with the terms of the Constitution itself. Legislation could not incorporate into Irish law a parallel quasi-constitution in the form of the Convention. The 2003 Act merely permits Irish Courts to have regard to Strasbourg decisions rather than compelling them to do so. The new regime will not dramatically alter the rights and protections afforded to Irish citizens and other persons by the courts, since it is generally acknowledged that Irish constitutional law already provides a higher degree of protection to the individual than that which exists in most member states of the Council of Europe.

The principle underlying the 2003 Act is to give further effect to the Convention in national law by enabling cases to be taken and remedies obtained before national courts in respect of violations of the Convention. Rights under the Convention are now enforceable in Irish courts. Irish courts are obliged to apply the Convention in all cases, and it may be pleaded as a cause of action or as a defence. When a court is interpreting any statutory provision or rule of law, it shall do so in a manner compatible with the State's obligations under the Convention (section 2). Where it is not possible in any case to interpret a statutory provision or rule of law in a manner compatible with the Convention, the High Court, or Supreme Court on appeal, can make a declaration that the provision or rule in question is incompatible with the provisions of the Convention (section 5). However, such a declaration will not affect the validity of the statutory provision or rule of law, though it may be the trigger for remedial action. It will be a matter for the Government to consider what steps should be taken to remedy the matter. In the absence of remedial legislation and administrative action to provide an effective remedy for a party to an action in which a declaration of incompatibility is made, the party in question may have direct recourse to the Court of Human Rights, since by that stage he will have exhausted domestic remedies. There is no entitlement to damages for loss suffered as a result of a statutory provision or rule of law being declared incompatible with the Convention. This is so, since the provision or rule of law in question, although incompatible with the Convention, remains constitutional. However, the injured party may apply to the Government, through the Attorney General, for an *ex gratia* payment in respect of such loss.

All public bodies, excluding the courts, are amenable to the Convention, in that they shall perform their functions in a manner compatible with the State's obligations under the Convention. A person who has suffered injury, loss or damage as a result of a public body acting in a manner incompatible with the Convention may bring an action for damages where no other remedy is available. Damages may be awarded in a case where a public body commits a breach of the Convention, unless it could not have acted differently under the law of the State. All such proceedings for damages against a public body must be commenced within one year of an alleged breach (section 3).

Of particular relevance to child care practitioners will be the manner in which the District Court deals with breaches of the Convention by health boards in carrying out their child-protection functions. For example, will the District Court be able to review a decision of a health board taken in relation to a child, where a parent or guardian alleges that he was denied a fair hearing under Article 6 of the Convention, or can the health board's decision only be reviewed by the High Court under its supervisory jurisdiction? Any undue delay by a health board in dealing with a child who may be at risk will amount to a breach of the child's right to respect for family life under Article 8 of the Convention (see *Glasser v United Kingdom* 2000, referred to in Chapter 13). Article 3 of the Convention places a positive obligation on health boards to take preventative measures to protect a child who may be at risk from another individual. To continue to allow a child at risk of being further ill-treated and neglected while a health board procures welfare reports may amount to breach of the child's right not to be subjected to inhuman or degrading treatment under Article 3. In *Z. and Others v United Kingdom* 2001, the Court of Human Rights held that there had been a violation of Article 3, in that the local authority had delayed unduly in taking children into care and had failed to protect them from severe neglect and abuse.

The EU Charter of Fundamental Rights

The Charter sets out the civil, political and social rights of European citizens and all those resident in the European Union. It was endorsed by all member states in December 2000. Article 24 of the Charter confers specific rights on all children. It provides that in all actions relating to children, whether taken by public authorities or private institutions, the child's best interests must be a primary consideration. Children have the right to such protection and care as is necessary for their well-being. They have the right to express their views freely, and to have such views taken into consideration in accordance with their age and maturity. Every child shall have the right to maintain on a regular basis a personal relationship and direct contact with both his parents, unless that is contrary to his interests. The explanatory note to the Charter states that Article 24 is based on the United Nations Convention on the Rights of the Child. It is a very welcome step in getting children's rights recognised in the European Union. However, the Charter does not have binding force at present.

A Constitution for Europe

Article 3, Part 1 of the draft Constitution for Europe includes children's rights in its internal and external objectives. The draft Constitution was adopted by the European Convention, comprising members from national parliaments, the European Parliament and Commission, in 2003. The EU Charter, including Article 24 relating to children's rights, has been incorporated in full in Part II of the draft Constitution. When the Constitution eventually takes effect, the EU Charter will become binding on all member states.

Conclusion

When taken in conjunction with the rights afforded to children under the
Constitution, as identified by our superior courts, the various international
instruments considered above do provide a comprehensive framework for the
care and protection of all children. Governments are required by the United
Nations Convention on the Rights of the Child to ensure that all actions
concerning a child take full account of his best interests. They must provide
children with adequate care when parents or others with legal responsibility
fail to discharge their duties. Despite the fact that the European Convention
on Human Rights makes no reference to the best interests of the child as
being a primary or paramount consideration in decisions regarding children,
the European Court of Human Rights in its judgments has on many occasions
referred to the United Nations Convention, and the overriding principle that
the best interests of the child shall be a primary consideration. When the new
European Constitution finally takes effect, the inclusion of children's rights
as an objective of the European Union will ensure that children are properly
recognised as European citizens.

CHAPTER 5

CHILD SEXUAL ABUSE: THE STATE'S RESPONSE

Introduction

The issue of child abuse, particularly the sexual abuse of children, has entered the public domain in the past twenty years or so. There is some controversy and debate as to the nature and ambit of the term "sexual abuse". Sexual abuse can cover a variety of acts from molestation to rape. *Children First* states that "sexual abuse occurs when a child is used by another person for his sexual gratification or sexual arousal or for that of others", and proceeds to give examples of child sexual abuse (Paragraph 3.5). The Statute of Limitations (Amendment) Act 2000 contains a definition of sexual abuse, and this is set out in Chapter 14. A number of high profile cases in the 1990s, such as the Kilkenny Incest Case 1993, the Kelly Fitzgerald Case 1996 and the Madonna House Affair 1996, created a social and political climate for public inquiries. These inquiries brought to light the misery suffered by children subjected to all forms of abuse and neglect, and alerted the public to the need for adequate child protection and welfare services.

The Kilkenny Incest case involved the physical and sexual abuse of a twenty-seven-year-old woman by her father over a fifteen-year period. In March 1993, her father was given a seven-year jail sentence, having pleaded guilty to six charges of rape, incest and assault from a total of fifty-six charges covering the period 1976 to 1991. The extensive media coverage which the case attracted caused public outrage, especially when it emerged at the trial that the abuse had gone on for so long despite the fact that the victim had a number of hospital admissions over the years for the treatment of physical injuries and had been in contact with professionals, including general practitioners, social workers and public health nurses. As a result of the publicity, the Minister for Health instituted an inquiry to carry out an investigation into the circumstances surrounding the case, to establish why the health services concerned had not taken action earlier to halt the abuse and to make recommendations for the future investigation and management by the health services of cases of suspected child abuse. The Report of the Kilkenny Incest Investigation 1993, in so far as it influenced the updating of child protection procedures, is referred to below.

The public outrage that followed the revelations contained in the various reports resulted in the Taoiseach making a public apology in May 1999 to the victims of childhood abuse for the collective failure of society as a whole to intervene to detect their pain and to come to their rescue. In making the apology, the State did not admit liability. However, the apology did signal the introduction of a number of measures designed to alleviate the effects of the abuse on victims and to prevent future abuse. These measures include the establishment of the Commission to Inquire into Child Abuse, the extension of the concept of disability to include the victims of childhood sexual abuse, the establishment of the Residential Institutions Redress Board, the introduction of a notification procedure or tracking system for convicted sex offenders and proposals on the mandatory reporting of instances of sexual abuse of children. Each of these measures is now considered in some detail.

The Commission to Inquire into Child Abuse

The Commission, chaired by a judge of the High Court, was established by the Commission to Inquire into Child Abuse Act 2000. The establishment of the Commission acknowledges the past failures of society regarding child abuse in institutions run by or on behalf of the State. The role of the Commission is to heal and offer some therapy to victims. It will afford individual victims the opportunity to overcome the lasting effects of childhood abuse. Announcing the establishment of the Commission, the Minister for Education said that the facts of abuse, however unpalatable, would be brought into the open, "so that we as a society can confront the truth and the lessons taught by past failures will be well learned to protect the children of the future".

The Commission has four main functions: to listen to the victims of childhood abuse in institutions who want to recount their experiences in a sympathetic forum; to fully investigate all allegations of abuse made to it, except where the victim does not wish for an investigation; to determine the extent to which institutions, management and regulatory authorities had responsibility for the abuse; and to publish a report on its findings to the general public. The report may identify institutions in which abuse occurred and the people responsible. It may also make findings in regard to management and regulatory authorities, and make recommendations on measures to alleviate the effects of abuse on victims and prevent future abuse in institutions. The institutions covered by the terms of reference of the Commission include industrial and reformatory schools, orphanages, hospitals, children's homes and any other places where children were cared for other than by members of their families.

The Commission will adopt a two-strand approach in pursuing its functions. A Confidential Committee is aimed at meeting the needs of victims who want to speak of their experiences but who do not wish to become involved in an investigative procedure. An Investigation Committee will facilitate victims who wish to both recount their experiences and have allegations of abuse fully inquired into. The two-strand approach allows serious allegations to be investigated, while also affording a sympathetic environment to those who wish to recount their childhood experiences. Victims of abuse will be offered counselling by a dedicated counselling service. While counselling and education for former detainees of the various institutions is important, justice and compensation for victims should clearly take priority.

Compensation for Persons who Suffered Abuse while Resident in Institutions

The Residential Institutions Redress Act 2002 provides for the making of financial awards to assist in the recovery of persons who as children were resident in institutions in the State, and who suffered injuries consistent with abuse received while so resident. A Residential Institutions Redress Board to make awards and a Residential Institutions Redress Committee as an appeals body to review awards will be established under the Act. The institutions covered by the Act include industrial and reformatory schools, orphanages, orthopaedic or psychiatric hospitals, special residential schools for deaf or blind children and children with intellectual disabilities, and children's homes for which public bodies had supervisory or inspection functions. Abuse is defined as covering sexual and physical abuse and any act or failure to act which results in injury.

The Residential Institutions Redress Board will not address issues of fault or negligence. Those accused of abuse will be afforded the opportunity of putting their side of the case. Hearings before the Board will be as informal as possible, subject to the right of the Board to require any person giving evidence before it to do so on oath. An applicant for compensation who has already received an award or a settlement in court arising out of the same circumstances may not receive an award under the Act. However, the making of an application in itself does not prevent the applicant from taking any other action in respect of the injuries suffered. An applicant must make an application for compensation within three years of an establishment day to be fixed by the Minister for Education. The Board may extend this time limit in exceptional circumstances, and will extend this limit where it is satisfied that the applicant was under a disability, for example a serious psychiatric illness, at the time when the application should have been made. An application may be brought on behalf of any person who would have qualified as an applicant, but who died since 11 May 1999 (the date of the Taoiseach's apology).

Extension of Limitation Period for Victims of Childhood Sexual Abuse

The Statute of Limitations (Amendment) Act 2000 extends the concept of disability contained in the Statute of Limitations 1957 to include a person bringing an action founded in tort in respect of an act of sexual abuse committed against him. As a result, persons suffering from a psychological injury as a result of being sexually abused during childhood, so that their will or ability to make a reasoned decision to institute proceedings in respect of such abuse is substantially impaired, are entitled to commence legal proceedings outside the limitation period prescribed by the 1957 Act. See further Chapter 6.

The Sex Offenders Act 2001

The 2001 Act is part of the Government's strategy for protecting the public from sex offenders, particularly those who prey on children and other vulnerable persons. The principal purpose of the Act is the protection of the public from the danger of further sexual offences. It is designed to act as a deterrent to unsuitable persons from seeking to gain access to children through the workplace, where relationships based on trust or fear can develop. The aim of the Act is to ensure that An Garda Síochána will at all times have up-to-date information on the whereabouts of convicted sex offenders. Among the key elements of the Act are a new notification procedure or tracking system for all convicted sex offenders, which will also apply to any sex offenders entering this jurisdiction from abroad; a new civil court order against sex offenders whose behaviour in the community gives the Gardaí reasonable cause for concern; a new system of supervision for sex offenders following their release from prison; and a new offence to cover sex offenders seeking employment involving unsupervised contact with children without telling of their conviction.

The notification procedure, or tracking system, will require convicted sex offenders to notify the Gardaí of their names and addresses and any changes to that information, including details of any trips abroad lasting ten days or more, in order to ensure that records in that respect are kept fully up to date. It is generally accepted that sexual offenders thrive on secrecy and have a propensity to move around. The requirement that offenders supply mandatory particulars to the Gardaí, which may have the effect of facilitating personal control and provide Gardaí with knowledge of an offender's whereabouts, was a first step in social control. While the notification requirements of the 2001 Act should not be viewed as a primary punishment, the Court of Criminal Appeal held in *The People (DPP) v NY* 2002 that the application of the Act constitutes "a real and substantial punitive element to which the court is entitled to have regard" for the purposes "of assessing the appropriate sentence on conviction".

The notification requirement will also extend to any sex offenders entering the jurisdiction from abroad. The offences that will trigger the notification requirement are, in the main, all those sexual offences committed against children. The duration of the notification requirement will depend on the length of sentence, as set out in the Act, from a minimum five-year period for those convicted and sentenced to a non-custodial sentence including a fully suspended sentence, to an indefinite period or lifetime notification requirement for those sentenced to more than two years. The finite periods are halved in the case of offenders who are under eighteen years of age at the time of sentencing. Failure to notify as required is an offence punishable by a fine or imprisonment for up to twelve months or both. It is intended that the Gardaí, in consultation with the relevant State agencies, such as the Probation and Welfare Service and the health boards, will undertake continuous risk assessment of those who are subject to the notification requirement.

The civil sex offender order will enable the Gardaí to apply to the courts for a sex offender order against any sex offender whose behaviour in the community gives reasonable cause for concern that an order is necessary to protect the public from serious harm. The order is geared towards persons whose behaviour, while not necessarily criminal, gives cause for concern. The order will prohibit the convicted sex offender from doing certain things as specified in the order, for example loitering around school playgrounds or other places where children congregate for no legitimate reason etc., and will last for a minimum of five years. Breach of an order without reasonable excuse is a criminal offence with a maximum penalty on indictment of five years' imprisonment.

The system of post-release supervision introduced will enable the court at the time of conviction to sentence a sex offender to a determinate sentence, with the latter part of it being served in the community under Probation and Welfare supervision. The combined custodial and non-custodial periods will not exceed the maximum custodial sentence available for the crime committed. The court, in addition to the supervision requirement, may impose additional requirements, including the requirement to attend psychological counselling or other treatment programmes run by the Probation and Welfare service or other bodies, or a requirement prohibiting a sex offender from doing things which the court considers necessary for the purpose of protecting the public from serious harm from the offender.

A new offence is created for sex offenders who seek or accept work involving unsupervised contact with children without informing the employer of their conviction. This offence is designed to act as a deterrent to unsuitable people from seeking to gain access to children through the workplace, where relationships based on trust or fear can develop. Under the provisions of the 2001 Act, the fact of conviction will not, in itself, render the person unsuitable to work. It will be a matter for the prospective employer or, in the case of the self-employed, the child's parent or guardian, on being informed of the conviction, to decide if the conviction is relevant to the work or position concerned. A conviction for this offence carries a maximum penalty on indictment of five years imprisonment.

In *Enright v Attorney General* 2002, the High Court turned down a challenge to the constitutionality of certain provisions of the 2001 Act by a man who had been convicted of the rape of a number of children and sentenced to twelve years' imprisonment. In view of the undisputed evidence that sexual offenders presented a significant risk to society by reason of their tendency to relapse, and the widely held international view that the condition was one which could not be cured, it was necessary to put in place measures of risk management of the condition, which facilitated personal and social control of the offender. The notification requirements did not restrict the applicant in his movements nor did they contain any special notification requirements to the public at large. The 2001 Act itself does not authorise the release to members of the public of any information received. In dealing with such information, the Gardaí would be bound by the Official Secrets Act 1963 and the provisions of the Garda code. However, in the context of child protection legislation, it may be necessary to release certain of the information to child care professionals.

Proposals for Mandatory Reporting of Child Abuse

Mandatory reporting is obliging certain persons to make a report to a designated authority, who in turn will investigate that report. As to what those mandated to report should in fact report, *Children First* suggests that reporters would be expected to make reports when they have "reasonable grounds for concern" (Paragraph 4.2.4). The issue of mandatory reporting of child abuse has come to dominate the minds of child care professionals, and now forms part of a highly politicised debate on how best to deal with what is in essence a highly sensitive matter. The fact that various professional and voluntary bodies involved in child protection have ended up on opposing sides of the debate makes it clear that opinion on the issue is very much divided. The Kilkenny Incest Investigation Report 1993 recommended the adoption of a system of mandatory reporting, as did the 1989 Law Reform Commission Report on Child Sexual Abuse. Official government policy on the matter is difficult to gauge at any given time, varying from a concern expressed by the Minister for Children in 1998 that mandatory reporting could be counter-productive, in that it could lead to less cases of child abuse being reported, to a commitment by the then Minister in July 2000 to bring a White Paper to cabinet which would propose the mandatory reporting of reasonable suspicions of abuse.

The opposing sides in the debate have put forward what they perceive to be the advantages and disadvantages of a system of mandatory reporting. Proponents of the system claim that mandatory reporting would lead to the discovery of hitherto unreported cases of child abuse. They also claim that mandatory reporting would assist the relevant professional personnel mandated to report by providing a clearer legal framework for reporting. The Protection of Persons Reporting Child Abuse Act 1998, together with the provisions for reporting of abuse and neglect in *Children First*, will ensure that those obliged to report will be clear about who to report to and in what format.

Those professionals who are opposed to mandatory reporting argue that it will result in an increase in the number of unsubstantiated cases reported. This could result in the child care system being swamped, thereby wasting valuable resources. Another possible disadvantage of mandatory reporting is that it might damage the professional/client relationship, and deter victims from disclosing cases of abuse. Critics argue that mandatory reporting may lead to innocent people being held to account and investigated based on flimsy suspicions. To overcome this major criticism, reassurances would be needed that all investigations would be handled with the greatest degree of sensitivity.

Recruitment of Staff to Be Involved with Children

It is essential that both statutory and voluntary organisations involved with children in any capacity have proper vetting procedures and good employment practices to ensure, in so far as possible, that children are protected from abuse. It is part of the remit of the Social Services Inspectorate (SSI) to make recommendations to health boards in relation to policies and practices on staff recruiting and staff vetting. Instances where Garda clearance and validated references have not been obtained or documented in respect of employees are highlighted by the Inspectorate in its reports, and recommendations are made around appropriate vetting of staff prior to their appointment. In its annual report for 2002, SSI refers to the fact that health boards have a responsibility to vet staff before they take up employment in children's residential centres to ensure, as far as possible, that people who are not suitable to work with children are not employed. According to records seen by inspectors, only one centre had completed adequate checks on all staff before employment. Five centres had obtained Garda clearance on all staff before employing them. Nine centres employed one or more staff for whom there were no records of Garda checks in the centres. Some were staff employed before the requirement for Garda checks were introduced. However, those staff ought to have retrospective Garda clearance. Seven centres had staff employed for whom Garda clearance was obtained only after they took up employment. The situation in relation to other centres was unclear in relation to Garda checks.

Directions on the recruitment and selection of staff to children's residential centres were issued by the Department of Health and Children in 1994. Under these directions, employers must obtain Garda clearance on all staff being considered for appointment to a children's residential centre. These directions were extended in 1995 to the recruitment of staff to any area of the health services, where they would have substantial access to children and vulnerable individuals. The directions stress that it is important that employers validate information supplied by candidates, and verify references proactively. Despite having these clearance arrangements available to them, employers should bear in mind that criminal record checks, while being capable in appropriate circumstances of making a significant contribution, are not the sole answer to ensuring that prospective employees are suitable for positions working with children.

Community and voluntary organisations not covered by the directions issued in 1994 and 1995 are now catered for in *Our Duty to Care,* a document issued by the Department of Health and Children 2002. The document stresses that safe practice starts with safe recruitment procedures. These involve applying thorough selection procedures, judging the suitability of applicants in relation to a broad range of matters, taking all reasonable steps to eliminate people who are not suitable for working with children and providing training. In addition, mindful of the fact that a large number of organisations with responsibility for child care, who engage staff, were not covered by Garda clearance arrangements, the Garda Commissioner set up a Central Vetting Unit in 2002. The primary role of the unit is to check prospective employees who as part of their duties will have substantial access to children.

Unlike the position prevailing in Northern Ireland, "lists" or registers of persons deemed unsafe or unsuitable to work with children are not maintained in this jurisdiction. In addressing a conference entitled "Beyond Borders – Protecting Children" in September 2002, the Minister for Children said that the introduction of such a register here "would present legal and constitutional difficulties". The Protection of Children and Vulnerable Adults Order 2003 authorises the Department of Health, Social Services and Public Safety in Northern Ireland (DHSSPS) to maintain a Pre-Employment Consultancy Service, compiled from information provided by the voluntary and statutory organisations, in relation to workers (paid employees and volunteers) who have been dismissed, transferred to other work or have resigned in circumstances where it is considered they posed a risk to children or adults with learning difficulties. The lists are not published. The relevant information is only furnished to those who need to know, for example a prospective employer. The purpose of the listing scheme is to protect children from those who are employed to work with them and to maintain public confidence in the care provided to children. Listing under the scheme involves a difficult balancing exercise between the safety of children and the rights of individuals to have their livelihoods and reputations safeguarded. An appeal lies to the High Court on a point of law. For a consideration of the legal implications of a similar listing scheme in England and Wales set up under the Protection of Children Act 1999, see *Secretary of State for Health v C.* 2002.

The Protection of Children and Vulnerable Adults Order 2003 also provides for the sharing of information with other jurisdictions. Organisations in other jurisdictions will be able to have checks carried out against the lists held by DHSSPS of those deemed unsuitable to work with children or vulnerable adults. This is a highly significant development, in that it will allow organisations which employ personnel who work directly with children in this jurisdiction to access Northern Ireland's vetting systems. This development will tighten up cross-border vetting procedures and will help to ensure that sex offenders in Northern Ireland will not be able to avoid vetting by moving between jurisdictions.

Bringing the Perpetrators of Child Sexual Abuse to Justice

The principal approach adopted by society in tackling the problem of child abuse has been to bring the perpetrators of such abuse to justice by means of the criminal law process, while at the same time protecting children from abuse by means of child welfare legislation. While a court in an individual case must give consideration to the community's right to have an alleged crime prosecuted in the usual way, the accused's right to fair procedures is superior to the community's right to prosecute. In *D. v DPP* 1994, Denham J said that if there is a risk that the accused will not receive a fair trial, "then there could be no question of the accused's right to a fair trial being balanced detrimentally against the community's right to have alleged crimes prosecuted". With regard to delay in cases where persons who are now adult are alleging indecent assault or rape as young children, Denham J said in *B. v DPP* 1997 that the test is whether there is a "real risk" that the accused, by reason of the delay, would not obtain a fair trial.

It is generally accepted that one consequence of physical or sexual abuse is that the victim may be reluctant, in varying degrees, to acknowledge what has occurred. The harmful consequences of the abuse may not be apparent in the immediate aftermath of the abuse, and may not become fully apparent until adulthood. Hence, the tendency of the victim to delay in making a complaint to the relevant authorities. 'Repressed memory syndrome' is simply an extreme form of this tendency. The syndrome can be described as a situation where the victim may experience the symptoms of abuse, but fail to recall the actual abuse itself. The theory behind the syndrome has been subject to much criticism and scepticism among psychologists and psychiatrists. This criticism relates to the fact that it is possible to implant a false memory of a traumatic event, and it is then open to the power of suggestion to invoke such a false memory. Unreliable evidence thus generated can present significant problems in the case of persons charged with child sexual abuse, in that it is more difficult for an accused to counter unreliable, and possibly false, evidence several years later. This could cause a danger to accused persons who are innocent. In *J.L. v DPP* 2000, the Supreme Court warned of the very real possibility of miscarriages of justice where prosecutions are based on recovered memories that are said to have been previously repressed.

The Supreme Court addressed the issue of repressed memory syndrome in *N.C. v DPP* 2001. Hardiman J referred to the continuing number of cases in which the courts had dealt with attempts to restrain the continuance of prosecutions in cases of alleged sexual abuse on the grounds of a lapse of time. The victim in the instant case claimed to have forgotten the assaults which had been perpetrated on her until she remembered them in the course of hypnosis. The unavailability of the hypnotist to give evidence was relied on heavily by the accused. The court held that where the delay in prosecuting indecent assault was partly explained by the fact that memory was lost or repressed and recovered during a consultation, the person conducting the therapy in the course of which a memory was recovered was an extremely important witness. This form of actually or allegedly recovered memory was a common feature of these cases. A person charged with very old offences on the basis of alleged recovered memory was entitled to seek to inform himself about every aspect of the therapy. If this could not be done, then there was no effective test or control of the mechanism of alleged recovered memory, and the situation would be fraught with the risk of unfairness. The death of a witness which left the complainant's account incapable of contradiction, or even exploration, demonstrated a severe risk of prejudice on trial.

In relation to delay in making a complaint of sexual abuse, the courts have been ready to identify the exercise of dominion by the alleged perpetrator over the complainant and, where this has been found to characterise the relationship, it has been held to explain the delay in recall. Where the dominion exercised over the complainant continued to have an effect over him to an extent that, even though he became conscious of the alleged abuse, such dominion rendered him incapable of making a complaint to the Gardaí, the court would seek some evidence of psychological disablement which created an incapacity on his part to approach the Gardaí until he had actually done so. In *P.C. v DPP* 1999, Keane CJ said that the issue in every case is whether the court is satisfied, as a matter of probability that the circumstances were such as to render explicable the inaction of the alleged victim from the time of the offence until the initiation of the prosecution.

The Law Reform Commission in its Consultation Paper on Child Abuse 2000 categorised this condition as "psychological incapacity" due to a lack of emotional strength, rendering the victim "unable to confront the abuser or to take any action against the perpetrator such as litigation". This psychological incapacity could be due to a number of reasons. Firstly, even when they reach majority, victims often continue to blame themselves for the abuse. Such self-blame is a strong inhibitor to disclosure. Secondly, complaining of abuse, particularly where the abuser is part of the family, or in a similar position of trust, takes considerable courage and emotional strength. Such strength is often lacking in victims of child sexual abuse. Thirdly, even where the abuse has ended, that does not necessarily mean that the 'relationship' between the abuser and abused has been terminated.

Conclusion

The high profile given to child sexual abuse by the media in recent times means that we are considerably more aware of the phenomenon than in the past. The various measures put in place by the State to lessen the effects of the abuse on the victims and hopefully, to prevent abuse in the future are both deserved and commendable. However, controversy seems to dog the best efforts of all involved to lessen the pain and suffering that the victims have been subjected to over a protracted period. On the question of compensating the victims for the abuse they suffered, a much less adversarial approach is needed. The recent controversy about funding for the Commission to Inquire into Child Abuse, resulting in the resignation of an imminent High Court judge as chairperson, amid accusation and counter-accusation that the Government was obstructing the smooth operation of the Commission, has led people to question the sincerity of the measures put in place to cater for the victims. While nobody really doubts that the State is sincere in its stated objectives of compensating the victims and trying to eliminate the conditions that gave rise to institutionalised sexual abuse, as a society we must accept that in the past the State pursued a protectionist approach, in order to minimise its responsibility to the very people to whom the Taoiseach apologised back in 1999. We must now face up to the past and eliminate forthwith the prevarication and delays that have caused the whole saga to continue.

Part Two

PROMOTING THE WELFARE OF CHILDREN

CHAPTER 6

PARENTAL RESPONSIBILITY

Introduction

Any consideration of legislation designed to cater for children who may be in need of care and protection necessarily requires an appreciation of the legal relationship that exists between a parent and child. It is not possible to describe the legal effect of State intervention in the family without some understanding of the nature of the parent and child relationship. Traditionally, this relationship has been considered by reference to the concept of parental rights and duties. We find reference in the Constitution and legislation to parents having rights and duties towards their children. However, there has been a shift in emphasis in recent times to defining the parent/child relationship more in terms of parental responsibility than parents having rights and duties towards their children. This is due in so small measure to the impact that ratification by the State of the United Nations Convention on the Rights of the Child has had on domestic policy in relation to the care and welfare of children. In emphasising children's rights as opposed to parental rights, Article 18 of the Convention provides that parents "have common responsibilities for the upbringing and development of children".

For the purposes of the Protection of Children (Hague Convention) Act 2000, the term "parental responsibility" is described as including parental authority or any analogous relationship of authority determining the rights, powers and responsibilities of parents, guardians or other legal representatives in relation to the person or the property of the child. As further evidence of this shift in emphasis, it is significant that in *North Western Health Board v H.W. and C.W.* 2001, Keane CJ, in commenting on "the emphatic language used by the Constitution in Article 41" to describe the family, said that parents did not think of their "rights" against their children, "but rather of the responsibilities which they joyfully assume for their children's happiness and welfare, however difficult the discharge of those responsibilities may be".

Guardianship

A guardian is a person legally entitled to parental rights and duties, in the sense that a guardian has parental responsibility in relation to a child. Guardianship is concerned with all matters concerning the child's physical, intellectual, religious, social and moral welfare. Custody is the most important parental right enjoyed by a guardian. Custody is the right to physical care and control of a child, and from it all other rights flow. Other rights include the right to determine where the child should live; the right to authorise medical treatment, in the case of a child less than sixteen years of age; the right to impose discipline; the right to educate the child; the right to apply for a passport for a child; and the right to bring and defend proceedings on behalf of a child. The duties include the duty to protect a child; the duty to control a child; the duty to maintain a child; and the duty to secure a child's education in a school approved by the State, where it is not possible to educate the child at home. This list is by no means exhaustive.

Married parents have equal constitutional rights to and are joint guardians of their children under Articles 41 and 42 of the Constitution. They also have the primary right to custody "for custody will normally be necessary for the effectuation of the parents' constitutional right and duty to provide for the religious and moral, intellectual, physical and social education of their children" (*G. v An Bord Uchtala* 1980). The mother of a non-marital child is sole guardian of and entitled to custody of her child (Article 40 of the Constitution). The father of a non-marital child has no constitutional rights in respect of his child (*State (Nicolaou) v An Bord Uchtala* 1966). However, he does have certain legal rights. Where he subsequently marries the mother, he automatically becomes a joint guardian by virtue of section 1 of the Legitimacy Act 1931. Otherwise, he may apply to the court to be appointed guardian of his child under section 12 of the Status of Children Act 1987. In *J.K. v V.W.* 1990, the Supreme Court held that the father has a defeasible right to apply to be guardian and not a right to be guardian. The court will only appoint him guardian where it is in the best interests of the child to do so. He may become guardian of the child by agreement with the mother under section 4 of the Children Act 1997. For this purpose, the father and mother must declare that they are the parents of the child, agree to the appointment of the father as guardian of the child and have entered into arrangements regarding custody of and, as the case may be, access to the child. They must also make a statutory declaration to the effect that they are the father and mother of the child. The Adoption Act 1998 confers on the natural father the right to be consulted in the adoption process. Subject to certain conditions, the father must be informed of the intention to place his child for adoption, so as to afford him the opportunity to apply to the court to be appointed guardian.

Custody

Custody is the right to physical care and control of the child. Where a parent is deprived of custody either by agreement, in the case of parents who are married to each other, or by court order in custody or child protection proceedings, that parent remains a guardian and retains a say in matters that are important to the child's welfare. A married couple may enter into a separation agreement providing for custody of and access to any dependant child of the family. However, the court will not enforce a custody agreement unless it is in the best interests of the child to whom it relates (*Cullen v Cullen* 1970). The Family Law Act 1995 provides for the making of preliminary orders and ancillary orders in the course of judicial separation proceedings as to custody and access or any other orders on any question affecting the welfare of a child. Where the court grants a decree of judicial separation, it may declare either spouse unfit to have custody, and where such spouse is a parent of a child of the family, he shall not be entitled as of right to custody of that child on the death of the other spouse. In the case of divorce proceedings, the court is empowered to make orders of a similar nature under the Family Law (Divorce) Act 1996.

Where a custody dispute arises between parents, section 11 of the Guardianship of Infants Act 1964 enables the court to make any order it thinks fit in relation to the welfare of the child. In resolving any dispute as to custody, section 3 of the 1964 Act requires the court to have regard to the welfare of the child as the first and paramount consideration. Other factors which might have a bearing on the welfare of the child are the conduct of the parents, the biological sex of a parent and the wishes of the child. As regards the conduct of the parents, the Supreme Court held in *MacD. v MacD.* 1979 that such conduct was relevant only in so far as it affected the welfare of children. Custody was awarded to the mother of two young children, despite the fact that she was in an adulterous relationship with another man. As regards the biological sex of a parent, the traditional view of the courts has been that the mother of very young children is the person *prima facie* entitled to their custody where parents were estranged. This "tender years" principle was questioned by McGuinness J in *D.F. O'S. v C.A.* 1999. Pointing to the fact that modern views and practices of parenting show the virtues of shared parenting, the learned judge said that "the older principles too often meant the automatic granting of custody to the mother virtually to the exclusion of the father". Nowadays, the courts favour making awards of joint custody, unless it is clear that it will not work, due the possible inability of the parents to co-operate in caring for the child.

Where a custody dispute arises between parents and outsiders, the case law indicates that it is only in exceptional circumstances that outsiders will be preferred to parents. The marital status of the parents will have an important bearing on how the court will resolve such a dispute. The landmark decision of the Supreme Court in *K.C. and A.C. v An Bord Uchtala* 1985 established the principle that it is only in exceptional circumstances (the "compelling reasons" test) that a marital or legitimated child will be removed from his parents.

There is no finality in the making of a custody order. This is so, as decisions relating to the custody of a child, especially a very young child, are never final but evolve with the child, retaining in changing times the fundamental concept of the welfare of the child. Section 12 of the 1964 Act enables the court to vary or discharge any previously made order. The parent deprived of custody can at any time in the future ask to have the original order varied or discharged on the basis of changed circumstances or new evidence of such matters as parental unsuitability.

Substitute Care

Because of the rise in broken marriages and unmarried relationships, and the economic pressure on mothers to remain in employment even while their children are very young, nowadays the task of caring for children is very often shared between parents who are living apart, grandparents and other relatives, and unofficial childminders. Parents may need to provide substitute care for their children because they are working, ill or simply going out for a social occasion. In *D. McA. v K. McA.* 2002, Herbert J in the High Court said that judicial knowledge may be taken of the fact that the weekday absence of both parents and the presence of childminders is part of a normal pattern of living. In the case before the court, which involved a custody dispute between parents, the judge said that in the absence of compelling evidence that it was not in the interests of the children, "it would be unjust and unrealistic" to expect either parent to assume a full-time role within the home. Many parents prefer to provide substitute care in their own homes if at all possible. There are no direct legal controls over this form of care, and there is no requirement for notification to or supervision by any public authority. Of course, childminders are subject to both the civil and criminal law, and may face prosecution or be subject to a civil suit for neglect, abandonment or exposure of a child to the risk of unnecessary suffering or injury to health. While there is obviously a need for some element of regulation of unofficial childminders, the imposition of too rigorous standards upon them will reduce the supply. This, in turn, might lead to parents turning to less satisfactory unregulated arrangements that are difficult to police.

Where it is not possible for parents to provide care in their own home, they must look to day care outside the home. Day care is usually provided by childminders in their homes and by private nurseries and playgroups. Nurseries and playgroups are generally regarded as more satisfactory than childminders, as they are easier to control than are people operating in private homes. The 1991 Act attempts to impose minimum standards on nurseries and playgroups providing pre-school services. Pre-school services are defined as embracing any pre-school, play group, day nursery, crèche, day care or other similar services which cater for pre-school children, including those grant aided by health boards (section 49). Persons carrying on pre-school services are obliged to notify the appropriate health board of their existence (section 51). They must take all reasonable measures to safeguard the health, safety and welfare of pre-school children attending the services, and comply with regulations made by the Minister (section 52). The health board, in turn, is required to arrange for the inspection of pre-school services (section 53). A health board may provide pre-school services in its area and make available information on pre-school services, whether provided by the board or otherwise (section 56). A person convicted of an offence under the 1991 Act is liable to a fine of £1000 or imprisonment of up to twelve months and, in addition, may be disqualified from operating a pre-school service for a specified period (section 57).

The Minister for Health and Children, in conjunction with the Minister for Education and Science and the Minister for the Environment, is required to make regulations for securing the safety and promoting the development of children attending pre-school services (section 50). The Child Care (Pre-School Services) Regulations 1996 and the Child Care (Pre-School Services) (Amendment) Regulations 1997 apply to pre-schools, playgroups, day nurseries, crèches and childminders looking after more than three children and other similar services that cater for children less than six years of age. Areas covered by the Regulations include development of the child, the health, safety and welfare of the child, adult/child ratios, record keeping, notification procedures, premises and facilities, child/space ratios and inspection. Pre-school providers are obliged to notify their local health board that they are carrying on or proposing to carry on a pre-school service. The health board must arrange for an inspection to be carried out by an authorised person. The process involves advisory visits, if required, and follow-up visits to ensure that any deficiencies identified during inspection are addressed within a specific time-frame as required. Complaints in relation to issues affecting the health, safety or welfare of children in a pre-school facility are dealt with by the pre-school advisory/inspection service of the local health board.

Despite the desirable objective of regulating the physical environment in which nurseries and playgroups provide pre-school services, the 1991 Act does not insist that the persons providing the services be professionally trained in the education and development of pre-school children. For this reason, there is a considerable risk that the people who agree to take children in will neither appreciate their needs nor be able to cater for them personally. The only control operates after the event, either through prosecution for neglect, abandonment or exposure to the risk of unnecessary suffering or injury to health, or procedures to remove the child because of ill treatment or neglect. Another main weakness in the system is the fact that persons looking after children from the same family, or not more than three children from different families in their (the childminder's) homes, are exempt from notification requirements (section 58). A review of the 1996 and 1997 Regulations, in terms of what has worked well and what aspects need to be strengthened or addressed, is currently taking place by a Review Group set up by the Minister for Children in 2001.

Medical Treatment

Section 23 of the Non-Fatal Offences against the Person Act 1997 fixes the age of consent to any surgical, medical or dental treatment at sixteen. If a child over sixteen does in fact consent, it shall not be necessary to obtain the consent of a parent or guardian. In the case of a child under the age of sixteen, consent can be given on his behalf by a parent or guardian. The parents not only have a right but it is also the duty of parents to give consent on the child's behalf if it is in the best interests of the child to do so. Sometimes a parent or guardian may be opposed to a child undergoing medical treatment on religious grounds or for other reasons where, for example, the treatment involves invasive surgery. If the parents refuse to consent, the court must be invited to override their refusal and to give approval for the treatment or surgery. In deciding whether to override the clearly expressed objections of parents to their child undergoing medical treatment, the question the court has to decide is whether it is in the best interests of the child that he should have the necessary treatment, and not whether the wishes of the parents should be respected.

In *North Western Health Board v H.W. and C.W.* 2001, the parents refused to allow the PKU (heel prick) test to be carried out on their one-year-old infant son, on the grounds that it was an invasive procedure. The test detects various disorders of the blood. The Supreme Court rejected the health board's challenge to the decision of the parents on the basis that, in matters regarding the welfare of their children, parents know best. If the responsibility for making decisions on medical tests and inoculations were transferred from parents to the State, it would herald in a brave new era (described by McCracken J in the High Court as "a Brave New World"). The court observed that parents daily make decisions regarding their children's welfare for which they were responsible, and liability rested with them. The court did not accept that the parents in this case had failed in their duty to their children. Their decision may have been ill advised and against the weight of the medical evidence to the effect that the PKU test is of benefit to babies. The court acknowledged the care and devotion shown by the parents to their child, and said that their decision could not be regarded as such a default of their moral and constitutional duty as to warrant State intervention. However, the court held that where parents refused to consent to medical treatment for their child, in exceptional circumstances the State could become "a default parent, and override the decisions of parents for the purposes of giving the required consent".

Where parents unreasonably withhold their consent to medical treatment for their child, the child protection procedure available under the Child Care Act 1991 can be invoked. In *A. and B. v Eastern Health Board* 1998 (the "C" case), the High Court held that the 1991 Act was "a perfectly appropriate umbrella" to determine in any given case whether a termination of pregnancy should take place. The case involved a thirteen-year-old girl who had become pregnant as a result of being raped. Her parents had refused to give their consent to the girl travelling to England for a termination of her pregnancy. The health board obtained an interim care order, and sought a direction from the District Court that the girl be allowed to have a termination. A psychiatrist gave evidence to the effect that the child was likely to commit suicide unless she had a termination of pregnancy. The court held that the termination of pregnancy was a medical procedure, and was also a medical treatment for her mental condition within the meaning of section 13 of the 1991 Act. Accordingly, the welfare of the child required that she be allowed to have her pregnancy terminated.

Discipline

Parents may prescribe standards of behaviour for their children and try to secure obedience to these standards. In this regard, they may discipline their children by administering reasonable corporal punishment. Parents are exempt from criminal liability in respect of the reasonable punishment of their children and the administering of reasonable corporal punishment has always been recognised as a defence to an action in tort for trespass to the person. What is reasonable will depend on the facts of an individual case. The punishment must be imposed for a good reason and must be proportionate to the child's "offence" and must take into account the child's age, understanding and physique. In *A. v United Kingdom* 1998, the European Court of Human Rights held that any form of corporal punishment meted out to a child must attain a minimum level of severity if it is not to fall foul of Article 3 of the European Convention on Human Rights. In that case, the court held that the punishment inflicted on a nine-year-old boy by his stepfather, by beating him with a garden cane, thereby causing extensive bruising to the child's buttocks, was unreasonable and amounted to torture or inhuman or degrading treatment within the meaning of Article 3. The court further held that "children and other vulnerable individuals in particular are entitled to State protection in the form of effective deterrents against such serious breaches of personal integrity". While not outlawing the use of corporal punishment, this judgment could be interpreted as indicating that the use of an implement to chastise a child is not permissible.

Article 37 of the United Nations Convention on the Rights of the Child is designed to protect the child from torture, inhuman and degrading treatment or punishment. Among the principal matters of concern included in the observations of the Committee on the Rights of the Child on Ireland's compliance with the Convention was "the lack of prohibition in legislation of corporal punishment within the family environment", which "contravenes the principles of the Convention". The Committee suggested that the State take all appropriate measures, including measures of a legislative nature, "to prohibit and eliminate the use of corporal punishment within the family environment" (CRC/C/15Add.85, 23 January 1998).

Education

Article 42 of the Constitution acknowledges that the primary and natural educator of the child is the family, and guarantees protection for the role of the parents in providing, according to their means, for the religious and moral, intellectual, physical and social education of their children. Education, in the sense described in Article 42, has been held to extend beyond a scholastic education, towards a broader conception of education for life. It encompasses the teaching and training of a child to make the best use of their inherent and potential capabilities, physical, mental and moral. In *Sinnott v Minister for Education* 2001, Denham J said that "educational rights are interwoven with the family, parental rights and duties, and the rights of the children". Parents are given a choice as to where they give the education to their children, provided that the children receive "a certain minimum education". In this regard, parents can educate their children at home, or in private schools, or in schools recognised or established by the State. The State is permitted to directly intervene in the education of children to ensure that they receive "a certain minimum education". However, it is only in exceptional cases where the parents, for physical or moral reasons, fail in their duty towards their children that the State, as guardian of the common good, shall endeavour to supply the place of parents. In the *Sinnott* case, the Supreme Court held that the State's obligation to provide free primary education ends when a child reaches eighteen years of age. In an earlier judgment in *O'Donoghue v Minister for Health* 1996, the Supreme Court held that the obligation to provide free primary education extended to persons with disabilities.

The minimum standard of education required by Article 42 has yet to be defined in legislation. In *Best v Attorney General* 2000, the Supreme Court addressed this issue. In this case, a mother was prosecuted for failing to send her children to school. She defended the charges brought against her, suggesting that her children were being educated at home. The Supreme Court ruled that a District Court Judge was not prevented from convicting the mother, even though the legislature had not defined what amounted to a suitable primary education. The factors to be taken into account when determining if a minimum education was provided in the home included the personality of the child, the response of the child compared with the child's response to any other education that he may have received, and any adverse effects on the child of continuing in home education. Education was viewed as a right of the child, and the right to educate a child at home could not be abused to the detriment of the child (*Re G. (Children)* 2001)

The somewhat emotive issue of home education has been finally addressed by the State in a structured fashion in the Education (Welfare) Act 2000, which fills the legal vacuum in which this issue has operated in the past. The Act provides for the setting up of a register of children being educated outside a recognised school. Where a parent wishes to educate a child at home, an application must be made to the Educational Welfare Board set up under the Act to have the child concerned registered in the register (section 14). The Board shall cause an assessment to be carried out by an authorised person, in consultation with the parent, for the purpose of determining whether the child is receiving a certain minimum education. If the Board is satisfied from the report and any representations made by the parent that the child is receiving a certain minimum education, it shall register the child in the register. If not satisfied by the level of education provided, the Board may direct that the child be enrolled in a recognised school. A parent who is dissatisfied with a decision of the Board may appeal to an appeal committee established under section 15 of the 2000 Act.

The Child Litigant

The Rules of The Superior Courts 1986 provide that, where it is necessary for a child to take legal proceedings, he may sue as plaintiff by his next friend, who is usually a parent or other guardian. Likewise under the Rules, a child may defend legal proceedings by a guardian appointed for that purpose. Before the name of any person shall be used in any cause or matter as next friend of any child, the written consent of that person must be obtained and given to the solicitor for the child and filed in the proper office. The role of the next friend is to look after the interests of the child. The next friend is entitled to consider whether or not a proposed settlement offered by a defendant in an action is reasonable. Although the next friend is entitled to consider whether a settlement is reasonable, he does not have authority to accept it on behalf of the child. The 1986 Rules provide that no settlement or compromise of the child's action may take place unless the court shall so direct. This rule is designed to ensure that the child's best interests are protected, while at the same time protecting the defendant by giving him a complete discharge in respect of the claim.

Limitation of Actions

The Statute of Limitations Act 1957, as amended by the Civil Liability and Courts Act 2004, provides that an action claiming damages for negligence, nuisance or breach of duty must be commenced within two years of the date on which the cause of action accrued. However, where the injured person does not know certain information at the date of accrual of the action, section 3 of the Statute of Limitations (Amendment) Act 1991 provides that the limitation period does not begin to run until the injured person has knowledge of the fundamental facts pertaining to his cause of action. This latter provision was introduced to remedy the anomaly that existed under the 1957 Act, whereby an injured person's cause of action could have been extinguished before he even knew that he had a cause of action. In the case of persons under a disability at the date that the cause of action accrued, such as children and persons of unsound mind, section 49 of the 1957 Act provides that the limitation period does not begin to run until the disability has come to an end. A child ceases to be under a disability when he reaches the age of eighteen. The Statute of Limitations (Amendment) Act 2000 extends the concept of disability to include persons suffering from a psychological injury as a result of being sexually abused during childhood, so that their will or ability to make a reasoned decision to institute proceedings in respect of such abuse is substantially impaired.

Dismissal for Want of Prosecution

The extended limitation period in the case of a child may result in an inordinate delay between the accrual of a cause of action and the commencement of proceedings. For this reason, the Supreme Court held in *O'Domhnaill v Merrick* 1984 that even though a claim was made within the extended limitation period, it could be struck out if it would be unjust to call on the defendant to defend himself after such an inordinate and inexcusable lapse of time. The court must strike a balance between the plaintiff's need to carry on a delayed action against a defendant and the defendant's basic right not to be subjected to a claim which he could not reasonably be expected to defend. The non-availability of witnesses and contemporaneous records are matters that must be taken into account. In the *O'Domhnaill* case, the proceedings were instituted some sixteen years after the plaintiff suffered injuries in a road traffic accident (see also *Toal v Duignan and Others (No. 2)* 1991).

In *Glynn v Rotunda Hospital* 2000, the High Court considered the case of a child plaintiff who had been born in 1981 and had suffered cerebral palsy with mental retardation. The proceedings were not commenced until January 2000. Certain documents relating to the birth, including neo-natal notes had only been discovered in 1998. The defendant sought to have the case dismissed for want of prosecution, claiming that a crucial medical witness was no longer available, while the midwife at the time of the birth could not recall the events in question. While accepting that much of the delay was inordinate and inexcusable, and that there would be difficulties for the defendant in conducting a proper defence, O'Sullivan J said that it had to be taken into account that the plaintiff was in her minority during the relevant period of delay, and that some of the material of relevance (although not of crucial relevance) was not available to the plaintiff's advisors during the relevant period of delay. The learned judge was not satisfied that allowing the case to proceed would lead to an unjust result. He held that the case should be permitted to proceed and the application of the defendant dismissed. On the other hand, in *Kelly v*

O'Leary 2001, the High Court held that a delay of fifty years was inordinate, and no evidence had been adduced to explain or excuse the delay. The case concerned a claim for damages for abuse by the plaintiff as a child while she was placed in an orphanage.

The Right to Apply for a Passport

In the *State (K.M. and R.D.) v Minister for Foreign Affairs* 1979, the High Court held that a child has a constitutional right, subject to public order and the common good, to travel and be issued with a passport for that purpose. This right is exercisable at the choice of a parent or guardian, subject to the power of the court "to deny that choice in the dominant interest of the welfare of the child". In the case of a marital child, a passport may issue to either parent on behalf of the child. However, in *Cosgrove v Ireland* 1982, the High Court held that where one of the parents of a child applied to the Minister for Foreign Affairs for the entry of that child on a passport, and the Minister was made aware of the objection of the other parent to that course and, in particular, of the objection of the other parent to the child being removed from the jurisdiction of the courts, the Minister had an obligation not to make the requested entry until directed by a court under the Guardianship of Infants Act 1964 to do so.

In *P.I. v Ireland* 1989, the Supreme Court considered the two judgments of the High Court mentioned above, and noted that it was the practice of the Minister, though without statutory obligation to do so, even though unaware of any objection, to require evidence of the consent of both parents in order to enter a child upon the passport of either of them. In that case, the Minister had issued a passport to the mother of a ten-month-old child with the name of the child entered on it. The mother had obtained this entry by forging the father's signature to the form of consent required by and submitted to the Department of Foreign Affairs. Differences arose between the parents and the mother left the father, taking the child with her. The father was granted access to the child under the 1964 Act and his solicitor wrote to the Passport Office asking that the child's name be removed from the passport. The letter did not advert to the fact that the entry on the passport had been obtained by fraud. The Minister replied stating that he did not have the power to remove the child's name. The mother thereafter removed the child to Canada. The father obtained an order from the Circuit Court attaching the mother for her refusal to comply with the orders as to access and was granted custody of the child. The Supreme Court dismissed the appeal of the father against the refusal of the High Court to grant an order of *mandamus* directing the Minister to remove the child's name from the passport issued to the mother. In doing so, the Supreme Court reserved the question as to whether the courts, even for the purposes of enforcing or facilitating decisions made by them within their jurisdiction, should in any circumstances direct the Minister to cancel a passport.

Maintenance

In the case of parents who are married to each other, the duty to maintain their children is governed by the Family Law (Maintenance of Spouses and Children) Act 1976, as amended. The Act enables the court to make a maintenance order in favour of an applicant spouse and any dependent children of the family, where it appears to the court that the respondent spouse has failed to provide such maintenance as is proper in the circumstances. A third party, even though such person does not have custody of the children, may apply for maintenance for dependent children where a spouse is dead, or has deserted or has been deserted by, or is living separately and apart from the other spouse. Where a spouse is ordered to pay maintenance to the other spouse and a dependent child, the order must specify what part of the payment is for the support of the child. In the case of a non-marital child, the mother of the child may apply to the court under section 11 of the Guardianship of Infants Act 1964 for an order requiring the father to pay maintenance for the child.

A dependent child is defined in the 1976 Act, as amended by the Status of Children Act 1987 and the Family Law Act 1995, as any child less than eighteen years of age of both spouses, or adopted by both spouses or in relation to whom both spouses stand *in loco parentis*, or a child of either spouse, or adopted by either spouse or in relation to whom either spouse stands *in loco parentis*, provided the other spouse is aware he is not the parent of the child and has consented to the child being treated as a member of the family. A child over eighteen and less than twenty-three years of age may be treated as dependent if he is in full-time education. In the case of a child suffering from mental or physical debility, dependency may be life-long.

In deciding whether to make a maintenance order, and in assessing the amount of maintenance that should be paid, the 1976 Act requires the court to take into account all the circumstances of the case, including (a) the income, earning capacity (if any), property and other financial resources of the spouses and of any dependent children, (b) the financial and other responsibilities of the spouses towards each other and towards any dependent children and the needs of any such children, including the need for care and attention and (c) the conduct of each of the spouses, where in all the circumstances it would be repugnant to justice to ignore such conduct. However, the conduct of a spouse having custody of the dependent children cannot be taken into account in determining the other spouse's liability to pay maintenance to the children.

The primary function of the 1976 Act is to ensure that proper and adequate maintenance will be available in accordance with the provisions of the Act to spouses and children. According to Walsh J in *H.D. v P.D.* 1978, the basic question to be decided was whether at any given time there was a failure by one spouse to provide reasonable maintenance for the support of the other spouse and any dependent children. The court, in assessing the amount of maintenance that should be paid in any given case, must give priority to the needs of the applicant spouse and any dependent children. The court must also ensure that the paying spouse will have sufficient resources left to live on. If there has to be any reduction in living standards, that reduction should be borne primarily by the respondent. This is particularly the case where his conduct has been the main cause of the marriage breakdown. Maintenance may be by way of secured or unsecured periodical payment or by way of lump-sum payment. The District Court cannot order a lump-sum payment in excess of £5,000. The 1976 Act provides that a maintenance order may later be revoked or varied at the request of the person paying, where new circumstances exist since the making of the order. Payments under a maintenance order are to be made to the District Court clerk for transmission to the maintenance creditor, unless the court otherwise orders.

Maintenance orders are enforced by means of an attachment of earnings order, a distress order on the maintenance debtor's goods or committal to prison. The attachment of earnings order is probably the most effective method of enforcing payment of maintenance. Such an order may be made on the application of either the maintenance creditor or the District Court clerk. There is now provision in the 1995 Act for the making of an attachment of earnings order on the occasion of the court making a maintenance order. The effect of an attachment of earnings order is a direction from the court to the maintenance debtor's employer to pay to the District Court clerk or the maintenance creditor the sum, known as "the normal deduction rate", that the court thinks is reasonable to deduct to meet the maintenance liability. The order must also specify the "protected earnings rate", which is the sum below which the maintenance debtor's earnings must not be allowed to fall. The court will not make an attachment of earnings order without the consent of the maintenance debtor, except where he has defaulted in making maintenance payments.

Financial and Property Provision on Judicial Separation and Divorce

Section 16 of the Family Law Act 1995 and section 20 of the Family Law (Divorce) Act 1996 empower the court to make certain ancillary orders, by way of financial and property provision, in favour of dependent members of the family on the occasion of granting a decree of judicial separation or divorce. The court can make periodical payments orders, secured periodical payments orders and lump-sum orders under section 8 of the 1995 Act (section 13 of the 1996 Act) on the application of any person on behalf of a dependent member of the family. Provision is also made in section 9 of the 1995 Act (section 14 of the 1996 Act) for the making of property adjustment orders, in the form of a transfer of property order, a settlement of property order, a variation of settlement order and an order extinguishing or reducing an interest in a settlement.

In exercising its powers to make provision for a dependent member of the family, section 16 of the 1995 Act (section 20 of the 1996 Act) requires the court to have regard to (a) the financial needs of the member, (b) the income, earning capacity (if any), property and other financial resources of the member, (c) any physical or mental disability of the member, (d) the manner in which the member was being and in which the spouses concerned anticipated that the member would be educated or trained, (f) the income and earning capacity of both spouses, their needs, obligations and responsibilities, and the standard of living enjoyed by the family prior to the institution of the proceedings or the separation, as the case may be, and (g) the accommodation needs of the member. Section 19 of the 1995 Act (section 23 of the 1996 Act) obliges the court to disregard the conduct of the applicant spouse when deciding to make a periodical payments order or lump-sum order in favour of a dependent member of the family.

Reciprocal Enforcement of Maintenance Orders

The Maintenance Orders Act 1974 provides for the enforcement in this jurisdiction of maintenance orders made in England and Wales, Scotland or Northern Ireland. The Maintenance Orders (Reciprocal Enforcement) Act 1972 allows for the enforcement in the United Kingdom of maintenance orders made in Ireland. In a global context, the Maintenance Act 1994, which is stated to be without prejudice to the provisions of the 1974 Act, consolidates the law relating to the reciprocal recognition and enforcement of maintenance orders. The 1994 Act gives legal effect to the 1990 Rome Convention between the member states of the European Communities on the simplification of procedures for the recovery of maintenance abroad and to the 1956 New York Convention on the recovery of maintenance abroad.

Section 4 of the 1994 Act provides for the establishment of a Central Authority to discharge the functions required of it under the Act, or required of a Central Authority under the Rome Convention, or of a transmitting agency or receiving agency under the New York Convention. The main purpose of the various conventions is to ensure co-operation by the various States Parties in the recovery of maintenance payments due. In this regard, the procedures to be followed on receipt of applications from reciprocating jurisdictions for recognition and enforcement of maintenance orders are set out.

Conclusion

To talk of parents having "rights" in respect of their children is somewhat misleading. Whatever rights they have are heavily qualified by the ability of the courts to intervene on the application of an interested person or health board. In matters such as education and medical treatment, the decisions of parents are capable of being overruled by the courts, acting in what they perceive to be the best interests of the child. Therefore, it is perhaps more accurate to refer to children's rights rather than parental rights. As against one another, parents have equal status, and any dispute between them as to the custody of a child must be decided in accordance with the welfare of the child. As against outsiders, they have a prior claim and important procedural rights if their right to custody is challenged. In essence, it is difficult to say that parents have "rights", although they have responsibilities towards their children, and these give rise to a prior claim and a considerable amount of power and authority.

CHAPTER 7

THE PROTECTION AND WELFARE OF CHILDREN

Introduction

The Child Care Act 1991 puts in place a statutory framework for the protection of children who might be at risk of abuse and neglect. The Act requires specified conditions to be fulfilled before the statutory agencies charged with the responsibility of supplying alternative care for children who might be at risk can intervene, and prescribes procedural safeguards for the various parties involved when action is taken. However, the decision to intervene in a particular case is left to the discretion of the particular agency involved in the case. The two main agencies involved in child protection are health boards and An Garda Síochána. Health board intervention takes the form of an application to the District Court for an emergency care order, a care order or a supervision order. In cases of serious and immediate risk to a child, where it would not be sufficient to await the making of a court order for the protection of the child, a member of An Garda Síochána may remove a child to safety.

The Duty to Promote the Welfare of Children

Section 3(1) of the 1991 Act imposes a duty on every health board to promote the welfare of children in its area who are not receiving adequate care and protection. The term "welfare" is not defined in the 1991 Act. Article 42.1 of the Constitution describes welfare as comprising "the religious and moral, intellectual, physical and social" welfare of a child. In *MacD. v MacD*. 1979, Finlay P, as he then was, considered the various categories of welfare referred to in both Article 42.1 of the Constitution and section 2 of the Guardianship of Infants Act 1964. He said that a dominant position must not be given to any of these categories. The whole question of welfare must be looked at globally, as the various categories of which it is composed are interrelated. Religious welfare is concerned with the education of the child in the practice of the religion in which he is being brought up. Moral welfare means the moral and ethical code of the religion in which the child is being brought up as judged against moral standards and values of the society of which he is a member. Intellectual welfare is concerned with the child's education. Physical welfare is concerned with the health, bodily comfort, nourishment and hygiene of the child. Social welfare means the type of welfare best suited to make a child a better member of the society in which he lives.

Section 3(2) of the 1991 Act provides that in the performance of its statutory function a health board, having regard to the rights and duties of parents, whether under the Constitution or otherwise, must regard the welfare of the child as the first and paramount consideration. In *MacD. v MacD.*, the Supreme Court, in endorsing the judgment of the House of Lords in *J. v C.* 1970, held that the requirement that the child's welfare shall be the first and paramount consideration must mean more than that the child's welfare is to be treated as the top item in a list of items relevant to the matter in question. The words "the first and paramount consideration" mean a process whereby, when all the relevant facts, relationships, claims and wishes of parents, risks, choices and other circumstances are taken into account and weighed, the course to be followed will be that which is most in the interests of the child's welfare. In requiring that other factors, such as the rights and duties of parents and the wishes of the child, be taken into account by a health board in the discharge of its statutory function, section 3(2) is making it clear that the word "paramount" does not mean exclusive.

The Wishes of the Child

Increasingly, the law has come to acknowledge that a child has the right to express his views in matters affecting his welfare. In *F.N. and Anor. v C.O. and Others* 2004, the High Court held that a child, in respect of whom a decision of importance is being taken, has a personal right, within the meaning of Article 40.3 of the Constitution, to have such decision taken in accordance with the principles of constitutional justice. Such principles of constitutional justice include the right of a child, "whose age and understanding is such that a court considers it appropriate to take into account his/her wishes", to have such wishes taken into account by a court in taking a decision as to the child's welfare. In performing its statutory function under section 3 of the 1991 Act, a health board is required, in so far as is practicable, to give due consideration, having regard to his age and understanding, to the wishes of the child. Also, in any proceedings under the 1991 Act, section 24 requires the court to give due consideration to the wishes of the child, having regard to the child's age and understanding. In imposing an obligation on health boards and the courts to have regard to the wishes of children in any decision making affecting their welfare, Irish legislation is reflecting the principles of participation and empowerment of children in decisions that may affect their lives set out in Article 12 of the United Nations Convention on the Rights of the Child, which Ireland ratified in 1992. Article 12 provides that ratifying states shall afford the child who is capable of forming his own views the right to express those views in all matters affecting the child, the views of the child being given due weight in accordance with his age and maturity. In particular, Article 12 stipulates that the child shall be provided the opportunity to be heard in any judicial and administrative proceedings affecting the child, either directly, or through a representative.

In the past, the courts have canvassed the views of children on many occasions in proceedings involving the welfare of children. However, recent judicial pronouncements seem to indicate a reluctance among the judiciary to interview children in chambers with a view to obtaining their wishes, partly because of the danger that children may be coached in what they are to say to the court. In *T.M.M. v M.D.* 1999, a child abduction case, the Supreme Court upheld the decision of McGuinness J in the High Court to interview an eleven-year-old girl, whom she considered "to have sufficient maturity so that it was appropriate to take her views into account". Stating that she had interviewed children on a number of occasions in regard to family matters, McGuinness J said that it is not a practice that she would undertake very often, as she was "well aware of the danger that children may be coached in what they are to say to the Court". She expressed herself certain that the child was not coached, and was sure she was expressing her sincere opinion. On appeal, Denham J expressed herself satisfied that the method by which the trial judge interviewed the child was appropriate, and said that "this is an area where the exercise of the discretion of the judge must be done with great care".

On the question of the trial judge seeing a child in chambers, in *A.S. (orse A.B.) v R.B.* 2001, Keane CJ issued a caveat in relation to such practice, pointing out that the only evidence which a trial judge can receive is evidence on oath or affirmation given in the presence of both parties or their legal representatives. The Chief Justice acknowledged, however, that interviews may be of assistance to the trial judge in ascertaining where the wishes of the children lie. Nowadays, in considering an application for a care or supervision order, a judge is more likely to seek social reports from experts in the field of paediatrics or child psychiatry under section 27 of the 1991 Act to decide the welfare of the child. Alternatively, the court may appoint a guardian *ad litem* under section 26 of the 1991 Act, and rely on his report to ascertain the wishes of the child (see Chapter 8).

A Positive Duty to Identify Children at Risk

In promoting the welfare of children, section 3 of the 1991 Act requires a health board to take positive steps to identify children who are not receiving adequate care and protection and to co-ordinate information from all relevant sources relating to children in its area. In *North Western Health Board v H.W. and C.W.* 2001, Denham J described the involvement of a health board in the care of a child in a family under section 3 as "a sensitive matter". Acknowledging that the board in the case "did not wish to be intrusive", she said that the board is a statutory body "given a statutory responsibility for the welfare of children in its area and potentially a liability for failure to ensure the welfare of the child". Section 8(2) of the 1991 Act lists children who might require care and protection as including the following:

(a) children whose parents are dead or missing,

(b) children whose parents have deserted or abandoned them,

(c) children who are in the care of a health board,

(d) children who are homeless,

(e) children who are at risk of being neglected or ill-treated,

(f) children whose parents are unable to care for them due to ill-health or for any other reason.

In placing a statutory duty on health boards to actively identify children who may be at risk, the 1991 Act is reflecting Article 19 of the United Nations Convention on the Rights of the Child, which provides that the State has an obligation to take all appropriate legislative and other measures to protect children from all forms of maltreatment perpetrated by parents or others responsible for their care. Such protective measures include preventative, investigative and treatment programmes, and follow-up of instances of such maltreatment with a view to judicial involvement. Article 34 requires the State to "undertake to protect the child from all forms of sexual exploitation and sexual abuse".

The Duty to Investigate

It is now generally acknowledged that inter-agency co-operation is vital if an effective system of investigation and intervention in child abuse cases is to operate. *Children First* provides a framework for inter-agency and multi-professional work practices. The aim of *Children First* is to assist people in identifying and reporting child abuse and, in particular, "to clarify and promote mutual understanding among statutory and voluntary organisations about the contributions of different disciplines and professionals to child protection (Paragraph 1.2.1). The Principles for Best Practice in Child Protection set out in *Children First* provide that effective prevention, detection and treatment of child abuse or neglect require "a co-ordinated multi-disciplinary approach to child care work and effective inter-agency management of individual cases". All agencies and disciplines concerned with the protection and welfare of children must work co-operatively in the best interests of children and their families" (Paragraph 1.9.1).

As part of its statutory child protection function under section 3 of the 1991 Act, a health board has a duty to investigate any allegation of child abuse or neglect made to it. As a result of carrying out an investigation, a health board may be satisfied that the provision of child care and family support services meets the needs of the case. However, if an investigation reveals that a child may need care or protection which he is unlikely to receive unless he is taken into care, section 16 of the 1991 Act imposes a duty on the health board to apply for a care or supervision order. However, as will be seen in Chapter 14, the decision to apply for a particular order is a matter for the discretion of the health board. In *M.Q. v Gleeson and Others* 1997, Barr J said that, in promoting the welfare of children in need of care and protection, a health board has a specific statutory obligation to identify the categories of children to whom it owes a duty of care under the 1991 Act. "That duty is not owed to all children in its area but only to those who are not receiving adequate care and protection." A health board is not confined to identifying children who are already at risk of abuse and require immediate care and protection. The duty also extends to children not yet identifiable who may be at risk in the future from a specific potential hazard to them which a health board reasonably suspects may come about in the future. "It is a present knowledge or reasonable suspicion of potential harm which is the essence of the health board's obligation to children."

The applicant in the *M.Q.* case had been accepted on a course leading to a qualification in child care. The Eastern Health Board furnished a report to the organisers of the course which contained allegations of child abuse against the applicant, as a result of which he was removed from the course. The court held that, on the basis that it had taken appropriate steps to inform itself, the health board would have been entitled to form an opinion that the applicant was unfit for child care work, and would have had an obligation to communicate its opinion to the organisers of the course. Barr J emphasised that "a health board has a child protection function which differs fundamentally from that of the prosecutorial function of the police and the DPP". In the case of a health board exercising its function under the 1991 Act, "the emphasis is on protection of vulnerable children", unlike the situation that exists in the prosecution of child abusers, where the objective is the detection and conviction of the abusers. There are many circumstances which may indicate that a particular person is likely to be, or has been, a child abuser, "but there is insufficient evidence to establish such abuse in accordance with the standards of proof required in a criminal or civil trial". The learned judge cited as an example the case of an abused child who, through fear, family pressure, age or mental capacity, may be unable to testify against the abuser. He also instanced the case of repeated physical injuries sustained by a child, where there may not be sufficient evidence to rule out accidents and to establish proof of abuse in law by a particular suspect. However, in such cases, there may be evidence sufficient to create, after reasonable investigation, "a significant doubt in the minds of competent experienced health board or related professional personnel that there has been abuse by a particular person". In those circumstances, the health board cannot "stand idly by but has an obligation to take appropriate action" to ensure that the abuser may not take up a position which may expose any other child to abuse by him.

Child Protection Conference

The child protection conference is a key part of the arrangements for inter-agency co-operation for the protection of children. It allows for an exchange of information to assist the health board in the discharge of its statutory responsibilities towards a particular child. Where appropriate, the child and his parents should be included. The purpose of a conference is:

(a) to enable the various professionals and the child's family to share and evaluate information and concerns,

(b) to outline a child protection plan to be completed following comprehensive assessment, and

(c) to identify tasks to be carried out by different professionals.

The child protection conference should not be seen as a pre-trial review or dress rehearsal for court proceedings. It may decide, however, to make a recommendation to the health board that it should consider care proceedings or other action in respect of a child. The conference should not be used as a substitute for normal consultation and supervision, inadequate inter-professional or inter-agency arrangements or relationships, or convened for any other reason not directly related to the requirements of the particular case. Guidance as to the role and procedures for child protection conferences is contained in *Children First* (Paragraph 8), and a protocol for the conduct of child protection conferences is set out in Appendix 6. The guardian *ad litem*, where one has been appointed, should be notified by the health board of the holding of a child protection conference, and given the option to attend. The perceived wisdom is that the guardian should not participate in the proceedings of a child protection conference. As the guardian's essential role is to give the child a voice, such participation might compromise the independence of the guardian in the eyes of the parents. Where the guardian feels that it might be of benefit to the child to attend, he should attend as an observer rather than a participant. This issue and other aspects of the guardian's role are considered in Chapter 8.

The importance of the child protection conference in the protection of children from abuse was emphasised by the Court of Appeal of England and Wales in re *A. (A Minor)* 1997. The case involved an application by the local authority for leave to disclose to a child protection conference certain litigation material, namely a statement of responsibility by the mother as to bizarre happenings in relation to a child who was in care on foot of an emergency protection order followed by a series of interim care orders. The mother had opposed the application of the local authority. In refusing an appeal by the mother against an order that the material be disclosed, Thorpe LJ said that the protection of children from abuse is not achieved simply by the family justice system or even principally by the family justice system. The Child Protection Conference is the first line of defence and embraces a range of difficult cases that never enter the family justice system. "It is absolutely essential that there should be the fullest co-operation between the two systems in those cases where both are involved".

Child Protection Plan

One of the tasks of the child protection conference is to discuss and outline a child protection plan to be completed following comprehensive assessment. The child protection plan is an inter-agency plan based on the outcome of assessment, together with the recommendations of the child protection conference, if one has been held. It is normally drawn up by the health board social worker in consultation with all parties involved, including the child and his parents/carers. It outlines the action which professionals and agencies directly involved with the family need to take in order to ensure the child's continued protection and well-being. The successful implementation of a child protection plan will depend on inter-agency and inter-professional co-operation, ongoing consultation with the child and his parents/carers, ongoing assessment and supervision, and support.

The Upbringing of Children within the Family

Section 3(2) (c) of the 1991 Act espouses the principle that it is generally in the best interests of a child to be brought up in his own family. Indeed, it could be said with some justification that the Act is founded on the premise of minimalist intervention by the State in the life of the child within the family unit. It is envisaged that a child should only be removed from the relative security of the family as a last resort, and then only in a child protection context. The requirement that a health board must actively seek out children who may be at risk is designed to ensure that the minimalist intervention approach will not act to the detriment of any child in need of care and protection. Where it is necessary for a health board to intervene to protect a child, it may be possible to avoid taking the child into care. Section 19 of the 1991 Act enables a court to make a supervision order on grounds identical to the making of a care order under section 18 of the Act. By means of a supervision order, the child can be monitored in the home by a social worker, thus eliminating the need to remove the child from the family.

The principle of minimalist intervention is reinforced by the Constitution and the special position afforded to the family under Articles 41 and 42. The United Nations Convention on the Rights of the Child is equally forceful in the view that the child is generally best served by remaining within the family unit. Article 9 of the Convention requires ratifying states to ensure that a child is only separated from his parents "when competent authorities subject to judicial review determine ... that such separation is necessary for the best interests of the child". To make it possible for children to grow up in their own families, a health board is empowered to provide assistance to parents in the upbringing of their children. The assistance shall be provided through child and family support services, which aim to promote the welfare of children in vulnerable families and minimise the circumstances in which a child may have to be received into care by a health board.

Family Support Services

In keeping with the general philosophy underlying the 1991 Act, section 3(3) requires health boards to provide child care and family support services for the purpose of preventing the need to take children into care. Health boards may also provide and maintain premises and make such other provision, as they consider necessary or desirable for such purposes. In this way, health boards are enabled to provide assistance to parents in the upbringing of their children to make it possible for the children to grow up in their own families.

Health boards are required by section 8 of the 1991 Act to prepare a report on an annual basis on the adequacy of the child care and family support services in their areas. In preparing a report, a health board should have regard to the needs of children in its area who are not receiving care and protection and, in particular, children whose parents are dead or missing; children whose parents have deserted or abandoned them; children who are in the care of the board; children who are homeless; children who are at risk of being neglected or ill-treated; children whose parents are unable to care for them due to ill-health or for any other reason. Notice of the preparation of the report must be given by a health board to any child care advisory committee in its area established under section 7 of the Act, and to such other bodies as the board sees fit who are involved in the provision of child care and family support services. A child care advisory committee shall be composed of persons with a special interest or expertise in matters affecting the welfare of children, including representatives of voluntary bodies providing child care and family support services. The health board must consider the views and general input of such committee or bodies in the preparation of the report. A copy of the report must be delivered to the Minister for Health and Children.

Children First offers guidance to health boards in the performance of their statutory responsibility to deliver support services. On the occasion of the launch of *Children First* in September 1999, the Minister for Children said that in recent years there has been "a major investment in child care and family support services to enable health boards to respond to child abuse and welfare concerns". In the preparation of *Children First*, the Working Group established by the Minister to review the 1987 Child Abuse Guidelines em-phasised the importance of support services to children and families. Chapter

7 of *Children First*, entitled "Support Services to Children and Families", affirms the statutory responsibility of health boards to provide support services to the families of children who may be at risk of abuse or neglect. Family support may be delivered formally through statutory and voluntary organisations or informally through extended families, friends and local networks. The principles that should inform best practice in child protection suggest that "early intervention and support should be available to promote the welfare of children and families, particularly where they are vulnerable or at risk of not receiving adequate care or protection". (Paragraph 1.9.1(iv)).

The importance placed by the Government on family support has been underlined in the publication of "A Guide to What Works in Family Support Services for Vulnerable Children" in 2000. The Department of Health and Children published the Guide as part of the Springboard community-based early intervention initiative. Springboard is specifically focused on supporting families with children who are at risk of going into care, dropping out of school and getting into trouble with the law. A key element of Springboard is its co-ordinated approach to supporting families in the community. The kind of support services envisaged include therapeutic work, parent education programmes, home-based parent and family support programmes, child development and education interventions, youth work and community development. The main aim of the Guide is to ensure that everyone involved in the provision of family support services is fully apprised about the ways of working with vulnerable families which, as a result of systematic research whether in Ireland or elsewhere, have been shown to be effective.

Conclusion

The 1991 Act sets out the rules regarding health board intervention for the protection of children in clear and straightforward terms. In doing so, the Act clarifies the rights of all parties, including the child, and seeks to maintain a fair balance between the right of the parents to custody of the child and the right of the child to be protected from abusive or neglectful parents. Although the 1991 Act prescribes the statutory procedures for health board intervention in the affairs of a family, the use of these procedures is a matter left to the discretion of a particular health board. The Act simply requires that the discretion be exercised in good faith after a consideration of all the relevant factors. The decision to take action should be based on the nature of the abuse or neglect, the response of the parents, the initial assessment of the parent's ability to change, their acceptance of responsibility and their willingness to co-operate with the health board.

CHAPTER 8

WELFARE REPORTS AND REPRESENTATION OF CHILDREN

Introduction

In proceedings involving the welfare of a child, the court will need a great deal of information about the child before it can reach a decision as to the order it should make. Welfare reports prepared by court welfare officers and social workers are the most effective method of procuring that information. From time to time the court will require reports from experts in the field of paediatrics or child psychiatry to arrive at a decision as to what is in the best interests of the child. The purpose of welfare reports is to assist the court, in conjunction with the other evidence at its disposal, in deciding the best outcome for the child in a complex and difficult case. Commenting on the corresponding power of the court to order welfare reports in matrimonial proceedings under section 47 of the Family Law Act 1995, in *S.O'F. v N.O'F*. 1999, Budd J said that one of the purposes of the section is to have an independent report and thereby "reduce the intrusion caused by more than one similar expert intervening and reporting on the child". In cases where a guardian *ad litem* has been appointed, the court may be prepared to rely on the guardian's report, without the need for a separate welfare report. However, as the role of the guardian *ad litem* is to represent the child and see things from his point of view, the court might feel that it requires an independent report which will provide information on matters of the family and the child's history and background.

Welfare Reports

In care proceedings or in relation to any matter concerning a child in the care of a health board, the court, of its own motion or on the application of any party to the proceedings, may procure a report from such persons as it may nominate on any question affecting the welfare of the child (section 27 of the 1991 Act). In deciding whether to obtain a report, the court must have regard to the wishes of the parties to the proceedings, but is not bound by those wishes. Any report obtained by the court has to be made available to the parties. The report may be received in evidence and the person making it may be called as a witness by the court or any party to the proceedings. The court may of course depart from the recommendations contained in a welfare report, bearing in mind that the court is the decision-maker and not the person making the report. In the course of a detailed judgment in *Re M.K., S.K. and W.K.* 1999, the Supreme Court emphasised that, while an expert can guide the court, it is the court that ultimately decides any given case. Where the court departs from the recommendations of a welfare report, it should give reasons for doing so. The judge should give a balanced view of his approach to the welfare report, stating not only why it was that he disagreed with recommendations in the report, but also a good and sound basis for doing so (see the English case of *Stephenson v Stephenson* 1985).

A welfare officer or social worker who prepares a report is an officer of the court appointed for the purpose of investigating circumstances relating to a child or a family, and reporting on those circumstances to the court. He must be independent of the parties and provide, on the basis of his investigations, a balanced view upon which the court can decide the welfare of the child. It is important to emphasise the fact that, while a welfare officer or social worker reporting to the court may provide a certain expertise which is invaluable to the court in its deliberations, such a person is in a different category to persons with expertise in general medical or psychiatric matters engaged by a party to the proceedings to advise and, if necessary, give evidence on behalf of that party. Where an expert is engaged by a party to prepare a report, that expert has to be given leave by the court to present the report and give evidence.

When dealing with welfare reports, caution should be exercised, since welfare professionals may be in a position to unduly influence the manner in which courts decide disputes over children. Expert witnesses are in a privileged position, as only experts are permitted to give an opinion in evidence. Whether a professional should be afforded the status of expert is a matter for the court in a given case. The credentials of an expert to express opinion should be carefully scrutinised, as a misleading opinion from an expert may prevent a proper determination of a particular case. A professional afforded the status of expert witness has a duty to be objective, as an absence of objectivity may result in a child being wrongly placed and thereby unnecessarily put at risk. In the English case of *Re X (Non-Accidental Injury: Expert Evidence)* 2001, the Family Division of the High Court was highly critical of an expert engaged by the parents to counter the expert evidence of four mainstream experts that the injuries sustained by an infant child were typical of non-accidental injury. The parents' expert suggested that the probable cause of the child's multiple fractures was a bone disease described as temporary brittle bone disease. The other experts contested that any such disease existed. In holding that the threshold criteria for making a care order were met in relation to each parent, Singer J said that the parents' expert had failed to act as an expert, in that he had provided a misleading opinion, failed to be objective, omitted factors which did not support his opinion and lacked proper research into the case in point.

As stated above, the court or any party to the proceedings may call the person making the report as a witness. Where the person making the report is unavailable to give evidence due to illness or other sufficient reason, the question arises as to whether a welfare report should be allowed in evidence without the person who prepared it being called as a witness and subjected to cross-examination. The court has to consider whether it is in the child's best interests that the case should be adjourned so that the witness could attend and give evidence. Adjourning a case for a considerable time to facilitate the attendance of that person may result in unjustifiable delay, which may have a detrimental effect on the child. Bearing in mind that where a judge has to arrive at crucial findings of fact, he should found them on sworn evidence rather than on an unsworn report, it is not unusual for judges to allow reports to go in without witnesses being called. In those circumstances, the reports should be given such weight as the presiding judge thinks fit, bearing in mind that the persons who prepared them have not been cross-examined.

As a great deal of responsibility is placed upon the authors of welfare reports, it is important that they should differentiate quite clearly between matters of which they have first-hand knowledge and matters which are merely hearsay or pure gossip, and also between statements of fact and expressions of opinion. In the English case of *Thompson v Thompson (1975)* 1986, the inexperienced welfare officer saw the mother only on two occasions, and relied on what he had been told as a result of extensive enquiries from at least twenty-one people outside the family to form an unfavourable opinion of the mother. The court said that it was "a classic example of the dangers of hearsay evidence – impossible to evaluate and impossible for the person concerned to refute". Whereas welfare reports must of necessity contain a certain amount of hearsay, a fact accepted by the courts, thanks to the judgement and discretion of welfare officers, it rarely leads to difficulty, "because care is taken to keep it to a minimum, and so far as possible to confine it to non-controversial matter".

Guardians *Ad Litem*

The 1991 Act enables the District Court to make major life decisions about children who are in need of care and protection, including a decision that a child be taken into care and the contact that is to take place between the child and his family. As these decisions will have far-reaching consequences for the child in question and his family, and can be painful and stressful for all involved, it is important that the child have independent representation. The principle of representation and participation in decision making, as reflected in Article 12 of the United Nations Convention on the Rights of the Child, requires the State to put in place a mechanism whereby the child's independent views on decisions affecting him is presented to the court. The provisions of the 1991 Act and the Children Act 1997, which allow for the appointment of a guardian *ad litem* for the child, are part of the State's response to its obligations under the Convention.

Where a child is not legally represented, section 26 of the 1991 Act enables the court to appoint a guardian *ad litem* to ensure that the child has the benefit of independent and impartial representation in care proceedings. A guardian *ad litem* may also be appointed in proceedings involving a child who is already in the care of a health board. Before appointing a guardian, the court must be satisfied that it is necessary in the interests of the child and in the interests of justice to do so. There is one significant drawback in the scheme, in that a guardian cannot be appointed where the child is already a party to the proceedings. Additionally, where a guardian has been appointed, that appointment is automatically terminated where the child is subsequently made a party to the proceedings. Usually, the guardian will be a social worker or other care professional, who is independent of all the parties involved. However, the courts have from time to time appointed personnel from the various voluntary organisations involved in child protection, as well as solicitors, psychiatrists and psychologists. The benefit of the guardian *ad litem* to the court lies in the independence of the role. The 1991 Act does not contain any guidelines as to the role of the guardian, nor has the matter been dealt with either in regulations or any other guidance document. In *Re M.H. and J.H., Oxfordshire County Council v J.H. and V.H.* 1988, Costello J said that the role of the guardian is to carry out an investigation of the child's circumstances and to advise the court on behalf of the child as to what should be done to promote his best interests.

In the absence of regulations and guidelines in this jurisdiction as to the role of the guardian *ad litem* in proceedings involving the welfare of a child, voluntary agencies such as Bernardos and the Irish Society for the Prevention of Cruelty to Children that operate guardian *ad litem* schemes have adopted the English model, as set out in the Children Act 1989 and regulations made giving effect to the statutory regime. The principal function of the guardian is to give the child such advice as is appropriate, having regard to his age and understanding, on all matters relevant to his interests in the proceedings. It is vital that the guardian should gain the confidence of the child, to the extent that the child is prepared to express freely his desires and wishes. In practice, the guardian will investigate all aspects of the child's life and family. This will usually involve conducting interviews with the child and other members of the child's extended family. Having concluded his investigations, the guardian will provide a report for the court.

This report of the guardian *ad litem* will inform the court of the wishes of the child, the options that are available to the court in respect of the child and the suitability of each of those options, including the appropriate order to be made. It is important that the guardian convey the child's exact thoughts and wishes to the court, even if the guardian disagrees with them. It is for the court alone to determine what weight should be given to the child's wishes. Where possible, the guardian should also strive to establish a good working relationship with the parents and the health board. In the majority of cases a guardian will support health board applications for care orders. However, information available from the Beacon Guardian *Ad Litem* Service operated by Bernardos makes it clear that the involvement of a guardian in care proceedings does not mean the unquestioned acceptance of health board plans. In many cases, guardians were instrumental in bringing about plans which were more specific and related to the child's needs. In some cases the involvement of a guardian instigated the process of care planning. A guardian should not compromise his independence by taking part in child protection, nor should he take part in a child protection conference except as an observer.

The general rule is that the report of the guardian *ad litem* is to be made available to all the parties to the proceedings. However, as the report when filed becomes a document held by the court, it attracts the usual confidentiality and must not be disclosed to a third party without the court's consent. *In Eastern Health Board v Fitness to Practice Committee of the Medical Council and Others* 1998, Barr J spoke of the confidentiality which documents used in *in camera* proceedings attract, and said that it would be a contempt of court to make these documents available to a third party without the leave of the court. As to the circumstances in which the court could authorise the disclosure of information contained in the report of a guardian *ad litem*, the judgment of Barr J suggests that a court could order disclosure if the interests of justice so required. Where disclosure is ordered, the court can attach such conditions to the order as it sees fit to protect the interests of the child concerned.

Also covered by the rule as to confidentiality is the information gathered by the guardian *ad litem* in the course of interviews and discussions with parents and other important persons in the child's life, for the purpose of reporting to the court. In *Oxfordshire County Council v P.* 1995, the English High Court ruled that the guardian *ad litem* had acted incorrectly in making a witness statement to the police without first having obtained the authorisation of the court. In the course of the statement, the guardian informed the police that a mother had admitted to her that she had caused injuries to her child by throwing him repeatedly onto a bed and possibly onto a wooden edge of a changing unit. According to Ward J, if the report of the guardian attracts confidentiality, "it must be a necessary inference" that the information collected by the guardian for the purpose of preparing his report must equally enjoy confidentiality.

It may be necessary for the court to terminate the appointment of a guardian *ad litem* before the conclusion of the proceedings. For example, the guardian may be unable to continue because of illness or a conflict of interest might arise. There will be occasions when the guardian will have to take action to protect the interests of the child, action of which the parties, and in particular the parents, are likely to disapprove. If a situation arises in which the guardian's relationship with the parties is likely to be adversely affected, it would be prudent and appropriate for the guardian to seek the guidance of the court. In *Re F. (A Minor)* 1997, the English Court of Appeal approved the decision of the trial judge to terminate the appointment of a guardian *ad litem* who had engaged a private investigator to satisfy himself that the mother of a child who was in the care of a local authority was living apart from the father, as she was required to by order of the court returning the child to her custody. Both the local authority and the father felt that the guardian had acted behind their backs. While not criticising the guardian's good faith or the end that he was seeking to achieve, which was more properly a step for the local authority to take if appropriate, the court held that "it was a step which in the circumstances resulted in the undermining of confidence and the diminution of the value of his contribution".

In *Re N. and L.* 2003, the Family Division of the High Court in Northern Ireland held that a guardian *ad litem* has the power to interview persons outside the jurisdiction. The children the subject of the proceedings were in care on foot of an interim care order, when the parents absconded with the children to Donegal. The guardian sought the leave of the court to visit the children outside Northern Ireland for the purpose of making appropriate investigations and to enable her prepare a report to the court advising on the interests of the children. In reaching its decision, the court said that if a child is to be denied direct access to the person who in fact is speaking for him at the trial, namely the guardian *ad litem*, "then a possible infringement of the child's rights", under both Article 12 of the United Nations Convention on the Rights of the Child and Article 6 of the European Court of Human Rights, could conceivably arise.

Legal Representation for the Child

A child does not automatically become a party to care proceedings under the 1991 Act. Under section 25 of the Act, it is a matter for the discretion of the court as to whether or not the child should be a party to the proceedings. The court has power to join the child as a party where it is satisfied, having regard to the age, understanding and wishes of the child and the circumstances of the case, that it is necessary in the interests of the child and in the interests of justice to do so. The child can be joined in the proceedings without the need to appoint a parent or other person as next friend to the child. Obviously, the concern of the court in any particular case will be to ensure that the interests of the child are properly represented. One way of ensuring this is to make the child a party to the proceedings with his own legal representation, if required. Where the court makes an order providing that the child is to be joined as a party to the proceedings, or where the child is already a party to those proceedings, the court may, if it thinks fit, appoint a solicitor to represent the child and give directions as to the performance of his duties. The costs and expenses of any solicitor so appointed shall be borne by the health board, unless the court directs that any other party to the proceedings should bear those costs. It is significant that prior to the coming into force of the 1991 Act there was no provision for separate representation for children, a situation described by O'Flaherty J in *M.F. v Superintendent Ballymun Garda Station* 1990 as "unique in that the fundamental rights of persons are in issue in litigation in which they are not represented".

A particular difficulty may arise in connection with legal representation where the child is too young to express independent views. Who should the solicitor look to for guidance in such an eventuality? The social worker involved in the case has a conflict of interest. The child's parent cannot offer impartial assistance or guidance, as very often the need for care proceedings in the first place stems from parental neglect, abandonment or abuse of the child. As the law presently stands, the solicitor cannot enlist the help of a guardian *ad litem* in obtaining the child's views. This is so, because an order joining the child as a party to the proceedings results in the termination of the appointment of the guardian *ad litem*. It is to be regretted that this state of affairs should exist, as obviously a great deal of trust will have been created between the guardian and the child. Bringing the relationship to an abrupt end may prove upsetting for the child. Obviously, this is a matter that the court will bear in mind when exercising its discretion as to whether the child should be granted legal representation. In particular, the court should ensure that the child is prepared for the severing of the relationship with the guardian, by explaining fully to him the wisdom of the decision to make him a party to the proceedings with separate legal representation.

Whether or not the child is a party to the proceedings, there is no need to bring the child before the court unless the court of its own motion, or on the application of any interested party, decides that this is necessary for the proper disposal of the case (section 30 of the 1991 Act). This provision is in accord with the views expressed by O'Flaherty J in *M.F. v Superintendent Ballymun Garda Station* 1990 that "a court is, prima facie, not a suitable environment" for a child in care proceedings. Where the child requests to be present in court during the proceedings or any part of them, the court shall accede to any such request unless it appears to the court that, having regard to the age of the child or the nature of the proceedings, it would not be in the child's best interests to do so. Although not specifically provided for, the inherent jurisdiction of the court in the proper conduct of the proceedings would enable it to take steps to remove the child, where the evidence and hostile environment of the courtroom might be injurious to the welfare of the child.

Conclusion

Bearing in mind that it will rarely be in the interests of a child to call him as a witness, the crucial question for the court is how can the child's own views become known. The court may interview the child for the purpose of ascertaining his views. However, recent judicial pronouncements indicate that interviewing a child is not the most desirable method of ascertaining a child's views, especially in the case of very young children. To avoid the necessity of having the child interviewed in open court or in chambers, all courts now have powers to call for independent reports on all matters relevant to the child's welfare. A report, whether from a court welfare officer or a guardian *ad litem*, should give straightforward information about the child and his family circumstances. A recommendation contained in such a report carries a great deal of weight, and there must be solid reasons for rejecting it.

CHAPTER 9

VOLUNTARY CARE AND HOMELESS CHILDREN

Introduction

In fulfilling its obligation under section 3 of the 1991 Act to promote the welfare of children in its area who are not receiving adequate care and protection, a health board has a number of options. Where there is a risk of substantial harm to the child if he remains in the custody of his parents, the health board should proceed to invoke the procedures of the 1991 Act that allow for the taking of a child into care on a non-voluntary basis. Alternatively, there may be a voluntary reception of the child into care under section 4 of the Act. However, where grounds for receiving the child into care do not exist, and it appears to a health board that a child is homeless, the board has a duty under section 5 of the Act to provide suitable accommodation for the child. The interplay between the sections is not clear, and in the absence of any statutory guidelines as to what course of action a health board should adopt, it would appear that the board has a fairly wide discretion in the matter. In practice, section 5 is designed to cater for adolescents rather than very young children, usually young people in the fifteen to eighteen age category, who need temporary accommodation as opposed to residential care. Crucial to the health board's deliberations in deciding what is appropriate for a particular child will be the fact that the board does not acquire parental responsibility for the child while providing him with accommodation under section 5.

Voluntary Care

Section 4 of the 1991 Act provides for the voluntary reception of children into care by health boards. It shall be the duty of a health board to take into care any child who resides in or is found in its area where it appears to the board that the child in question requires care or protection that he is unlikely to receive unless he is taken into care. It should be emphasised that the duty imposed on a health board extends not only to children who reside in its functional area, but also to children found in its area, regardless of where they reside. Before taking a child into voluntary care, the health board must be satisfied that the child in question requires "care or protection". Section

8(2) of the 1991 Act suggests certain criteria for determining whether a child is receiving care and protection, but the list is not exhaustive, and the health board retains considerable discretion in the matter. Included in the list are children whose parents are dead or missing; children whose parents have deserted or abandoned them; children who are homeless; children who are at risk of being neglected or ill-treated; and children whose parents are unable to care for them due to ill-health or for any other reason. Indeed, there appears to be no reason why a health board could not avail of section 4 to take a child into care at the request of a parent or the child.

As a prerequisite to invoking the power to take a child into voluntary care, a health board must inquire into the particular circumstances of the case to see if any of the criteria set out above are satisfied, always bearing in mind that the underlying philosophy of the 1991 Act is that children are best cared for by remaining within the family unit. There is no guidance as to the extent of the investigations to be carried out. Section 4 merely requires that the child "appears" to the health board to require care or protection that he is unlikely to receive unless he is taken into care. In this regard, the health board enjoys a considerable amount of discretion. Provided this discretion is used to promote the welfare of the child, and the board acts within its powers under the Act, any decision arrived at will not be reviewed by a court.

A child cannot be taken into voluntary care against the wishes of a parent having custody of the child or any person acting *in loco parentis*. Neither can a health board maintain a child in its care if the parent having custody or a person acting *in loco parentis* wishes to resume care of the child. It should be emphasised that it is only a parent who has custody of a child that can remove the child from voluntary care. For example, where legal custody has been granted to one parent in proceedings under the Guardianship of Infants Act 1964, as amended, the non-custodial parent cannot unilaterally remove the child from care. This is so, even if the non-custodial parent is deemed suitable by the health board to have care of the child, bearing in mind the principle that the welfare of the child is the first and paramount consideration. The health board might overcome this problem by placing the child with the non-custodial parent as a "foster parent" or "relative" within the meaning of section 36 of the 1991 Act. In this way, the health board could retain the overall control of the child and fulfil its statutory obligation to promote the welfare of the child without breaching the terms of section 4 of the 1991 Act.

The fact that a health board cannot maintain a child in its care against the wishes of a parent or person acting *in loco parentis* could prove problematic in practice, where a health board considers that the discharge of the child would be against the child's best interests. This eventuality is not covered by section 4 of the 1991 Act. Clearly, the health board should not return the child regardless of the fitness of the parent or person acting *in loco parentis* to have care of the child, or of any possible threat to the welfare of the child. Although the High Court held in *P.S. v Eastern Health Board* 1994 that no duty of care is imposed on a health board for breach of its functions under the 1991 Act, a health board could be held vicariously liable for the actions of an employee, such as a social worker or other care professional, in negligently releasing the child, against his best interests, into the care of a parent or other person (*X. v Bedfordshire County Council* 1995). Bearing this in mind, a health board would have to consider the possibility of applying for an emergency care order with a view eventually to taking the child into care on a permanent basis on foot of a care order, or make the child a ward of court. In *Southern Health Board v C.H.* 1996, the health board had a six-year old girl made a ward of court to prevent the father removing her from voluntary care on the grounds that the child alleged that the father had sexually abused her.

Whenever a child is taken into voluntary care, the health board has a duty to maintain him in its care for so long as his welfare requires it and while he remains a child. For so long as the child remains in care, the health board must take all the necessary steps to promote the child's welfare. In the provision of care, the health board must have regard to the wishes of a parent having custody of the child or of any other person acting *in loco parentis*. The child should also be consulted, and the care professional dealing with the case should give due weight to the views of the child in accordance with his age and maturity. Subject to these considerations, however, decisions as to how a child should be looked after while in care are a matter for the health board alone. The usual range of options, such as residential care and placement with foster parents or relatives, are available to the health board in discharging its duty to safeguard and promote the welfare of the child while he remains in care.

Where a child is taken into voluntary care because it appears that he is lost, that a parent having custody of him is missing or that he has been deserted or abandoned, the board must endeavour to reunite him with that parent where this appears to the board to be in the child's best interests (section 4(4) of the 1991 Act). The wording of the sub-section gives a health board considerable discretion on the question of rehabilitating a child with his family. A health board only has a duty to reunite a child with his parents where such a course is consistent with the child's welfare. Should a health board decide that rehabilitation with the family is not in a child's best interests, it should take the appropriate steps to obtain a care order, with a view to the child remaining in care in the long term. On the other hand, a health board might take the view that the child could be reunited with the parents in circumstances where the board would have the child visited periodically to satisfy itself as to his welfare and give advice to the parents. In these circumstances, the board should apply for a supervision order under section 19 of the 1991 Act.

Homeless Children

The Youth Homeless Strategy 2001 states that youth homelessness is different from adult homelessness in a number of ways. The key difference is that the vast majority of children under the age of eighteen have a place of residence from which to operate. This may be their home, or an alternative form of accommodation supplied by a health board or a voluntary agency. In essence, when a young person becomes homeless, it is because he can no longer operate from this base. The term "out of home" rather than homeless is sometimes used when referring to children who are homeless, as this takes cognisance of the fact that there is a place of residence available which has become, for whatever reason, a place where the young person feels that he can no longer live. Homelessness is more than lacking in material items; it is also a cause of mental distress characterised by insecurity and low self-esteem. The Report of the Forum on Youth Homelessness 2000 defines homelessness as including "young people who look for accommodation from the Eastern Health Board Out of Hours service" and "those in insecure accommodation with relatives or friends regarded as inappropriate, that is to say where the young person is placed at risk or where he or she is not in a position to remain".

It is significant that the National Children's Strategy 2000, in acknowledging that some children have additional needs to the basic needs of all children, provides that "children will have access to accommodation appropriate to their needs" (Paragraph 5.2). It identified the development of a national strategy on youth homelessness as a priority in addressing youth homelessness, and envisaged the adoption of a plan for addressing youth homelessness and stated that measures to eliminate youth homelessness will be fast-tracked. The Youth Homeless Strategy 2001 aims to achieve a more co-ordinated and planned approach to tackling the issue of youth homelessness. The Strategy places particular emphasis on prevention and on the importance of supporting schools, communities and the young people themselves and their families. Where a young person becomes homeless, the Strategy stresses the need for a prompt child-focused, high-quality service, which will address the individual needs of the young person. The primary goal of the Strategy is to reduce and, if possible, eliminate youth homelessness through preventative strategies and, where young people become homeless, to ensure that they benefit from a comprehensive range of services aimed at re-integrating them into their community as quickly as possible.

The Youth Homeless Strategy contains twelve key objectives under three broad categories, namely preventative measures, responsive services and planning and administrative supports. Following a consultation with relevant statutory and relevant bodies, each health board will be required, within three months of the publication of the Strategy, to develop a two-year strategic plan to address youth homelessness in line with specific actions. Other bodies in the public sector, including schools, the National Education Welfare Board, local authorities and the City and County Development boards, are required to either support the actions of the health boards or take specific steps themselves. At national level, given the cross-sectoral dimensions of youth homelessness, the National Children's Office will have responsibility for driving and co-ordinating the actions necessary to ensure the successful implementation of the Strategy.

Services for homeless children are generally provided as part of the child protection and welfare services of health boards. The obligation to provide suitable accommodation for homeless children is contained in section 5 of the 1991 Act. Section 8 of the Act includes homeless children among the categories of children to whom a health board owes a duty under section 3, as children who are not receiving adequate care and protection. In its report, "Out On Their Own: Young People Leaving Care in Ireland" 1998, Focus Ireland states that section 5 is weak and that there is a need for ministerial order to define clearly the rights of young homeless people to accommodation, and to strengthen the obligation on health boards to provide accommodation. Whether a child is homeless or not is a question of fact to be decided by a health board after carrying out an assessment of the needs of the child. Where it appears to a health board that a child in its area is homeless, the board shall inquire into the child's circumstances. If, as a result of such inquiry, the board is satisfied that there is no accommodation available which the child can reasonably occupy, then, unless the child is received into care under the provisions of the Act, the board shall take such steps as are reasonable to make suitable accommodation available to the child. While there is no specific requirement in section 5 that the wishes of the child be taken into account when considering whether he needs to be accommodated, it is in keeping with the requirement in section 3 that the child's views be ascertained, if he is able to express them. Clearly, in the case of a young person aged fifteen and over, the board would be remiss in not taking his views into account.

Although section 5 of the 1991 Act clearly envisages that a health board will inquire into the circumstances of each individual case to see if a child needs accommodation, no regulation is imposed as to the method or extent of the investigations that should be undertaken. At present, there is no code of treatment for homeless children being accommodated by health boards, unlike children who are accommodated under section 36 of the Act following their reception into care. This is so, as the health board does not acquire parental responsibility by providing accommodation. While the child's daily care is in the hands of the health board, the board can only make major decisions or continue to care for the child with the consent of a parent or guardian. In the absence of statutory guidelines, *Children First* contains guidance for health board personnel in dealing with homeless children. These suggest that where a health board considers a child to be homeless following a thorough investigation of the circumstances of the child and his parents, and the facts do not warrant the obtaining of an emergency care order or a voluntary reception of the child into care, and there appears to be no suitable accommodation for the child, then the board has a duty to provide the child with a place to stay that is suitable to his needs. The placement should be short term, pending the completion of a full assessment. In carrying out its investigation, the health board must contact the child's parents, where possible, with a view to obtaining their views. The child's views should also be obtained (Paragraph 10.3).

Section 5 of the 1991 Act is framed in terms of a duty rather than a discretion. However, the duty only arises "where it appears" to a health board that there is no accommodation available which a child can reasonably occupy, suggesting that there is a wide margin of discretion available to the board when discharging its duty. Provided the health board considers the best interests of the child, the wisdom or otherwise of its decision will not be reviewed by a court. Of course, where it is alleged that a health board is in breach of its duty to provide suitable accommodation, the duty can be enforced by an order of *mandamus* in judicial review proceedings. In *P.S. v Eastern Health Board* 1994, the applicant, a fourteen-year-old boy, had lived away from home for many years and had been homeless for long periods. He had severe behavioural problems and was out of control, requiring that he be detained in a secure unit for therapeutic treatment. Stating that "the purpose of the section was to ensure that accommodation would be given", the court held that the health board was in breach of section 5 for failing to provide any accommodation for a considerable period of time in the past. The court held that the then current accommodation of the boy in a house in Dublin under the supervision of a social worker could not be regarded as suitable accommodation, and that there was a statutory duty on the health board to find a suitable alternative which would provide "substitute parental training and education".

Conclusion

A great many admissions to voluntary care are for genuinely short-term reasons, the most common being short-term parental illness. Sometimes, there may have to be a more prolonged separation of parent and child, for example where a single parent is unwilling or unable to provide for a child. The essence of voluntary care is that parents can use the service secure in the knowledge that they do not run any greater risk of losing their children than they would if they had made private arrangements for the care of the children. Where grounds for receiving a child into voluntary care do not exist, but the child is homeless, a health board has a duty to provide suitable accommodation for the child. The child may in fact have a family home, but the circumstances in the home may be intolerable. Unfortunately, because of a shortage of proper accommodation, in many cases homeless children are placed in unsuitable accommodation, with the result that they return to a life on the streets, dependent for their well-being on the voluntary agencies that try to cope with the problem of homelessness generally.

CHAPTER 10

ADOPTION

Introduction

Adoption was permitted for the first time in this country by the Adoption Act 1952, a time when many attitudes and practices were very different to those that exist today. Since then there have been amending Acts in 1964, 1974, 1988, 1991 and 1998. The principal object of adoption is to provide a permanent, secure and loving home for the child whose natural parents are unable or unwilling to look after him themselves. Adoption is a very final decision, as it is a total severance of any ties the child has with the birth family. On the making of an adoption order the birth parents lose all legal rights over the child and are relieved from all duties towards the child. These rights and duties are transferred to the adoptive parents. The child is regarded in law as the child of the adoptive parents as if he were born to them in marriage. An adoption certificate is made out, and, in effect, the child begins a new life.

All applications for adoption are made to the Adoption Board (An Bord Uchtala), an independent statutory body set up under the Adoption Act 1952. The Board has the sole and exclusive power to make an adoption order. The Board consists of a chairperson and eight ordinary members appointed by the Government. The primary function of the Board is to grant or refuse applications for adoption orders in relation to Irish adoptions, to register and supervise the adoption societies and to grant declarations of eligibility and suitability in relation to foreign adoptions. While it has usually been presided over by a judge, the Board is not a court, and its membership includes a majority of persons who are not judges. No court has the power to make an adoption order. The High Court is given jurisdiction in respect of applications to dispense with parental consent under section 3 of the Adoption Act 1974, and to order the Adoption Board to make an order authorising the non-consensual adoption of a child under section 3 of the Adoption Act 1988. There are proposals presently under consideration for updating the provisions relating to the structure and functions of the Adoption Board.

The Provision of Adoption Services

Section 34 of the 1952 Act provides that only registered adoption societies and health boards are legally entitled to place children for adoption. This measure is designed to regulate adoption practice and prevent commercial trafficking in adoption, which might result from the fact that at any given time there are far more people wishing to adopt children than there are children available for adoption. This fact is starkly illustrated by statistics available from the Adoption Board, which show that in 2001 only 81 Irish children were available for adoption through the societies and health boards. In the same year the Board made orders recognising 179 foreign adoptions.

Section 6 of the Child Care Act 1991 requires a health board to provide an adoption service, either itself or through a registered adoption society. A health board may take a child into care with a view to adoption, but cannot maintain the child in care against the wishes of a parent or person acting in *loco parentis*. Where a child eligible for adoption is in the care of a health board, section 36 of the Child Care Act authorises the board to place the child with a suitable person with a view to adoption. While there may be some children in care who are eligible for adoption at any given time, a major cause for concern is the large number of children in care who are not eligible for adoption. In its Report, Adoption Law: the Case for Reform 2000, the Law Society referred to a sizeable reservoir of Irish children in long-term care or fostering arrangements who would benefit from living in a stable family environment. Some of these children have suffered such a high degree of neglect and abuse that they will not be able to safely return home. For others, their parents have many problems, often related to drug and alcohol addiction, which mean that despite repeated efforts to help them, it is simply not feasible for them to take on the commitment that parenting requires.

Eligibility Requirements for Adoption

Who May Adopt?

Section 10 of the Adoption Act 1991 provides that the following persons are eligible to apply to adopt a child:

(a) a married couple living together. This is the only situation in which the law permits the adoption of a child by more than one person,

(b) a married person may only adopt alone where the other spouse consents, unless (i) the spouses are living apart under a decree of judicial separation or a deed of separation, (ii) the other spouse has deserted the prospective adopter or (iii) the conduct of the other spouse has justified the prospective adopter leaving the family home and living apart (constructive desertion),

(c) the mother, father or relative of the child. A relative includes a grandparent, brother, sister, uncle or aunt of the child and/or the spouse of any such person, relationship to the child being traced through the mother or the father,

(d) a widow or widower,

(e) a sole applicant who does not come within the classes of persons defined at (c) and (d) above may only adopt where the Board is satisfied that, in the particular circumstances of the case, it is desirable to grant an adoption order,

(f) the law does not permit two unmarried persons to adopt jointly.

An applicant or applicants for adoption must be ordinarily resident in the State and have been so resident for at least a year before the date of the making of the adoption order. An applicant must have attained the age of twenty-one years. A married couple adopting a child to whom they are not related must both be at least twenty-one years of age. Where a married couple is adopting the child, and one of them is the father or mother or a relative of the child, only one of them must have attained the age of twenty-one years. The law does not lay down upper age limits for adopting parents. However, the Adoption Board points out that age is a significant factor when assessing a couple's suitability to adopt, and most adoption agencies apply their own upper age limits. Where the prospective adopter(s), the child and the birth parent(s) are not all of the same religion, section 4 of the Adoption Act 1974 provides that the birth parent(s) must know the religion, if any, of each of the adopting parents when giving consent to the child's adoption.

The suitability requirements for prospective adopter(s) are set out in section 13 of the 1952 Act. The Adoption Board cannot make an adoption order unless it is satisfied that each of the prospective adopters is a suitable person to have parental rights and duties. They must each be of good moral character and financially capable of looking after the child's temporal needs. The prospective adopter(s) should be chosen carefully and, as far as possible, "matched" with the child, thus minimising the risk that the placement will break down. In order to establish their suitability, a detailed assessment is carried out by social workers of the adoption agency dealing with the case. This process includes interviews and visits to their home. They will also have to undergo a medical examination.

If the prospective adopter(s) are accepted by the adoption agency and have a child placed with them, the next step is to apply to the Adoption Board for an adoption order. The Board operates a fairly rigorous vetting procedure. Applicant(s) for adoption will have to undergo a detailed assessment to establish their suitability as prospective adopter(s). In this regard, the Board's social workers will visit the applicant(s) home and interview them, and ultimately report to the Board on their suitability. When the Board is satisfied that an adoption is ready to be finalised, it will invite the applicant(s) to attend before it with the child for the hearing of their application. At the oral hearing the applicant(s) are asked certain questions on oath in order to establish their identity and eligibility to adopt. The other persons entitled to attend and be heard at the oral hearing are set out in section 5 of the Adoption Act 1998, and they include the mother of the child, the father of the child or the person who believes himself to be the father, any guardian or person who has control of the child, a representative of an adoption agency that has at any time been connected with the child, and any other person whom the Board decides to hear. If, following the oral hearing, the Board is satisfied as to the eligibility and suitability of the applicant(s) to adopt, it will make an adoption order in their favour

Who May Be Adopted?

Section 10 of the 1952 Act permits the adoption of orphans and children born outside marriage. A child born outside marriage, who is legitimated by the subsequent marriage of his birth parents, is eligible for adoption under section 2 of the Adoption Act 1964, provided his birth has not been re-registered. In exceptional cases, the High Court may make orders under section 3 of the 1988 Act authorising the adoption of both marital and non-marital children whose parents have failed in their duty towards them, in circumstances amounting to abandonment of parental rights. The child must be resident in the State, be at least six weeks old and under the age of eighteen years. The child need not have been born in the State. Where the child is over the age of seven years at the date of the application for adoption, the Adoption board must take his wishes into account, having regard to his age and level of understanding. The Board is not bound to agree with the child's wishes.

Placement for Adoption

Section 34 of the 1952 Act provides that it is unlawful for any body of persons to make arrangements for an adoption unless it is a registered adoption society or a health board. Section 7 of the 1998 Act permits a parent to place a child for adoption with a relative of the child. A relative is defined in section 2 of the 1998 Act as a grandparent, brother, sister, uncle, or aunt of the child, whether of the whole or half blood or through marriage, and includes the spouse of any such person, relationship being traced through the mother or father of the child. Section 7 of the 1998 Act also makes it unlawful for a person other than a relative to receive a child for the purpose of adoption otherwise than from an adoption agency. The main purpose of this provision is to ensure that the people who arrange adoptions and place children are suitably qualified and experienced and not just acting for profit. The case of *Eastern Health Board v E., A. and A.* 1999 vividly illustrates the scope for abuse of the system without proper regulation. The owners of a pregnancy counselling agency persuaded a twenty-one-year-old unmarried woman to place her new born child with them for adoption. In the course of *habeas corpus* proceedings brought by the health board, the High Court held that the placement was unlawful, as being in contravention of section 7 of the 1998 Act.

The natural father of a non-marital child must now be consulted in the adoption process. This improvement in the father's position is a result of the decision of the European Court of Human Rights in *Keegan v Ireland* 1994, which held that Ireland was in breach of Article 6 (the right to a fair hearing) and Article 8 (the right to family and private life) of the European Convention on Human Rights in allowing the applicant's child to be placed for adoption without his knowledge and without giving him a say in the adoption process. As a result of this judgment, the 1998 Act now provides a consultation procedure, thus ensuring that a concerned father has a say in a process that may result in him losing parental rights and duties in respect of his child. Section 7B of the 1952 Act (as inserted by section 4 of the 1998 Act) provides that a child under four weeks old may not be placed for adoption unless the father indicates beforehand that he has no objection to the placement, or the provisions of section 7F apply. The four-week period is designed to give the father an opportunity to apply to be appointed guardian by order of the court under section 6A of the Guardianship of Infants Act 1964. The placement must be postponed until the guardianship proceedings have been disposed of.

The circumstances in which the placement can go ahead without consulting the father are set out in section 7F of the 1952 Act. Consultation is not necessary where:

(a) the identity of the father is unknown to the agency arranging the placement, and the mother refuses to identify him,

(b) the agency is unable, after taking such steps as are reasonably practical, to contact the father whose identity is known to it,

(c) the nature of the relationship of the mother and father, or the circumstances of the conception are such that it would be inappropriate to contact the father, for example in the case of rape,

(d) the mother makes a statutory declaration to the effect that she does not know the identity of the father.

Agreement to Place Child for Adoption

Where the mother or guardian of a non-marital child proposes to place the child with an adoption agency for adoption, section 39 of the 1952 Act requires the agency to fully explain the effect of an adoption order to them and ensure that they understand same and sign a document to that effect. Invariably, in practice, it is the mother who contacts the agency with a request to arrange a placement. It is essential that the agreement to place the child is full, free and informed. The mother must have full knowledge of the consequences of the agreement to place the child for adoption. The circumstances must be such that neither the advice of the agency involved nor the circumstances in which the mother found herself as a result of her pregnancy deprived her of the capacity to make a fully informed free decision.

In *M. O'C. v Sacred Heart Adoption Society* 1996, the Supreme Court considered the requirements of a valid placement. The court held that the mother has a constitutional right to her child under Article 40 of the Constitution, although it is not essential that it be categorised as such when the effect of placement is being explained to her. The mother must be aware that the placement does not amount to an extinguishment of her rights to the child, which subsist right up to the time the adoption order is made. She must be aware of the two-stage nature of the adoption process, which involves her consent to placement in the first place, followed by her consent to the making of the adoption order. It must be explained to the mother that she can withdraw her consent to placement, or refuse to consent further to the adoption. However, it must be made clear to her that, on the application of prospective adopters, the court can dispense with her consent under section 3 of the 1974 Act where it is in the best interests of the child to do so.

Consent to Adoption Order

The two-stage nature of the adoption process requires the mother or guardian to consent to the making of an adoption order. The consent cannot be given until the child is at least six weeks old, and it can be withdrawn at any time before the adoption order is made. Because of the almost irrevocable effect of an adoption order, the consent must be given freely with a full understanding of what is involved. The consent must be unconditional. Thus, the mother cannot consent to her child being adopted on condition that she can continue to see him or be kept informed about his upbringing and well-being, or, as happened in the *State (McG.) v A.H. and M.H.* 1983, that the child be placed with prospective adopters outside the county in which she lived. In the case of the natural father, his consent will only be necessary where he is a guardian of the child. This is so as, unlike the mother, he has no automatic constitutional right to guardianship. He can apply to the court to be appointed joint guardian with the mother (section 6A of the Guardianship of Infants Act 1964), or he may become guardian without the need for a court application by agreement with the mother (section 4 of the Children Act 1997).

Dispensing with Consent

Section 14 of the 1952 Act requires the Adoption Board to obtain the consent of the mother or guardian before making an adoption order in respect of a non-marital child. The Board may dispense with the consent of any person whose consent is required if it is satisfied that that person is incapable by reason of mental infirmity of giving consent or cannot be found. The consent of a ward of court shall not be dispensed with except with the sanction of the court.

Section 3 of the 1974 Act empowers the High Court to dispense with the consent of any person whose consent is required to the making of an adoption order relating to a child and who has agreed to the placing of the child for adoption, where such person fails, neglects or refuses to consent or withdraws a consent already given. The court will only make an order dispensing with consent where it is in the best interests of the child to do so. The term "best interests" implies a consideration of long-term factors affecting the child's future in addition to matters which would affect the child's present welfare. In *G. v An Bord Uchtala* 1980, the Supreme Court held that, when considering an application under section 3 of the 1974 Act, the court must first decide whether the mother has agreed to place her child for adoption. It is only where it is found that that she has so agreed that the court can proceed to consider the question of the best interests of the child. Indeed, the vast majority of the cases have turned on the question as to whether the mother, in all the circumstances, did agree to place her child for adoption.

Where the natural mother's consent to place her child for adoption is subsequently withdrawn, at a time when arrangements have proceeded to the extent that the child has been living with the prospective adopters for some time and is happy with them, the court is faced with a difficult task in dealing with the competing interests of the mother and the prospective adopters. On the one hand, the court has to respect the mother's right to refuse or withdraw her consent to the adoption of her child. The court should only override such refusal or withdrawal where the particular circumstances of the case make it clear that it is necessary in the best interests of the child. The importance of the blood link between mother and child was recognised by the Supreme Court in *G. v An Bord Uchtala* 1980. However, where the child has formed a strong and loving bond with his adoptive parents and with members of their extended family, the probable and possible effects of the child being removed from the adoptive parents could be to cause him long-term psychological damage. In *J.B. and D.B. v An Bord Uchtala* 1998, McGuinness J said that the extent to which the child has bonded with the adoptive parents "must weigh heavily with the court". In reliance on the evidence of a very experienced psychiatrist that the removal of the child from his adoptive parents might cause him to suffer acute anxiety in the short-term and long-term psychological damage, the learned judge made an order under section 3 of the 1974 Act dispensing with the mother's consent.

As an adoption order is an interference by a public authority with the exercise of the right to respect for family life under Article 8 of the European Convention on Human Rights, the European Court of Human Rights held in *Silver v United Kingdom* 1983 that the interference must meet a pressing social need and be proportionate to that need. Clearly, the decision of a court to dispense with the consent of the natural mother is an interference with her

Article 8 rights. However, where the court decides that an adoption order is best for the child in all the circumstances, it is difficult to see how this can infringe the child's rights under Article 8. The balancing exercise required in considering the rights of the mother and child under Article 8 does not differ in substance from the like balancing Act undertaken by the court under section 3 of the 1974 Act when deciding whether adoption would be in the best interests of the child.

Involuntary Adoption

Prior to the enactment of the Adoption Act 1988 only non-marital or orphaned children could be adopted. The children of married parents who formed part of families whose rights arose under Articles 41 and 42 of the Constitution could never be adopted, even in cases where they had been left in the care of foster parents for many years and where there was little or no likelihood that they would ever return to the care of their parents. Other children who had been for a long period in the care of foster parents could not be adopted because their unmarried parents had never agreed to place them for adoption in the first place. In *Northern Area Health Board v An Bord Uchtala* 2003, McGuinness J said "it was with a view to curing this mischief that the Oireachtas enacted the 1988 Act". The Act extends the categories of children who may be legally adopted to marital children and non-marital children who have not been placed for adoption. Such children may now be adopted in very restricted and exceptional circumstances, where their parents for physical or moral reasons have failed in their duty towards them and such failure amounts to an abandonment of parental rights.

Under section 3 of the 1988 Act, on an application made to it by or on behalf of the persons in whose favour the Adoption Board has made a declaration under section 2 of the Act that it would be proper to make an adoption order, the High Court can make an order authorising the Adoption Board to make an adoption order where it is satisfied:

(1) that–
   (a) for a continuous period of not less than twelve months immediately preceding the time of the making of the application, the parents of the child, for physical or moral reasons, have failed in their duty towards the child,
   (b) it is likely that such failure will continue without interruption until the child attains the age of eighteen years,
   (c) such failure constitutes an abandonment on the part of the parents of all parental rights, whether under the Constitution or otherwise with respect to the child, and
   (d) by reason of such failure, the State, as guardian of the common good, should supply the place of parents;

(2) that the child–
  (a) at the time of the making of the application, is in the custody of, and has a home with the applicants, and
  (b) for a continuous period of not less than twelve months immediately preceding that time, has been in the custody of and has a home with the applicants; and

(3) that the adoption of the child by the applicants is an appropriate means by which to supply the place of the parents, the court may, if it so thinks fit and is satisfied, having had due regard for the rights, whether under the Constitution or otherwise, of the persons concerned (including the natural and imprescriptible rights of the child), that it would be in the best interests of the child to do so, make an order authorising the Board to make an adoption order in relation to the child in favour of the applicants.

In considering any application made to it under section 3 of the 1988 Act, the court shall, in so far as is practicable, give due consideration, having regard to his age and understanding, to the wishes of the child concerned. In *Northern Area Health Board v An Bord Uchtala*, the Supreme Court approved the decision of the trial judge to interview the twelve-year-old girl the subject of the proceedings informally in chambers in the presence of the court stenographer and two solicitors. The judge did not ask the child to take an oath. He found her to be "a happy, intelligent and open child" giving no discernible indication of any physical disability or speech or learning impairment resulting from her cerebral palsy. He was satisfied that the court should attach considerable weight to her wishes "having regard to her age and to her degree of understanding in this matter".

Section 4 of the 1988 Act obliges the court to hear the parents of the child and any other person who, in the opinion of the court, ought to be heard by it. Where the parents fail or refuse to give evidence at the hearing, having been requested by the court to do so, the court may make an order despite the absence of the evidence of the parents. Where the identity of the parents is not known to the applicants or to the Adoption Board, and all appropriate measures have been taken to identify them, or where their whereabouts are not known at the time of the making of the application or during the twelve months immediately preceding that time, and all appropriate measures have been made to ascertain those whereabouts, the court may make an order notwithstanding the absence of their evidence. In *Northern Area Health Board v An Bord Uchtala*, the Supreme Court was satisfied that the High Court had fulfilled the requirement of seeking and hearing the evidence of the parents of the child the subject of the proceedings. The court heard the evidence of the mother of the child but did not deem it necessary to consider the natural father further, being satisfied on the evidence that he had never acknowledged the child as his daughter. The father did not appear in the proceedings before the Adoption Board or the court, despite being informed in advance.

Abandonment of Parental Rights

Before making an order under section 3 of the 1988 Act the court must be satisfied that there has been a failure of parental duty, for physical or moral reasons, in circumstances amounting to abandonment of all parental rights. In *Re Adoption (No. 2) Bill* 1987 (1989), the Supreme Court held that the failure of parental duty must be total in character, and "no mere inadequacy of standard in the discharge of parental duty" would suffice to establish a failure of duty. The failure must arise for physical or moral reasons, and need not necessarily in every case be blameworthy. A failure "due to externally originating circumstances such as poverty" would not constitute a failure within the meaning of section 3. The failure of parental duty must be such as to constitute an abandonment of all parental rights. The mere failure of parental duty is not of itself evidence of abandonment. Abandonment could be established by evidence of the conduct of the parent or parents concerned. A mere statement by a parent or parents that they wish to abandon a child would not necessarily constitute proof in a particular case of the fact of abandonment, but may do so. The Supreme Court held in *Northern Area Health Board v An Bord Uchtala* that "physical reasons", as a cause of failure of parental duty, includes both physical and mental disability.

In *Southern Health Board v An Bord Uchtala* 2000, the Supreme Court said that the word "abandonment" is used in section 3 as "a special legal term". The section does not require that there be an intention to abandon. While there may be cases under section 3 where there is simple abandonment of a child and an intention to abandon the child, these are not the only circumstances where the section may be applied. Denham J said that the word "abandon" has a special legal meaning, and can be used "where, by their actions, parents have failed in their duty so as to enable a court to deem that their failure constitutes an abandonment of parental rights". The evidence in the case established that, while in the custody of his parents, the child had suffered fractures to his left arm, which were not of recent origin, and had bruising all over his body. A doctor who examined the child on his admission to hospital was of the opinion that the injuries were non-accidental. There was psychiatric evidence that the child was suffering from post-traumatic stress disorder, and the psychiatrist was of the view that the child should not be exposed to his parents until his late teens or early twenties, and then only if he wished to see them. The High Court was satisfied that the parents had failed in their duty to the child in circumstances amounting to abandonment of all parental rights.

The fact that a parent has played little or no part in the upbringing of a child may or may not, in the circumstances of a particular case, be evidence of failure of parental duty amounting to an abandonment of all parental rights. In *Western Health Board v An Bord Uchtala* 1996, the parents of the child were husband and wife, but separated because the wife was having an affair with another man. Subsequently, the husband had intercourse with his wife without her consent and a child was conceived. The separated father in the case played no part whatever in the upbringing of his child. However, he was unaware during that period, apart from a lingering suspicion, that the child was his. When he realised following a paternity test that the child was his, he took positive action to assert his right to custody of the child by issuing proceedings under the Guardianship of Infants Act 1964. Throughout the hearing of the case he asserted that his aim was to regain custody of his child. The application for an order under section 3 of the 1988 Act was dismissed by the High Court on the basis that, while it was established that the father had failed in his duty towards his child, and that such failure would continue until the child attained the age of eighteen years, the court was not satisfied that he had abandoned his parental rights. On appeal, the Supreme Court upheld the decision of the High Court.

However, in *Northern Area Health Board v An Bord Uchtala*, the fact that the natural mother of a non-marital child had played virtually no part whatsoever in the upbringing of her child was crucial to the court deciding that her failure of parental duty amounted to an abandonment of all parental rights. McGuinness J distinguished the *Western Health Board v An Bord Uchtala* case from the case at hearing, as the mother had agreed to the continuing care of her daughter by her foster parents over virtually the child's entire life to date. The mother was happy that this situation should continue. She had allowed and willingly continued to allow her daughter to become a member of the family of the foster parents. "She has, in my view, abandoned the custody and care of her daughter to Mr and Mrs H". Referring to the fact that the mother would continue to leave to the foster parents the crucial decisions regarding the child's health and education and the carrying into effect of those decisions, together with the "by no means insubstantial costs that arise from them", McGuinness J was of the view that "this situation amounts in a real and objective sense to abandonment of her rights as a parent". The learned judge was also of the view that the infrequent visits by the mother to her daughter, largely initiated by others, "are not inconsistent with the reality of her abandonment of her position as a parent".

Access to Birth Records of Adopted Persons

Every person born in this country has a birth certificate, which gives the name(s) of his parent(s), as well as other details such as when and where he was born. When an adoption order is made, an entry is made in the Adopted Children Register showing the adopters as the parents of the child. The Registrar of Births issues an adoption certificate which takes the place of the child's birth certificate. The Registrar is obliged to maintain a cross-referencing index, so that the connection between each entry in the Adopted Children Register and the corresponding entry in the Register of Births can be traced, if required. The index is not open to public inspection, and no information from the index can be given to any person without the consent of the Adoption Board (section 22 of the 1952 Act). Under section 8 of the Adoption Act 1976, the court may order the release of information from the index where it is in the best interests of the child in question.

Even at the present time, a culture of secrecy surrounds the whole adoption process in this country. The long-standing practice of anonymity in adoption proceedings must be related back to a time, in the not-too-distant past, when the stigma of an unwanted pregnancy outside marriage forced many young mothers to place their children for adoption. They did so on the strict understanding, and with the necessary assurances from adoption agencies, that their identity would never be revealed. The arguments in favour of anonymity were compelling, as any revelation of identifying information might compromise the natural parent(s) relationships with existing spouses and partners. Mindful of the huge sensitivities involved in legislating for the release of identifying information which might enable adopted persons to establish contact with birth parents, and *vice versa*, in recent years there has been an emerging trend of openness in adoption practice. In *Northern Area Health Board v An Bord Uchtala*, McGuinness J said that "the old insistence on secrecy and a complete exclusion of the natural mother" had virtually gone, and it is not uncommon for adopted children to continue to meet their birth parents from time to time.

Following on from a comprehensive consultation process conducted by the Department of Health and Children with all those persons and bodies most closely involved in the adoption process, the Minister for Children published proposals for an Adoption Information and Post-Adoption Contact Bill. The Bill provides for a structured system of search and reunion, which will enable adopted persons to have access to their birth records and, perhaps, trace their birth parents. A State-funded tracing and reunion service, available to adopted persons and birth parents, will be set up under the Bill. A National Search Service, operated by a newly constituted Adoption Board will help to speed up tracing queries. A national Files index, managed by the Adoption Board, will ensure that there is speedy access to personal information.

In the case of adoptions since the enactment of the Adoption Act 1952, the Bill proposes that an adopted person, on reaching the age of eighteen, will have a right to a birth certificate and personal information from the file maintained in respect of him. A birth parent will have the right to an adoption certificate when an adopted person reaches the age of eighteen. In the case of adoptions that take place after the proposed legislation takes effect, an adopted person, from the age of eighteen, will have the right to his birth certificate, personal information from files and relevant information about birth parents. A birth parent will have the right to information about the child's progress and well-being while the child is under eighteen, and the adoption certificate when the child reaches eighteen. An adoptive parent will have the right to non-identifying information on matters such as medical and family background while the child is under eighteen.

A Voluntary Contact Register will be established and operated by a reconstituted Adoption Board. Any party seeking contact with another can place his name on the contact register and he will be assisted with reunion. Any contact has to be made through the placement agency. As contact and reunion can be a very difficult and stressful process, counselling will be available to both adopted people and birth parents, if they wish. A Contact Veto Register will be established so that people who do not want to be contacted can register that wish. Any attempt to make contact without consent will attract a sanction.

Intercountry Adoption

Prior to the enactment of the Adoption Act 1991, intercountry adoption was not regulated by statute in this country. The 1991 Act, as amended by the Adoption Act 1998, deals almost exclusively with the recognition of foreign adoption orders and procedures to be followed by Irish adopters. It provides that the Adoption Board will approve prospective adopters of foreign children and issue declarations of eligibility and suitability in advance of their adopting overseas. In effect, it gives applicants the statutory right of assessment, to be carried out by a health board or registered adoption society, as to suitability and eligibility (section 8). The 1991 Act also makes provision for a child adopted abroad to be registered on a Register of Foreign Adoptions (section 6). Provided certain requirements as to domicile (section 2), habitual residence (section 3) or ordinary residence (section 4) are met, foreign adoptions coming within the definition of a "foreign adoption" in section 1 of the 1991 Act, as amended by section 10 of the 1998 Act, are to have the same effect as adoption orders made under Irish Law. To come within the terms of the definition, the child must be under eighteen years of age; the adoption must have been effected in accordance with the law of the foreign country, and the necessary consents or dispensations must have been obtained; the adoption must have substantially the same effect as an adoption order made by the Adoption Board; the adoption must have been effected for the purpose of promoting the interests and welfare of the child; no payment, other than reasonable expenses, must have been made by the adopters.

Irish legislation and policy making in intercountry adoption is bound by two international conventions, the United Nations Convention on the Rights of the Child (UNCRC) and the Hague Convention on the Protection of Children and Co-operation in respect of Intercountry Adoption 1993. Ireland ratified the UNCRC in 1992. Legislation is being prepared at present so that the Hague Convention can become part of domestic law. The Hague Convention can be seen as a companion instrument to the UNCRC, fleshing out the bare bones of Article 21(c) of the UNCRC, which requires that ratifying states "ensure that the child concerned by intercountry adoption enjoys safeguards and standards equivalent to those existing in the case of national adoption". Under both the UNCRC (Article 22) and the Hague Convention (Preamble and Article 4), intercountry adoption is to be a last resort where a suitable placement cannot be found in the state of origin.

The Hague Convention has brought regulation to an area rife with abuses. The purpose of the Hague Convention is to regulate and control intercountry adoption and prevent trafficking in children. It sets up a Central Authority in each State to be responsible for handling intercountry adoptions. Under the Hague Convention, the Central Authority plays a key role in protecting children who are involved in intercountry adoption. Central Authorities are responsible for establishing the adoptability of children, matching children with prospective adoptive parents, ensuring that the adoption is legally and procedurally valid, ensuring that the consent of birth parents has been given and that the prospective adopters have been approved in their own country. Article 32 of the Hague Convention forbids improper financial gain and allows only costs and expenses to be paid. Article 8 places responsibility on Central Authorities to ban improper gain.

Conclusion

Adoption law and practice have come a long way since 1952, when the stereotype of the unmarried mother giving her baby to childless strangers may have applied. Indeed, adoption was at one stage the only option for many young women because of society's attitude to children born outside marriage. Important developments in adoption law and practice have meant that marital children may now be adopted in restricted circumstances, and persons who want to adopt foreign children can have such adoptions recognised by the State. However, in order to truly reflect the growing trend towards openness in the modern adoption system, there is a need to put in place a structured system for search and reunion to meet the growing pressure from adopted persons to have access to information about their birth family. The proposed Bill on adoption information and post-adoption contact will lead to a new, modern, open adoption system.

CHAPTER 11

ENFORCEMENT OF DUTIES OF HEALTH BOARD

Introduction

In general, where a statute confers a discretion upon an administrative body (such as a health board), the court has power to, but will not, review the exercise of that discretion, on the grounds that the Oireachtas has conferred the discretion on the administrative body and not upon the court. In entrusting health boards with child care and child protection functions under the 1991 Act, the Oireachtas has marked out an area in which, subject to the enacted limitations and safeguards, decisions for the child's welfare are removed from the parents and from supervision by the courts. The court will interfere, however, if a health board can be shown to be acting outside its statutory powers, or can be shown not to be exercising those powers in good faith, or to have been exercising its discretion improperly.

Judicial Review

Judicial review is a process by means of which an aggrieved person can seek relief against decisions made by public bodies in exercise of the powers conferred on them by statute. Judicial review, as the words imply, is not an appeal from a decision but a review of the manner in which the decision was made. It should not be seen as a substitute for an action for damages, nor is it a substitute for a general complaints procedure or an enquiry. The scope for challenging decisions made by public bodies by way of judicial review proceedings is confined to those cases where reliance can be placed on want of jurisdiction, or excess of jurisdiction. There must be some departure from fair procedures or natural justice, or some error of law apparent on the face of the record, in arriving at the decision.

Should the members of a child's family wish to formally challenge the decisions of a health board on any matter relating to the statutory function of the board, they can do so by means of judicial review. In the case of a complaint against a health board, the complainant is required to show that the decision of the board is flawed on account of some error of law or some procedural failure. The High Court, as part of its supervisory jurisdiction, can review the procedures operated by a health board in discharging its parental role towards children in care under the 1991 Act. In general, the courts will not review the exercise of a discretionary power conferred on an administrative body by statute. In *A. v Liverpool City Council* 1982, the House of Lords held that a court has no general power to review decisions made by a local authority as to the welfare of a child in its care. The House of Lords did, however, recognise that there are exceptions to the general rule, where the court could intervene to see whether the local authority had contravened the law by acting in excess of the powers (*ultra vires*) that parliament had conferred on it. The court could also intervene where the local authority was not acting in good faith or was exercising its discretion improperly. The process of judicial review takes the form of the High Court making orders of *certiorari, mandamus* and *prohibition.*

Certiorari

Certiorari is frequently invoked where a court or other public body has not applied principles of natural justice and fair procedures, or where there is bias in the decision-making process. An order of *certiorari* has the effect of quashing any decision of an inferior court or public body made in excess of jurisdiction. In *Eastern Health Board v McDonnell* 2000, the health board alleged that the District Court had acted *ultra vires* in imposing conditions that restricted the operation of the board in caring for a child in its care. In refusing an application for *certiorari*, McCracken J held that it was the function of the courts and not of health boards to ensure that the constitutional rights of children in care were vindicated. Similarly, in *Donnelly v Ireland* 1998, the Supreme Court upheld the decision of the trial judge to refuse to quash the conviction and imprisonment of the applicant for the sexual assault of a fourteen-year-old girl. The court held that the procedures set out in the Criminal Evidence Act 1992 regulating the giving of evidence by means of video link were constitutional.

Mandamus

A person or body can be compelled to carry out a constitutional or legal duty by an order of *mandamus*. The power of the courts to review the exercise by a health board of its statutory function under the 1991 Act was considered by the High Court in *P.S. v The Eastern Health Board* 1994. The case involved the obligations of the board to promote the welfare of a homeless child under section 3 of the 1991 Act, and to provide suitable accommodation for him under section 5 of the Act. The court held that any breach by the board of its obligations under the Act could be remedied by judicial review. Although no express remedy is given in the Act, "it is perfectly clear that the duty under section 5 would be enforceable by *mandamus*". In *F.N. v Minister for Education* 1995, the High Court held that the State has a constitutional duty to provide secure accommodation for the special needs of a child in urgent need of special treatment which could be enforced by an order of *mandamus*.

Prohibition

An order of *prohibition* prevents a court or other body or person exercising a power that it does not possess. In the *State (Williams) v Kelleher* 1983, an order of prohibition made against a District Judge prevented the continuance of the preliminary investigation of an indictable offence because the proper documents had not been served on the accused before the investigation.

Procedure

Order 84 of the Rules of the Superior Courts 1986 sets out the procedure involved in judicial review proceedings. The prior leave of the court is a prerequisite to bringing an application for judicial review. This is meant to ensure that frivolous applications are not allowed to proceed. The court may not grant leave to apply unless it is satisfied that the applicant has *locus standi,* i.e. a sufficient interest in the matter the subject of the application. An application for leave to apply must be made by motion *ex parte* (without notice to the respondent) in the High Court. The notice of motion must give details of the relief sought and the grounds on which it is being sought, and must be supported by a verifying affidavit. Where leave to apply is granted, a copy of the order is served on the respondent. The respondent must file in the Central Office of the High Court a statement, verified by affidavit, setting out the grounds for opposing the application. The remedies are interchangeable, with the result that there is no longer any need for the applicant for judicial review to state exactly the type of order sought. It is sufficient to apply for judicial review. If the application is successful, the court will grant the appropriate order of *certiorari, mandamus* or *prohibition.*

Liability of Health Board in Damages

Breach of Statutory Duty

Where a statute imposes a statutory duty on a public authority, it usually confers discretion on the authority as to the extent to which, and the methods by which, such statutory duty is to be performed. In general, a public authority cannot be liable in damages for doing that which Parliament has authorised. There can be no liability in negligence, where the decisions of a public authority fall within the ambit of the statutory discretion, even if the authority has to choose between several alternatives open to it. In this regard, the wording of section 3(1) of the 1991 Act, which requires a health board "to promote the welfare of children in its area who are not receiving adequate care and protection", would indicate that a health board enjoys a wide area of discretion in discharging its statutory function. There are other remedies, by way of judicial review, or through extra judicial routes such as the Ombudsman for Children, available to those persons who may feel aggrieved by the decision of a health board to take a child into care.

The House of Lords held in *X. (Minors) v Bedfordshire County Council* 1995 that legislation designed to enable a local authority to carry out a statutory child protection function does not confer a remedy in damages for breach of statutory duty. In *Barret v London Borough of Enfield* 1999, the House of Lords was of the view that social workers and other professionals dealing with child abuse and neglect cases on behalf of a local authority would be inhibited in the proper performance of their primary functions for the benefit of society as a whole "if they are required to look over their shoulder to avoid liability in negligence". In *P.S. v The Eastern Health Board* 1994, the High Court considered the liability of the health board in damages under section 5 of the 1991 Act for its failure to provide suitable accommodation for a fourteen-year-old boy who was homeless. The court held that the purpose of section 5, which places a statutory duty on a health board to provide accommodation for homeless children, was to ensure that accommodation would be provided and not that compensation would be paid for a failure to provide accommodation.

Despite the generous degree of discretion afforded to public bodies, such as health boards, in the exercise of their statutory functions, there can be no question of such bodies enjoying blanket immunity from action for breaches in respect of the performance of their public duties. The European Court of Human Rights held in *Osman v United Kingdom* 1998 that any rule or principle of law that would exclude all claims against a public authority (in that case the police) for the negligent exercise of its powers would fall foul of Article 6 of the European Convention on Human Rights, which provides for the right to a fair hearing. In the context of a health board exercising its child protection functions under the 1991 Act, the court held in *Z. and Others v United Kingdom* 2001 and *T.P. and K.M. v United Kingdom* 2001 that no such immunity existed in relation to a local authority exercising its child care and child protection functions.

Common Law Duty of Care

Despite the generous degree of discretion afforded to a health board in the exercise of its child protection function, there are circumstances where a health board can be held liable at common law for the negligent exercise of its statutory discretion. Where the decision complained of is so unreasonable that it falls outside the discretion conferred by the statute, the common law liability should not be excluded. If the public authority exceeds its powers, the authority is not exercising a statutory power, but purporting to do so and the statute is no defence. In *Barrett v London Borough of Enfield,* above, the defendant council took the plaintiff into care when he was ten months old, where he remained until he was seventeen years old. The plaintiff alleged that the council was in breach of a common law duty of care owed to him, as a result of which he suffered deep-seated psychiatric problems caused by the defendant's negligence. In the course of his judgment, Hutton LJ said that when the decisions taken by a local authority in respect of a child in its care are alleged to constitute negligence at common law, the trial judge, bearing in mind the room for differences of opinion as to the best course to adopt in a difficult field, and that the discretion is to be exercised by the authority and its social workers and not by the court, "must be satisfied that the conduct complained of went beyond mere errors of judgment in the exercise of a discretion and constituted conduct which can be regarded as negligent".

Vicarious Liability of Health Board

Vicarious or indirect liability arises in situations where an employer or principal may be liable for the negligence of an employee or agent acting in the ordinary course of employment. As to whether an employee is acting in the ordinary course of his employment, the test is whether there is a sufficient connection between the work he was employed to do and the wrongful acts complained of. In *Delahunty v South Eastern Health Board and Others* 2003, a housemaster in an industrial school sexually assaulted the plaintiff who was visiting a friend in the school. At the time of the assault, the plaintiff was a twelve-year-old boy. The High Court held that there was not a sufficiently close connection between the employment of the employee as a housemaster in an industrial school and the assault on the plaintiff as to fix liability on his employers. The plaintiff had been a visitor in respect of whom the housemaster had no duties. Where a person is employed by a health board to carry out professional services as part of the fulfilment of the board's statutory duty, there is no overriding reason in principle why that person should not owe a duty of care and why, if the duty of care is broken by that person, the board as principal should not be vicariously liable. The health board will be vicariously liable if the existence of a duty of care does not conflict with the proper exercise by the board of its statutory powers and discretions. In *X. v Bedfordshire County Council,* above, the House of Lords, while recognising that those engaged in the provision of child care services should not be hampered by the imposition of such a vicarious liability, held that a local authority may be vicariously liable for the negligence of its employees or agents in discharging its duties under child care legislation.

In *Phelps v The London Borough of Hillingdon* 2000, an educational psychologist employed by the local authority had failed to appreciate or assess the child's learning difficulties and her dyslexia. The House of Lords held that if a breach of the duty of care to the child by such an employee is established, *prima facie* a local or education authority is vicariously liable for the negligence of its employee. The court was "very conscious of the need to be cautious in recognising such a duty of care where so much is discretionary in these as in other areas of social policy". While it was important that those engaged in the provision of educational services under statute "should not be hampered by the imposition of such a vicarious liability", the recognition of the existence of the duty of care does not necessarily lead, nor is it likely to lead, to that result. Nor does the recognition of the existence of a duty of care of itself impose unreasonably high standards. There is no negligence if the professional in question "exercises the ordinary skill of an ordinary competent man exercising that particular art".

Damages for 'Nervous Shock'

Where a child in the care of a health board suffers psychiatric injury as a result of being abused in residential care or while being cared for by foster carers or relatives, the health board may incur liability in damages for nervous shock or psychiatric illness, which is reasonably foreseeable. In *Curran v Cadbury (Ireland) Ltd* 2000, McMahon J, in the Circuit Court, having carried out an extensive review of the authorities in the matter, held that a defendant might be liable for damages for nervous shock if the plaintiff is within the range of persons who is likely to be affected by the defendant's actions or omissions, and to whom a duty is owed, and it is reasonably foreseeable that failure to take care on the part of the defendant will result in psychiatric illness. Moreover, liability will arise in circumstances where no physical injury results from the lack of care.

However, the duty to compensate for nervous shock in negligence cases only extends to recognised psychiatric illnesses, such as post-traumatic stress disorder (*Mullally v Bus Eireann* 1992). Compensation is not available for general grief or sorrow, or for a condition which is brought about over a period of time, for example the wear and tear which caring parents might suffer if they have to look after a child severely injured in an accident. Of course, in some cases it will be difficult to distinguish between acute grief and psychiatric injury. In *Alcock v Chief Constable of South Yorkshire* 1992, the House of Lords defined shock as the "sudden appreciation by sight or sound of a horrifying event, which violently agitates the mind". The person claiming must have seen or heard the incident or come across it in the immediate aftermath. It does not include psychiatric illness caused by the accumulation over a period of more gradual attacks of the nervous system.

Whereas, *Curran v Cadbury (Ireland) Ltd* involved a claimant who was directly involved in the accident, two earlier Irish decisions involved claimants not directly involved. In both *Mullaly v Bus Eireann* 1992 and *Kelly v Hennessy*

1995, persons who were not directly involved in the accident claimed damages for psychiatric illness they suffered from witnessing horrific scenes in the immediate aftermath of the accident. Understandably, in the 'immediate aftermath' cases there may be policy reasons put forward which might prevent the plaintiff from recovering. Typically, such policy reasons might include 'floodgate' fears (the possibility of encouraging time-wasting claims), evidentiary problems of proving psychiatric illness and the possibility of fraud. If there are no policy reasons operating against the plaintiff, liability must follow. As to the possible liability of a health board for psychiatric injury suffered by a child in its care or an aftermath victim, such as a parent or a foster parent or relative with whom a child has been placed, see the decision of the House of Lords in *W. v Essex County Council and Another* 2000.

Conclusion

The general nature of the duties imposed on health boards by the 1991 Act, in the context of a national system of child care and protection, and the remedies available by way of appeal and judicial review, indicate that the Oireachtas did not intend to create a remedy by way of damages for breach of statutory duty. The 1991 Act is concerned with conferring discretionary powers of administrative duties in the area of social welfare, where damages have not normally been awarded in cases of breach of statutory duty. However, a health board may incur liability for breach of a common law duty of care where it acts in a manner that is unreasonable and outside the scope of the discretion conferred on it by statute.

CHAPTER 12

RECORD KEEPING, CONFIDENTIALITY AND SHARING INFORMATION

Introduction

The primary responsibility for safeguarding children rests with their parents. However, where parents cannot ensure that their children are safe from danger in the home and free from risk from others, it may be necessary for statutory agencies to intervene to ensure that children are adequately protected. Safeguarding children depends upon effective information sharing, collaboration and understanding between families, agencies and professionals. For this reason, it is essential that all agencies involved in child protection maintain accurate records and share and help to analyse information, so that informed assessments can be made of each child's circumstances.

The Keeping of Records

Accurate records of the reporting and investigation of suspected cases of child abuse are an essential component of an effective child protection system. Records should be clear, use straightforward language and be concise and accurate. They should clearly differentiate between facts, opinion, judgements and hypothesis. Well-kept records are essential to good child protection practice. Records should be contemporaneous, and should include details of contacts, consultations and any actions taken. The importance of a "central recording system which could have collated and highlighted the repeated injuries and raised suspicions as to their non-accidental nature" was highlighted in the Report of the Kilkenny Incest Investigation.

The necessity to maintain accurate records was also highlighted in *M.Q. v Gleeson and Others* 1997. Barr J said that a health board, as part of its child protection function, is entitled to keep records of allegations of child abuse, whether substantiated or not, and, indeed, has an obligation to do so in the interests of professional competence. The only exception would be where, on investigation, an allegation is found to be positively false. However, where records are kept, they must accurately record all complaints received. Where a complaint has been made which after reasonable investigation has been found to be false, the fact that a false allegation has been made should be recorded, but the name of the alleged abuser should not appear. The board's assessment of the weight it attaches to each allegation of child abuse should be stated and should be objectively based. In serious cases, the complaint should be put to the alleged abuser in the course of the investigation and he should be given an opportunity to respond to it. An exception may arise where the board official dealing with the case "has a reasonable concern that to do so might put the child in question in further jeopardy".

Children First offers advice on the handling of information stored electronically. The Data Protection Acts 1988–2003 should be adhered to at all times in the keeping of records. The Acts apply to the automatic processing of personal data. The Acts give the right to individuals to establish the existence of personal data relating to them and to have inaccurate data rectified or erased. Data controllers are obliged to ensure that personal data kept by them are processed fairly, accurate and up to date, kept for lawful purposes and for no longer than is necessary for those purposes, and not used or disclosed in any manner incompatible with those purposes. The Acts also require both data controllers and data processors to protect the data they keep, and imposes on them a special duty of care in relation to the individuals about whom they keep such data.

Access to Records

Since information compiled and maintained by public bodies could be used to affect prejudicially the persons to whom the information relates, it is important that the persons affected have the right, subject to certain restrictions in the public interest, to access that information. The Freedom of Information Acts 1997–2003 give members of the public the right of access on request to records held by any public body concerning them, the right to have official information about themselves amended where it is incorrect, incomplete or misleading and the right to reasons regarding acts of public bodies affecting the persons concerned. The right of access to public records has been broadly interpreted, and the exceptions have been narrowly interpreted. In *N. McK. v The Information Commissioner* 2004, the High Court held that access to appropriate records shall be granted where the requester is a parent or guardian and where the record relates to a minor. The only relevant qualification is that the provision of access to such records be in the interests of the minor.

The records to which the right of access relate are, in general, records created after 21 April 1998. Old records are subject to the right of access where they relate to personal information about the person seeking access which are being used, or which it is proposed to use, in a manner that affects, or may affect, prejudicially the interest of the person concerned. In the event of a refusal of access, the decision may be appealed to an Information Commissioner appointed under Part IV of the 1997 Act. The role of the

Information Commissioner is to ensure that the rights afforded to members of the public under the Act are vindicated and to promote an attitude of openness by public bodies. The Commissioner can compel a public body to make records available. A decision of the Commissioner is binding, subject to a right of appeal to the High Court on a point of law.

Section 15 of the 1997 Act requires a public body, including a health board, to prepare, publish and make available a reference book containing an outline of its structure and organisation, functions, powers and duties, and the services it provides, a general description of the classes of records it holds and the manner in which the records may be accessed, and the personnel responsible for affording access. In preparing a reference book, a health board shall have regard to the fact that the purpose of the book is to assist clients in ascertaining and exercising their rights under the Act. Section 16 of the Act requires health boards to prepare, publish and make available a document setting out the rules and procedures used by them for determining whether records or information should be made available to clients.

Section 26 of the 1997 Act allows a request for information to be refused where the information was given to the health board in confidence, and its disclosure would be likely to prejudice the giving to the board of further similar information. The refusal to allow an applicant access to records held by a health board may constitute an interference with the applicant's right to respect for his private life under Article 8 of the European Convention on Human Rights. In *M.G. v United Kingdom* 2002, the European Court of Human Rights held that the file held by the local authority in respect of the applicant "provided a substitute record for the memories and experience of the parents of a child who was in care", since the information compiled and maintained by the local authority related to the applicant's basic identity. In deciding whether to release confidential records, a fair balance had to be struck between the vital interest of the applicant in receiving information necessary to know and understand his childhood and early development, and the fact that confidentiality of public records was important for receiving objective and reliable information, and such confidentiality could be necessary for the protection of third persons.

Confidentiality and Exchange of Information

Personal information about children and families held by professionals is subject to a duty of confidence and should normally not be disclosed without the consent of the subject. However, the need to maintain confidentiality must be balanced against the necessity to protect the welfare of the child and the public interest. The law permits the disclosure of confidential information necessary to safeguard a child. In *Eastern Health Board v Fitness to Practice Committee of the Medical Council and Others* 1998, Barr J said that a crucial public interest, such as "the protection of vulnerable children, takes precedence over the interest of the protected person in the non-disclosure of the information in question". As inter-disciplinary and inter-agency work is an essential process in the task of attempting to protect children from abuse, there must be the free exchange of information between the agencies involved in order to facilitate that work and the protection of children. Information regarding concern or assessment of child abuse should be shared on a need-to-know basis, in the interests of the child. While it is essential that ethical and statutory codes concerned with confidentiality and data protection be adhered to, the sharing of information by the various agencies in order to protect a child who is at risk could not be considered a breach of confidentiality. Too narrow a definition of confidentiality should not be allowed to impede the effective communication of information.

In the *Eastern Health Board* case, above, the health board sought judicial review of orders made in proceedings taken by the Medical Council against a doctor, whereby the board was directed to produce medical records in its possession relating to certain children. The board claimed that the records were covered by the *in camera* rule. The primary reason for the rule in such cases is "to provide protection for minors from harmful publicity arising out of the disclosure of evidence and other related matters in protected proceedings". Barr J held that there is not an absolute embargo in all circumstances on the publication of information deriving from proceedings held *in camera*. If justice requires disclosure of information protected by the rule, the court should take all reasonable measures to protect the interests of minors and others who are intended to have the benefit of the rule in the given case. The court has power to impose such terms in that regard as it deems necessary in the circumstances. In the matter under review, involving complaints of a serious nature alleging professional negligence and/or incompetence by a doctor as a medical specialist in the area of diagnosis of child abuse, "there is an imperative public interest that such complaints should be fully investigated by the Committee as the body having statutory authority to carry out such inquiries".

In view of the ease of travel between the member states of the European Union, it is crucial that social workers work together even in different jurisdictions to ensure the safety of children. In *Re L. (Disclosure to Third Party)* 2002, the Family Division of the High Court in Northern Ireland ordered a Health and Social Services Trust to release two medical reports, which dealt with the background to allegations of sexual abuse of a child, to the child protection unit of a local authority in England. The court was satisfied that there was real and cogent evidence of a pressing need for the requested disclosure. Whilst persons who give evidence in child proceedings can normally assume that their evidence will remain confidential, they are not entitled to assume that it will remain confidential in all circumstances. In deciding whether or not to grant permission for disclosure to third parties, the court has to exercise its discretion, in the process of which it has to carry out a balancing exercise of competing rights and interests.

The Dissemination of Information to Third Parties

Where a health board intends making the results of its investigation into allegations of child abuse available to any third party having an interest to receive them, it is important, in the interests of fairness, that the alleged abuser be given an opportunity to answer complaints made against him. This raises the question of the duty owed by the board to the alleged abuser. In *M.Q. v Gleeson and Others* 1997, Barr J referred to the two cardinal rules of natural or constitutional justice that govern the duty owed by the board to the applicant, and cited the Supreme Court cases of the *State (Gleeson) v Minister for Defence* 1976 and *Beirne v Commissioner of An Garda Síochána* 1993. The first rule provides that a person charged with wrongdoing should be informed of what is being alleged against him, and the second rule requires that he be given a reasonable opportunity to make his defence. A health board should be mindful of the fact that unfounded complaints of child abuse have the "potential for great injustice and harm", both to the person complained of and to the particular child or children whom it is sought to protect and other members of the family concerned. Barr J described the potential for injustice and harm to the family unit as follows:

> A false complaint of child abuse, if incorrectly interpreted by a health board, could involve the destruction of a family as a unit by wrongfully having the children it comprises taken into care. It may also destroy or seriously damage a good relationship between husband and wife or long-standing partners.

As regards the dissemination by a health board of information or records in its possession, regard should be had to the High Court decision in *Eastern Health Board v Fitness to Practice Committee of the Medical Council and Others*. In the course of his judgment, Barr J said that where a health board has medical records in its possession which it required in the course of exercising its child protection function, and the said records relate to matters which were the subject matter of *in camera* proceedings before the courts of this jurisdiction, it would be a contempt of court to disseminate information derived from those proceedings without prior judicial authority.

Privilege and Statutory Immunity in Reporting Child Abuse

In discharging its statutory powers and functions in promoting the welfare of children, a health board should be mindful of the fact that unfounded and unreasonable allegations of child abuse against a person may involve the board and the investigating personnel in defamation proceedings. Defamation consists of the publication of a false statement about a person, which is likely to injure that person's good name and general reputation or lower that person in the eyes of right-thinking members of society. Publication consists of the communication of the statement to a third party. There are a number of possible defences to the tort of defamation, including justification (the truth), qualified privilege and fair comment.

The defence having most relevance to the reporting and investigation of incidents of child abuse is qualified privilege. This defence is available where a person under a duty or interest to report a matter does so to a person or authority having a corresponding duty to receive the report. The duty or interest in question may be legal, moral or social. Malice defeats the defence of qualified privilege. In *Hynes-O'Sullivan v O'Donnell* 1988, Henchy J said, "an occasion of qualified privilege cannot exist unless the person making the communication has a duty or interest to make it and the person to whom it is made has a corresponding duty or interest to receive it". The case established that the person to whom the communication is made must have an actual duty or interest to receive it. An honest but mistaken belief that the recipient of the communication has a duty or interest in receiving it is not enough. Clearly, a health board has a statutory function in the area of child protection, and, accordingly, in the absence of malice, it has a duty or interest in communicating information in relation to the abuse of a particular child or children. Those who would have a corresponding duty or interest to receive that information would include members of An Garda Síochána, doctors, child care professionals, schools and teachers. Each case would depend on its own particular circumstances.

The Protection for Persons Reporting Child Abuse Act 1998 provides immunity from civil liability to any person who reports child abuse "reasonably and in good faith" to designated officers of health boards or any member of An Garda Síochána. In effect, even if a suspicion of child abuse proves unfounded, a plaintiff taking action would have to prove that the defendant had not acted reasonably and in good faith. Significant protection is provided for employees who report child abuse against all forms of discrimination, including dismissal. The Act creates a new offence of false reporting of child abuse, where a person reports an incident of child abuse to the appropriate authorities "knowing the statement to be false". This offence is designed to protect innocent persons from malicious reports.

Conclusion

Professionals can only work together effectively to safeguard children if there is an exchange of relevant information between them. Very often, it is only when information from a number of sources has been shared that it becomes clear that a child is not at risk. However, any disclosure of personal information to others must always have regard to both common law and statute. To ensure that professionals have access to the relevant information, it is vital that accurate, up-to-date records exist. Judgments made, actions and decisions taken should be carefully recorded. The subject of a record does have the right in law to request access to the information recorded at any stage. A request for information can only be refused where the need to protect a confidential source of information outweighs the interest of the applicant in obtaining information about his childhood and early development.

PART THREE

STATE INTERVENTION TO PROTECT CHILDREN

CHAPTER 13

EMERGENCY PROTECTION OF CHILDREN

Introduction

The emergency protection of children considered to be at risk requires that those professionals charged with protecting the children have sufficient powers to act swiftly and decisively. At the same time, even where there is reasonable cause to suspect that there is immediate and serious risk to the welfare of a child, the potential for damage to the long-term welfare of the child by precipitate action must always be borne in mind. The various procedures and protocols for emergency intervention and summary removal of a child from the family contained in *Children First* are designed to prevent precipitous action by An Garda Síochána and the health boards. It is also important that the legal position of the various parties involved in the emergency proceedings be made clear, in particular the right of the child's parents to challenge the emergency intervention in the life of the family. The special position afforded the family by the Constitution dictates that all concerned exercise the utmost caution.

Removal of Child to Safety by Member of An Garda Síochána

Section 12 of the 1991 Act enables a member of An Garda Síochána, without warrant, to remove a child to safety where the member has reasonable grounds for believing that:

(a) there is an immediate and serious risk to the health or welfare of a child, and

(b) it would not be sufficient for the protection of the child from such immediate and serious risk to await the making of an application for an emergency care order by a health board.

For the purpose of removing the child to safety, the member of An Garda Síochána may be accompanied by such other persons as a social worker, as may be necessary, and may, without warrant, enter any house or other place (if need be by force) and remove the child to safety. The power to remove a child to safety is without prejudice to any other powers exercisable by An

Garda Síochána in the general area of law enforcement. The drastic nature of this summary power bestowed on a member of An Garda Síochána dictates that it is only as a last resort that the procedure should be availed of. It must really be a matter of life and death, so to speak, as in the case referred to later, where a garda sergeant in Waterford relied on the procedure to take a child to safety for the purpose of life-saving medical treatment. In any subsequent judicial review of the decision to intervene under the section, it would have to be shown that the urgency of the situation justified departure from the procedures for emergency action to protect a child outlined in *Children First*.

Where a member of An Garda Síochána removes a child from the custody of his parents, the parents at that stage are, in effect, being denied their constitutional right to due process and fair procedures. However, there is authority, most notably the judgment of Barrington J in *Clancy v Ireland* 1989, to the effect that there is no obligation to apply fair procedures in respect of a decision which is only preliminary to a full hearing, where the person affected will be afforded fair procedures. Since the parents must be heard in the subsequent care proceedings, they will be given the opportunity to make their case fully. In any event, where there are allegations of child abuse and the circumstances suggest that urgent action should be taken to protect a child, *Clancy v Ireland* is also authority for the proposition that there may be factors which amount to a "permissible delimitation" of constitutional rights in the interests of the common good, where to afford the parents fair procedures might defeat the purpose and object of the emergency provisions of the 1991 Act. It is significant that in *M.Q. v Gleeson and Others* 1997, Barr J acknowledged that an exception to the obligation to comply with the requirements of constitutional justice and fair procedures may arise where to do so "might put the child in question in further jeopardy".

A child who is removed by a member of An Garda Síochána to safety must, as soon as possible, be delivered up to the custody of the health board for the area in which the child is for the time being. The health board to whom the child is delivered must, unless it returns the child to the parent having custody of him or a person acting *in loco parentis*, apply for an emergency care order at the next sitting of the District Court held in the same district. Where the next sitting of the District Court in the same district is not due to be held within three days of the delivery up of the child to the health board, an application may be made to any judge of the District Court. It shall be lawful for a health board to retain custody of a child pending the hearing for an emergency care order.

Chapter 9 of *Children First*, acknowledging that a health board and An Garda Síochána are the key agencies empowered by law to carry out the assessment and investigation of suspected child abuse, establishes a protocol for inter-agency co-operation. Where emergency intervention is necessary, and An Garda Síochána has to take immediate action to protect a child without first notifying the health board, it is essential that the health board be informed by means of a Standard Notification Form (Form 9.2) as soon as possible of any actions taken. Similarly, where a child's immediate safety is deemed to be at risk, and the health board is obliged to take immediate protective action, it is essential that An Garda Síochána be informed by means of a Standard Notification Form (Form 9.1) as soon as possible of any actions taken or planned.

Emergency Care Order

Where a child's immediate safety is deemed to be at risk, a health board has a statutory obligation to take immediate protective action. The emergency care order is designed to cover the situation where immediate intervention is required to remove a child in immediate and serious risk from the home. It should be seen as a short-term measure that may or may not lead to an application for a care order. *Children First* suggests that if a report made to a health board indicates the presence of immediate and serious risk to a child, urgent action must be taken to protect the child. This may mean securing the co-operation of a protective carer, family member or other responsible adult in the child's home "whose capacity to protect the child can be defined and agreed" (Paragraph 8.9.1). If it is not possible to have the child protected at home, he may need to be removed to an appropriate location, "preferably with the consent of the parents/carers, but if necessary using legal measures under the Child Care Act 1991" (Paragraph 8.9.2).

Section 13(1) of the 1991 Act provides for the making of an emergency care order where a judge of the District Court is of the opinion, on the application of a health board, that there is reasonable cause to believe that:

(a) there is an immediate and serious risk to the health or welfare of a child which necessitates his being placed in the care of a health board, or

(b) there is likely to be such a risk if the child is removed from the place where he is for the time being.

For the purposes of making an emergency care order, the court need only be of the opinion, as opposed to being satisfied (which is the requirement for the purposes of making an interim care order, a care order or a supervision order), that the threshold conditions for the making of an order exist. Paragraph (b) above is designed to cover the situation where a child is in voluntary care, and a health board has reason to fear that a parent who seeks the return of the child might pose a risk to the child. This was the position that pertained in *C.H. v Southern Health Board* 1996, where the health board obtained a place of safety order (emergency protection) under the Children Act 1908 to counter the father's attempt to regain custody of his daughter who was in voluntary care. The health board's decision was influenced by the fact that the father had spent two years in prison following the child's admission to voluntary care, coupled with the fact that the child had made allegations of sexual abuse against the father.

Compelling Reasons for Removing Child from Family

Because of the special position afforded to the family by Articles 41 and 42 of the Constitution, State intervention to remove a child from the custody of its parents is only justified in exceptional cases under Article 42.5, where the parents for physical or moral reasons fail in their duty to the child. The Supreme Court held in *K.C. and A.C. v An Bord Uchtala* 1985 that there is a constitutional presumption that the welfare of both marital and legitimated children is to be found within the family, and that this presumption can only be rebutted where there are "compelling reasons" why a child should be removed from the custody of its parents. Any statutory provision authorising the removal of a child from its family must require the agency charged with the removal to reach the conclusion that no other action will suffice to protect the child's constitutional rights. The underlying theme of the 1991 Act, which emphasises that a child is best cared for by remaining within the family, would seem to meet this requirement.

The case law of the European Court of Human Rights makes it clear that exceptional circumstances must exist before an emergency care order can be made. In *P., C. and S. v United Kingdom* 2002, the court, in acknowledging that it had been proper for the local authority in its child protection function to obtain an emergency protection order, held that the removal of a baby from its mother at birth required exceptional justification. As such justification was not forthcoming, the court concluded that this step could not be regarded as "necessary in a democratic Society" for the purposes of safeguarding the child. Accordingly, there had been a breach of the applicant's right to respect for family life under Article 8 of the European Convention on Human Rights.

In recognising that removing children from their parents or home "can be very stressful and requires sensitive handling", *Children First* states that the likely effect of separation must be balanced against the danger of leaving the child at home; "all means of protecting the child at home must be considered first" (Paragraph 8.9.3). A less damaging means of protecting the child would be for the abuser to leave the home, as opposed to the child being removed. Of course, this could only happen where there is someone else in the home that could be trusted to provide the necessary parenting and protection for the child. In the *State (D. and D.) v G. and Midland Health Board (No.2)* 1990, the Supreme Court held that where there is a suspicion that a child is being ill-treated or abused by one parent only, "there is a very definite and positive obligation" on the court to consider whether the welfare of the child requires its removal from the custody of the innocent parent. Such a removal could only be justified "if the innocent parent was unwilling or, as might well be the case, unable to protect the child from the risk of harm from the other parent".

In *South Western Area Health Board v J.C. and E.C.* 2002 (Circuit Court), the court accepted the expert evidence that the mother was unable to make "a responsible reaction to the genuine and properly held concerns of all, including this court, for the future well-being of their children". The evidence established that the father was a paedophile and child sex abuser, that the children had been exposed to sexual abuse in the home at the hands of the father and that the mother was not capable of protecting the children from such abuse.

Effect of an Emergency Care Order

An emergency care order places the child in the care of the health board for up to eight days. There is no provision for an extension of that period. One can only assume that this limitation was imposed to ensure that a child is not removed from the custody of his parents for longer than is necessary to enable the health board to complete its investigation into the child's circumstances. A removal for longer than was reasonably necessary to enable a health board to consider the welfare of the child could not be justified under Article 42.5 of the Constitution. In the *State (D.C.) v Midland Health Board* 1986, Keane J said that a statutory provision, which allowed for a child's removal from the custody of his parents for longer than the minimum required to assess the child's welfare, would be a breach of the parents' constitutional rights. The limited duration of an emergency care order may not be sufficient to enable the health board assess the difficulties in the family which have placed the child at risk. Accordingly, if the health board wants to pursue care proceedings it has the option of applying for an interim care order.

For the purpose of executing an emergency care order, a judge of the District Court may issue a warrant to a member of An Garda Síochána authorising him to enter (if need be by force) any premises where a child is and to deliver the child into the custody of a health board. Another member of the force and such other persons as may be necessary may accompany the garda. Where the relationship between a parent and a health board has broken down, the removal of a child can be a difficult exercise and very stressful for all concerned. It requires sensitive handling. Section 34 of the 1991 Act makes it an offence for the person who has custody of the child, having been given or shown a copy of the warrant, to refuse to deliver up the child. A person who is present in court when the warrant is issued will be deemed to have notice of it. The penalty prescribed is a fine not exceeding £500 and/or imprisonment for up to six months. Failure to obey a warrant may also be a contempt of court.

An emergency care order shall be made by the judge of the District Court where the child resides or is for the time being. Where a judge is not immediately available, any judge of the District Court may make an order. An application for an emergency care order may be made *ex parte* (without prior notice to a parent or carer) and elsewhere than at a public sitting of the District

Court where the urgency of the matter so requires. An appeal from an emergency care order shall not stay the operation of the order. It shall not be necessary in any application or order to name the child if such name is unknown.

The Court's Power to Give Directions

Section 13(7) of the 1991 Act provides that where the court makes an emergency care order, it may of its own motion, or on the application of any person, give such directions (if any) as it thinks proper with respect to:

(a) whether the address or location of the place at which the child is being kept is to be withheld from the parents of the child, or either of them, a person acting in *loco parentis* or any other person,

(b) the access, if any, which is to be permitted between the child and any named person and the conditions under which the access is to take place,

(c) the medical or psychiatric examination, treatment or assessment of the child.

In considering the corresponding provisions of the Children Act 1908 in the *State (D. and D.) v G. and the Midland Health Board (No. 2)*, above, the Supreme Court held that the decision to exclude knowledge as to the child's whereabouts from one or both of the parents, a person acting in *loco parentis* or any other person should not be taken lightly. In delivering the judgment of the court Finlay CJ said:

> Such an exclusion of knowledge should not, however, be lightly undertaken, having particular regard for the fact that questions of proper access and communication between such parents and the child may in some instances still be a very necessary ingredient in the welfare of the child.

Similar sentiments were expressed by O'Flaherty J in *M.F. v Superintendent Ballymun Garda Station* 1990, when he said that unless "very exceptional circumstances can be established justifying a different course", parents should be informed of the location of the place of safety where the children were detained pending the hearing of the application for a fit person order under the Children Act 1908. The mother of five children, who had been moved to a place of safety pursuant to section 20 of the 1908 Act, was unable to ascertain their whereabouts, despite attending six times at the offices of the social worker having charge of the case in order to see them. At no time during the period when she was denied access to her children did anyone contact her either on behalf of the health board or An Garda Siochana. The learned judge accepted that there had not been any deliberate attempt by the board or any of its social workers to keep the whereabouts of the children from the mother, and that the failure to do so resulted from a breakdown in communications. The importance of access to children in care is dealt with in Chapter 19.

As regards the power to direct medical or psychiatric examination, treatment or assessment, Section 13(7) can be seen as dealing with the interaction between the powers of the health board entitled to make decisions as to the child's welfare in the interim, and the needs of the court to have access to the relevant information and assessments so as to be able to make the ultimate decision. The purpose of the section is to enable the court to obtain the information necessary for its own decision whether or not to make a care order, and, where necessary, to override the views of the health board. In the context of the court giving a direction for treatment or assessment of children who have been the victims of abuse, it may be necessary from time to time to draw a distinction between the word "treatment" and the word "assessment". The purpose of an assessment is investigative, i.e. to explore what has happened. On the other hand, the purpose of treatment is therapeutic, i.e. to help the child come to terms with past experience.

The use of the emergency provisions of the 1991 Act to override the wishes of parents who refused to consent to medical treatment for a child is illustrated by a case reported in the *Irish Independent* on 4 March 2000. A Waterford garda sergeant had made use of section 12 of the Act to remove to safety and deliver up to the health board a two-year-old child who had suffered critical injuries in a car crash and was in urgent need of a blood transfusion. The health board had obtained an emergency care order to enable it consent to the child having a blood transfusion, thereby overriding the religious-based objections of the parents who, as members of the Jehovah's Witnesses sect, refused to consent to medical treatment involving the use of blood products. As to the power of a District Court to give directions that a child undergo medical treatment, see the case of *A. and B. v Eastern Health Board* 1998, discussed further in Chapter 8, where the court ordered that a thirteen-year-old girl, who was pregnant and suicidal as a result of having been raped, be permitted to travel abroad to have her pregnancy terminated.

Duty to Inform Parent of Emergency Intervention

Where a child is received into care by a health board from a member of An Garda Síochána or as a result of an emergency care order, the board is required by section 14 of the 1991 Act as soon as possible to inform or cause to be informed a parent having custody of the child or a person acting *in loco parentis* that this has happened, unless the parent or person is missing or cannot be found. There is no need to inform the parent or person acting *in loco parentis* of the placing of the child in the custody of a health board if the parent or person is given a copy of the emergency care order or is present in court on the making of the order. Section 15 of the Act obliges a health board to provide or make arrangements with the registered proprietors of residential centres or other suitable persons for the provision of suitable accommodation for the care of children in emergencies.

Conclusion

Emergency intervention by means of an emergency care order seems to have become the normal way of beginning care proceedings, at least in child abuse cases. The fact that a child can be removed and kept away from home, even for a limited period, without any opportunity to challenge the order or test the evidence, is a cause for concern. At the same time, there are occasions where children undoubtedly need emergency protection, and the emergency care order may enable a crisis to be resolved without having to take the drastic step of commencing full care proceedings. The purpose of limiting the duration of an emergency care order to eight days is to eliminate unnecessary delay, which can be so damaging for the child and so prejudicial to the parents. Any provision that permitted the child's removal from the custody of his parents for longer than was necessary to assess the child's welfare would clearly fall foul of the Constitution.

CHAPTER 14

CARE ORDERS

Introduction

In considering whether to initiate care proceedings, it should be borne in mind that intervention by the State into matters of the family may often call for immense caution and restraint. This is so because of the special position of the family under Articles 41 and 42 of the Constitution. In *M.Q. v Gleeson and Others* 1997, Barr J spoke of the damage that a false complaint of child abuse might inflict on the family unit "by wrongfully having the children it comprises taken into care". The potential damage to the family that even the making of an application for a care order can cause means that such a step should not be taken lightly.

The need for caution and restraint is also reflected in the provisions of Article 8 of the European Convention on Human Rights and its requirement of respect for family life. The essential object of Article 8 is "to protect the individual against arbitrary interference by public authorities" (*Glasser v United Kingdom* 2000). Mutual enjoyment by parent and child of each other's company constitutes a fundamental element of family life under Article 8, which is interfered with if a child is taken into public care. For this reason, the disruption of family life by taking a child into care is only justified where there are very pressing grounds for intervention by the State. The use of a care order should be seen as a measure of last resort. In *K. and T. v Finland* 2000, the reasons used to justify the care order were insufficient and amounted to an infringement of Article 8. The taking of a child into care should be regarded as a temporary measure, and that parent and child should be reunited as soon as possible where reunification is clearly in the best interests of the child (see *Soderbuck v Sweden* 1999 and *Johansen v Norway* 1996).

The Decision to Apply for a Care Order

Section 16 of the 1991 Act places a duty on the health board to apply for a care or supervision order, where it appears to a health board that a child in its area requires care or protection which he is unlikely to receive unless a court makes a care order or supervision order in respect of him. However, the decision to invoke the child protection machinery of the 1991 Act is generally a matter for the discretion of the health board concerned. At the same time, the use of the word "duty" makes it clear that the reasons for not bringing proceedings should be persuasive, bearing in mind that the health board's decision may be subjected to the process of judicial review. Also, the health board should be mindful of Article 3 of the European Convention on Human Rights, which imposes an obligation on State Parties to take preventative measures to protect children from harm and ill treatment. In *Z. and Others v United Kingdom* 2001, the European Court of Human Rights held that a local authority has a positive duty to see that appropriate measures are taken to protect a child at risk.

As regards the exercise by a health board of its discretion, it is worth noting the remarks of McGuinness J in *Comerford v Minister for Education* 1996, where she said that the health board might have moved earlier to take the applicant and the other children into care "given the level of neglect and lack of supervision by the parents which has caused immense problems to all the children". However, the learned judge accepted that the health board had to bear in mind "the extremely strong rights given to parents and the family in the Constitution and the comparative lack of express constitutional rights for the child as against the parents". The health board also had to bear in mind the provisions of section 3 of the 1991 Act that required it to "have regard to the fact that it is generally in the best interests of a child to be brought up in his own family".

Even though the court has no general power to direct a health board to apply for a care order or supervision order, it does have the power in certain family proceedings to direct the board to consider applying for such an order (section 20 of the 1991 Act, as amended by section 17 of the Children Act 1997). Where in the course of proceedings involving issues of guardianship, custody and access to children, and proceedings for the delivery or return of a child, it appears to the court that it may be appropriate for a care order or supervision order to be made, the court may, of its own motion or on the application of any person, adjourn the proceedings and direct the health board to undertake an investigation of the child's circumstances. For the purposes of its deliberations, the court can order that social reports be prepared by probation and welfare officers or any other suitably qualified person. The person who prepares a report can be called as a witness in the proceedings. A copy of any report obtained by the court shall be furnished to the parties involved in the proceedings, and may be admitted in evidence.

Where the court gives a direction under section 20 of the 1991 Act, the health board is obliged to undertake an investigation of the child's circumstances and consider whether it should apply for a care order or supervision order, or provide services or assistance for the child or his family, or take any other action with respect to the child. As a result of its investigation, the health board is perfectly entitled to decide not to apply for a care order or supervision order. It must inform the court of its reasons for so deciding and give details of any service or assistance it has provided, or it intends to provide, for the child and his family, and any other action it has taken, or proposes to take, with respect to the child. Whether or not a health board decides to apply for a care order or supervision order, it may find itself having to care for the child in any event, as section 20 of the 1991 Act enables the court to give directions as to the care and custody of, or to make a supervision order in respect of, the child pending the board finalising its investigation.

Grounds for Making a Care Order

Section 18(1) of the 1991 Act provides that the court may make a care order where it is satisfied that:

(a) the child has been or is being assaulted, ill-treated, neglected or sexually abused, or

(b) the child's health, development or welfare has been or is being avoidably impaired or neglected, or

(c) the child's health, development or welfare is likely to be avoidably impaired or neglected.

The court must also be satisfied that the child requires care and protection which he is unlikely to receive unless a care order is made. In other words, the court must be satisfied not only that the particular threshold for making a care order has been crossed, but also that the harm being suffered is attributable to the actual or anticipated care being received by the child while in the custody of a parent or guardian. As to whether a child in a given case is receiving adequate care and protection from his parents in the home, this is an issue that is likely to be dominated by the evidence as to the abilities and conduct of the parents and the relationship between the child and those parents.

In the absence of any statutory definitions of the various categories of child abuse set out in section 18 of the 1991 Act, it is likely that the definitions contained in Chapter 3 of *Children First* will be used in practice. An *assault* is a form of physical abuse, which is defined as "any form of non-accidental injury or injury which results from wilful or neglectful failure to protect a child". *Neglect* is defined in terms of an omission, as a result of which the child suffers "significant harm or impairment of development", by being deprived of food, clothing, warmth, hygiene, intellectual stimulation, supervision and safety, attachment to and affection from adults and medical care. Subjecting a child to emotional abuse could be described as a form of neglect. *Harm*, in turn, is defined as "the ill-treatment or the impairment of the health or development of a child". The threshold of significant harm is reached "when the child's needs are neglected to the extent that his well-being and/or development are severely affected". *Sexual abuse* can cover a variety of acts from molestation to rape. The Statute of Limitations (Amendment) Act 2000 contains a definition of sexual abuse, which is likely to be adopted generally for child protection purposes. An act of sexual abuse is defined as including any act of causing, inducing or coercing a person to participate in any sexual activity, or to observe any other person engaging in any sexual activity, or any act committed against, or in the presence of, a person that any reasonable person would, in all the circumstances, regard as misconduct of a sexual nature.

The words "health, development or welfare", as used in section 18 of the 1991 Act, are in common usage in health care practice, and the court will have regard to the practical situation. Health includes physical and mental health. Development covers physical, intellectual, emotional, social and behavioural development. Emotional deprivation could be dealt with on this ground. Welfare must be taken in its widest sense, as embracing the intellectual, physical, social and moral well-being of a child. The words "health, development and welfare" are not mutually exclusive, and it is open to a health board to satisfy the court that a child's need for care and protection is caused by a combination of factors. The use of the words "avoidably impaired or neglected" in section 18 implies that the impairment or neglect can be avoided by proper care, and this is to be judged objectively. Clearly excluded, however, is the situation where, for example, a child is suffering from a degenerative disease or some ailment that is not susceptible to medical treatment.

The Standard of Proof Required

In care proceedings, the court is concerned with the question of protecting the child, rather than with who was responsible for his maltreatment. While there may be insufficient evidence to secure a conviction in criminal proceedings (because an offence must be proved beyond reasonable doubt), the court may still make an order which is designed to secure the protection of the child. Accordingly, where there is reasonable cause to suspect abuse or neglect, it is invariably worth bringing care proceedings, since a court in civil proceeding may make a finding of fact (that a particular event happened) by applying the balance of probabilities test. If the evidence shows a balance in favour of the event having happened, then it is proved that it did in fact happen.

The standard of proof required to establish the first two grounds set out in section 18 of the 1991 Act, namely that the child "has been or is being" assaulted, ill-treated, neglected or sexually abused, or that the child's health, development or welfare "has been or is being" avoidably impaired or neglected, is that of the preponderance or balance of probabilities. In other words, the health board instigating care proceedings on one of these grounds must prove that it is more likely than not that the relevant ground is met. The more improbable the event, the stronger must be the evidence that it did occur before, on the balance of probability, its occurrence will be established. The third ground in section 18 enables a court to make a care order solely on the basis of anticipated abuse or neglect. The court must be satisfied that the child's health, development or welfare "is likely" to be avoidably impaired or neglected. Here the court is concerned with evaluating the risk of something happening in the future. The word "likely" is used in section 18 in the sense of a real possibility, "a possibility that cannot sensibly be ignored having regard to the nature and gravity of the feared harm in the particular case" (see *Re H. and others (Minors) (Sexual Abuse: Standard of Proof)* 1996). There must be facts from which the court can properly conclude that there is a real possibility of future harm. Unresolved doubts and suspicions cannot by themselves form the basis of a conclusion that the condition is satisfied. In *O'D. v O'D. and Others* 1994, the mother alleged that the father had sexually abused the child, a fact denied by the father. Geoghegan J refused to grant the father unsupervised access to the child, being satisfied that there was a "real possibility" that the father had sexually abused the child. The learned judge said that it was not necessary for the court to make a finding of fact as to whether there was or was not sexual abuse. "Any substantial risk that there was such abuse must be taken into account". Even though a bare allegation is not enough, "a genuine risk falling well short of probability" has to be taken into account.

Where a child suffers non-accidental injuries at the hands of his parents, but the court is unable to identify which parent was the perpetrator, or, indeed, whether both parents were perpetrators, the child should not be left at risk simply because it is not possible for the court to be sure which parent inflicted the harm. In *Re O. and N.* (minors) 2003, the House of Lords referred to such cases as the "uncertain perpetrator" type of case. The court held that, in the absence of any other explanation provided by either parent and accepted by the medical experts, neither parent should be free from blame, and the injuries should be deemed to have been caused by either or both of them. In *Lancashire County Council v B.* 2000, a child was looked after by a carer (who had a child of her own) in the carer's home while the parents were at work. The child sustained serious non-accidental head injuries when she was seven months old. It was not possible to decide on the evidence who was at fault. The House of Lords held that the child must not be left at risk "simply because it is not possible for the court to be sure which part of the care network has failed".

The relevant date with which the court had to be satisfied that the threshold conditions existed was the date at which the health board initiated the procedure for protection under the 1991 Act. Accordingly, where, at the time the application for a care order was considered by the court, there were in place interim arrangements for the protection of the child by the health board, which had been continuously in place for some time, the relevant date was the date at which the procedure for protection was initiated. The House of Lords held in *Re M. (A Minor) (Care Order: Threshold Conditions)* 1994 that any other construction of the words used in the corresponding section 31 of the English Children Act 1989 would mean "that if a child suffers harm and is rescued by a local authority, a care order cannot be made" because it can no longer be said that the child is suffering harm.

The Processing of a Care Order Application

Participation in Care Proceedings

Those persons who are full parties in the proceedings, such as respondents to an application for a care order, are entitled to legal representation, to call evidence and to cross-examine witnesses. Other persons who are not parties to the proceedings, but who have an interest in the outcome, must be given notice of the proceedings. They do not have the rights of parties to the proceedings, but may acquire them by making application to the court to become parties. It is also possible for the court to confer party status on a person without a specific application having to be made. The child the subject matter of the proceedings is not a party thereto, but may be joined as a party under section 25 of the 1991 Act, and the court may appoint a solicitor to represent the child. Where the child is not a party, the court may appoint a guardian *ad litem* for the child under section 26 of the Act to ensure that the child's voice is adequately aired in the proceedings. This matter is dealt with further in Chapter 8.

All persons involved in child protection proceedings must be afforded fair procedures and constitutional justice. A fair trial requires a hearing in the presence of the parties at which all evidence should be produced to the parties who, in turn, should have the opportunity to challenge evidence by cross-examination, if appropriate. The European Court of Human Rights held in *McMichael v United Kingdom* 1995 that, as a matter of general principle, the right to a fair – adversarial – trial means the opportunity to have knowledge of and comment on the observations filed or evidence adduced by the other party. In the instant case, the lack of disclosure of such vital documents as social reports affected the ability of participating parents to influence the outcome of the hearing.

Where care proceedings in respect of children and criminal proceedings in respect of their parents are both pending, there is no bar on hearing the care proceedings in advance of the criminal proceedings. Although care proceedings could understandably be perceived as adversarial by parents who were at risk of losing their children, the objective was not to punish the parents but to seek to achieve what was best for the children. In *Southern Health Board v C.H.* 1996, the Supreme Court said that in care proceedings "the judge is in essence required to inquire as to what is in the best interests of the child", while at the same time "the right of the father must be safeguarded, as far as practicable". But when the consequences of any encroachment on the respective rights is concerned, "the child's welfare must always be of far greater concern to the court".

In *Re L1 and Anor (Care Proceedings)* 2003, the Family Division of the High Court in Northern Ireland, citing with approval the judgment of Butler-Sloss LJ in *Re T.B. (Care Proceedings: Criminal Trial)* 1995, held that there was no reason why the care proceedings should be adjourned pending the completion of the criminal proceedings. The welfare of the child should take precedence over the detriment of the family who are coming up for trial. The mother was charged with criminal offences in relation to serious non-accidental injuries to her two-and-a-half-year-old child. The court rejected the argument of the mother that she would suffer prejudice in the criminal trial if the care proceedings took precedence, as there was a risk of self-incrimination if she made a statement or gave evidence in the care proceedings, thereby compromising the mother's right to a fair trial under Article 6 of the European Convention of Human Rights. The court pointed out that a statement or admission made in care proceedings is not admissible in evidence against the person making it in proceedings for an offence other than perjury. The purpose of this protection against incrimination is to encourage frankness and candour on the part of the witness in the care proceedings in the best interests of the child.

Evidence

In deciding whether a health board applying for a care order has shown that one of the grounds for making an order exists, the court must have regard to the evidence adduced. The court must have before it facts on which its conclusion can properly be based. There must be facts, proved to the court's satisfaction if disputed, on which the court can properly conclude that the child is suffering harm, or that there is a real possibility that the child will suffer harm in the future. Because of the far-reaching consequences that the making of a care order may have for the child and the parents, the legislation has prescribed that a court may only make a care order on the basis of proven facts. Unproved allegations of maltreatment could not form the basis for a finding by the court that the child has suffered harm. More is required than mere suspicion, however reasonably based that suspicion might be.

Evidence of maltreatment may be forthcoming from a number of sources. The child may have made a complaint of abuse to a doctor, social worker or other child care professional. The pre-trial interviewing of children with a view to gathering evidence of abuse, and the involvement of children as witnesses in court proceedings, is considered in Chapter 3. The doctor who examined the child may be called on by the health board to give evidence as to his findings. In the *State (D. and D.) v Groarke* 1990, the Supreme Court held that in order to determine with safety whether the conclusion reached by a doctor, who had formed an opinion that a child had been sexually abused by her father, was a sound conclusion which would warrant the taking of a child into care, it would be necessary for the court to have before it the evidence on which such a conclusion was based. The evidence on which the doctor based such a conclusion included an interview which she had with the child who was questioned by her with the aid of anatomical dolls, which was recorded on video, and a physiological examination of the child which had been carried out whilst the child was anaesthetised by the doctor and another doctor jointly.

Before a doctor or any other professional witness is allowed to give opinion evidence, it is for the court to decide whether the witness should be given the status of an expert with the privilege and influence which that status brings. This is particularly the position where a medical witness offers a diagnosis of injury which is controversial and at variance with the mainstream experts in a particular case. In *Re M.K., S.K. and W.K.* 1999, Barron J considered at some length the role of the expert witness. He said that expert opinion is essential in assisting the court to determine whether there has been abuse, whether it is presently continuing and whether it will continue into the future. The role of the expert is to draw the attention of the court to circumstances in which it is likely that what the child has said at interview is true. Although the expert can guide the court in such matters, the learned judge pointed out that "it is the trial judge who ultimately decides any given case", and went on to emphasise that "the court should be careful to ensure that the trial is not seen as a trial by expert witnesses". The weight to be attached to the evidence of an expert depends on the level of his qualification. "In the ordinary case, the extent of the expertise of the witness goes to the weight of the evidence". Where a court is being asked to alter the custody of a child, "it should not be asked to nor should it act upon the evidence of some one with little or no expertise in the field of child psychology, even though such a person may technically be an expert".

Delay

It is now generally accepted that delay in proceedings relating to the care of children is ordinarily inimical to their welfare. Children cannot put their development on hold while adults take an undue amount of time in making decisions about them. In *Re M.K., S.K and W.K.*, Denham J observed that "delay in proceedings relating to the welfare of children is a matter of concern". Referring to the fact that the children the subject of the proceedings had been in care on foot of an *ex parte* application at the commencement of the proceedings for over three years, the learned judge expressed her concern at the very considerable delay that had occurred as follows:

> Time is of the essence in child custody cases. Childhood exists for only a short and finite time. Custody and care arrangements of themselves create dynamics which have a profound effect on children and their families. The long-term effects can be immense. Consequently, I voice

my unease at the length of time, the delay, which exists between the judgment of the High Court and the appeal.

The usual reasons for delay in care proceedings are lack of court time, a proliferation of experts' reports and the need to have assessments carried out on children. Careful preparation of the health board's case at pre-trial stage, with a view to resolving a divergence of professional opinion on the need for assessment, may help to avoid the possibility of delay. There should be ample opportunity for the experts to get together well in advance to discuss their respective positions to see to what extent they truly do disagree. All delay or drawn out legal proceedings militate to the disadvantage of the child unless there are countervailing advantages. However, planned and purposeful delay may be beneficial, particularly where the court adjourns proceedings for the purpose of having a child assessed to assist it in its deliberations. In *S. O'F. v N. O'F.* 1999, the High Court refused to extend the time to lodge an appeal against an order of the Circuit Court, refusing an application by the respondent to appoint a second medical expert to examine and assess a child in judicial separation and custody proceedings. The Circuit Court had appointed an expert, whose report was before the court. In upholding the decision of the trial judge, Budd J said that one of the purposes of section 47 of the Family Law Act 1995, which provides for the procuration of social reports, was to have an independent expert's report, and to reduce the intrusion caused by more than one similar expert interviewing and reporting on the child.

Delay in care proceedings may amount to a violation of Article 6 (the right to a fair hearing) and/or Article 8 (respect for family life) of the European Convention on Human Rights. It is significant that Article 6 requires that any hearing to determine the child's welfare should take place "within a reasonable time". In *Glasser v United Kingdom* 2000, the European Court of Human Rights said that the reasonableness of the length of proceedings is to be considered in the light of the criteria laid down in the court's case-law, "in particular the complexity of the case, the conduct of the applicant and that of the relevant authorities". On the latter point, the importance of what is at stake for the applicant in the litigation has also to be taken into account. "It is, in particular, essential that custody and access cases be dealt with speedily". In *H. v United Kingdom* 1988, the Court of Human Rights held that the delays in the proceedings had failed to show respect for the applicant's family life under Article 8. "Exceptional diligence" is required in care proceedings, since any procedural delay could lead to a *de facto* determination of the matter in issue, before the domestic court had the opportunity to conduct a full hearing of the case.

Legal Effect of Care Order

In making a care order, the District Court assumes a supervisory role, in that it has overall care of the child in respect of whom the order was made. When a child is taken into care on foot of a care order, the health board in whose favour the order is made is given parental responsibility for the child. While a care order is in force, the health board shall have the like control over the child as if it were his parent (section 18). With certain exceptions, the health board is given the power to determine the extent to which parents or guardians are to be involved in the life of the child. The decision-making power as to the care and residence of the child and the promotion of the child's health, development or welfare is vested in the hearth board, and not in the court. In this regard, the health board may decide the type of care to be provided for the child, and may consent to medical treatment for the child and the issue of a passport to the child. Any consent given by a health board in accordance with the section shall be sufficient authority for the carrying out of a medical or psychiatric examination or assessment, the provision of medical or psychiatric treatment, the issue of a passport or the provision of passport facilities, as the case may be. This provision should remove any possible doubt that might exist as to the effectiveness of a specific consent given by a health board in relation to a child in its care. In *Western Health Board v K.M.* 2000, Finnegan J, in the High Court, held that the power of a health board to consent to the issue of a passport for a child was to enable him travel abroad for a limited period only. A limited period will most likely refer to a trip abroad beneficial to the child, such as a holiday, attendance for medical examination or treatment where that is necessary. However, a child could not be sent abroad where the effect of so doing would be the abandonment by a health board of the control which a care order vests in it.

Once a child is taken into care, section 36 of the 1991 Act requires the health board to provide care for the child by either placing him in residential care, with foster parents, with a relative or with a suitable person for adoption. The selection of an appropriate placement for the child is a matter for the health board in question. The court cannot direct a particular type of placement, be it with foster parents, in a residential home or otherwise, unless it is satisfied that the placement contemplated by the health board might adversely affect the child's welfare. The placement of a child in care requires a health board to continue to exercise "control and supervision" over a particular placement. For this reason, the Supreme Court held in *Western Health Board v K.M.* 2001 that a health board does not have statutory power to place a child with relatives or foster parents outside the State. The District Court may direct such a placement, and may limit the period for which the child is to be placed, since section 47 of the 1991 Act gives the overall control of children in care to the District Court. However, such an order "should be made rarely and with considerable caution" and only "where the evidence before the court indicates that such a placement is truly in the best interests of the child". Emphasising that the supervisory role of the District Court should be maintained to the greatest degree possible, the Supreme Court stressed that all the relevant factors should be carefully weighed. Among the factors that should be considered are the constitutional rights of the child and his parents; whether the rights of the child are paramount in the jurisdiction in which it is proposed the child will live; whether the country concerned is a signatory to the Hague and/or Luxembourg Conventions on Child Abduction; the extent of the co-operation between the respective child care authorities in both countries; the feasibility of access to the child by parents in terms both of distance and of expense; the possibility of the reciprocal enforcement of undertakings to make the position of the child and the relevant health board more secure.

The Health Board's Plans for the Child

A health board's proposals for dealing with a child placed in its care must be set out in a care plan prepared in accordance with the Child Care Regulations 1995, governing placement in residential care, foster care or the care of relatives. A care plan is an essential part of the management and planning for a child's placement in care. It enables the court and everyone else to know and consider the local authority's plans for the future of the child if a care order is made. The care plan is to include the aims and objectives of the placement and the supports to be provided for the child, his carers and parents. It also covers access and care plan review arrangements. As it is likely to be in the best interests of the child that the parents are encouraged to take an active role in planning for the child, the Regulations also provide for consultation with the child's carers, the child and his parents, where it is practical to do so. In practice, health board personnel make every effort to consult with all the important people in the child's life.

The extent to which the court can become involved in the formulation and implementation of a care plan was considered by the High Court in *Eastern Health Board v McDonnell* 2000. The health board contended that once a permanent care order has been made, the child is then committed to the care of the board and the powers of the court under the 1991 Act cease. The board further contended that administratively there could be serious problems caused if more than one body were to be responsible for the detailed and day-to-day welfare of the child once the child is in care. McCracken J held that the 1991 Act confers ultimate responsibility for the welfare of the child on the court, and that the court cannot pass or delegate that responsibility to a health board. Accordingly, it was clear from sections 24 and 47 of the 1991 Act that the court is entitled to give directions in relation to the care of the child, not only in proceedings before the court, but also in situations where the child was already in the care of the health board.

Despite the fact that the overall control of a child in care is given to the District Court, McCracken J emphasised in *Eastern Health Board v McDonnell,* above, that the court should not interfere in all the day-to-day decisions made by a health board. Rather, the court should only interfere "whenever any matters of concern are brought to the attention of the District Court, which could reasonably be considered adversely to affect the welfare of the child". While the judgment makes it clear that the plans and proposals of the health board for care of the child have to be produced to the court, this is not to suggest that the board is forever tied to them. Essentially, the management of a particular case is a matter for the health board rather than the court. Once a child is in care, the health board has a duty to promote his welfare. If the welfare of the child requires a departure from the proposals in the care plan, the health board should feel free to take that course.

The implications of the judgment of McCracken J for health boards, social workers and other child care professionals are quite significant. In a given case the court may require a health board to justify its long-term plans for a child, including the aims and objectives of a proposed placement and arrangements for access, in considering whether to make a care order. In the instant case, the District Court ordered that the social worker assigned to the case should not be a new recruit, because of the complexity of the case, and that there should be no change of the social worker without the prior approval of the court. The District Court further ordered that there should be no change of foster parents without its prior approval, and it gave detailed directions as to the manner in which access should take place and be supervised. The question of access is regulated by section 37 of the 1991 Act, and is considered further in Chapter 18.

Supervision Order as Alternative to a Care Order

Where the court is satisfied that one of the grounds for the making of a care order exists, but that it is not necessary or appropriate to make such an order, and it is desirable that the child should be visited periodically in his home by or on behalf of the health board, section 18(5) of the 1991 Act enables the court to make a supervision order under section 19 of the Act. As a measure of interim relief pending the hearing of an application for a care order, the court, of its own motion or on the application of any person, may give directions as to the care and custody of the child or make a supervision order in respect of the child. A supervision order authorises the health board to intervene in the life of the child, without the necessity to remove the child from the home. In deciding what type of order to make in a given case, the court must be mindful of what are two very different orders. Of particular significance is the fact that a care order gives the health board prime responsibility for the child, subject to the overall control of the court. A supervision order does not give parental responsibility to the health board. A particular difficulty for the court arises when all the parties involved agree that the child should remain at home with his parents, despite the inherent risks involved.

Interim Care Orders

Section 17 of the 1991 Act empowers the court, on the application of a health board, to make an interim care order placing a child in the care of a health board pending an application for a care order. Before making an interim care order, the court must be satisfied that:

(a) an application for a care order has been or is about to be made,

(b) there is reasonable cause to believe that any of the grounds for the making of a care order under section 18(1) exist or have existed, and

(c) the protection of the health or welfare of the child requires him to be placed or maintained in the care of a health board pending the determination of the application for a care order.

Although an interim care order can be made whether or not an emergency care order is in place, very often the route into care for a child begins with a health board invoking the emergency procedure provided by the 1991 Act, followed by an interim care order. An interim care order can be made at any stage in care proceedings where, for whatever reason, the court requires more time in order to decide how best to deal with a particular case. The health board may have had to initiate care proceedings before it had time to prepare its case fully, and the court may consider that it requires further evidence, by way of report or otherwise, to decide the matter finally.

The Effect of an Interim Care Order

As the title suggests, an interim care order is a short-term measure only. It is a temporary holding measure, designed to enable the court to safeguard the welfare of the child until such time as the court is in a position to decide whether it is in the best interests of the child to make a care order. The effect of an interim care order is that the child must be placed or maintained in the care of a health board for a period not exceeding twenty-eight days, or where the health board and the parent having custody of the child or a person acting *in loco parentis* consent, for a period exceeding twenty-eight days. An extension or extensions of the initial period for which an interim care order is made may be granted, on the application of any of the parties, where the court is satisfied that the grounds for an interim care order continue to exist. An extension in excess of twenty-eight days can only be granted with the consent of a parent or a person acting *in loco parentis*. An application for an interim care order or an extension thereof can only be made on notice to a parent or person acting *in loco parentis*, except where the court, in the interests of justice or the welfare of the child, directs otherwise. Accordingly, in exceptional circumstances, an interim care order could be made on foot of an *ex parte* application without prior notice to a parent or other person.

The making of an interim care order is essentially an impartial step, favouring neither one side nor the other. It should not be seen as affording a tactical advantage to the health board over the parents, nor should it be seen as pre-empting the making of a care order at a later stage. At the same time, the making of an interim care order is likely to have a severe impact on the life of the family. Where the court makes an interim care order, the health board is given complete discretion to deal with the child as it thinks fit, subject to direction by the court. In this regard, it should be pointed out that in view of the decision of the High Court in *Eastern Health Board v McDonnell*, above, the court has the power to override the views of the health board for the purpose of enabling it to discharge properly its function of deciding whether or not to accede to the application to take the child away from its parents by obtaining a care order.

The Court's Power to Give Directions on Making an Interim Care Order

Where an interim care order is made following an emergency care order, the court may order that any directions in force under section 13 of the 1991 Act shall continue, subject to any variations made by the court. Where no such directions are in force, or where an application for an interim care order is not an interim measure following on from an emergency care order, the court may give directions under section 13. The directions that can be given include the withholding of the location of the child, arrangements as to access and the medical or psychiatric examination, treatment or assessment of the child. In *A. and B. v Eastern Health Board* 1998, the health board applied for and obtained an interim care order in respect of a thirteen-year-old girl. The child was one of twelve children of a travelling community family who had been allegedly raped by an adult and become pregnant. The girl was very severely traumatised by the alleged rape. The health board sought a direction that she be medically examined. On the basis of psychiatric evidence that the girl was likely to commit suicide unless she had a termination of her pregnancy, the court ordered that she be afforded the right to travel abroad to obtain a termination of her pregnancy, which procedure was medical treatment for her mental condition for the purposes of the 1991 Act.

In many cases the determination of the question whether the court should make a final care order requires information to be gathered as to the child's circumstances and for that information to be placed before the court to enable it make its decision. In the period during which this information is being obtained, the child may be at risk. For this reason, section 18 of the 1991 Act provides that on application being made to it for a care order, the court can make an interim care order committing the child to the care of the health board, and give such directions as are mentioned in section 13 of the Act as its sees fit. This is so, as the threshold applicable to an interim care order is lower than that for a care order, in that the court only has to be satisfied that "there is reasonable cause to believe" that any of the grounds for the making of a care order exist or have existed. Accordingly, the court could make an interim care order and direct that the child be assessed as to his circumstances either by a doctor, social worker or other care professional. In *Re C. (A Minor)* 1997 Brown-Wilkinson LJ described the power to give directions on making an interim care order under the corresponding provisions of the English Children Act 1989 as "the interaction between the powers of the local authority entitled to make decisions as to the child's welfare in the interim and the needs of the court to have access to the relevant information and assessments as to be able to make the ultimate decision".

Variation and Discharge of Orders

The court is given specific power under section 22 of the 1991 Act, of its own motion or on the application of any person, to vary or discharge a care order or supervision order, or any condition or direction attaching to such an order. In the case of a care order, the court may discharge the care order and replace it with a supervision order in respect of the child. As regards the court's power to discharge a care order, the court would have to be satisfied on the clearest possible evidence that there has been a change in circumstances sufficient to justify removing the protection and professional control afforded by the care order. Before the court could consider replacing a care order with a supervision order, it would have to be satisfied that the health board was in a position to guarantee the safety and welfare of the child in his home by a regime of supervision and family support. Very often the reason for discharging a supervision order is that the social worker is being denied full access to the child, or is being wilfully obstructed by parents in carrying out the necessary level of supervision and support. Where those circumstances exist, the health board can return to court and ask for the discharge of the supervision order, to be replaced by a care order. If the circumstances require emergency intervention to protect the child, the health board could enlist the assistance of An Garda Síochána under section 12 of the 1991 Act or apply for an emergency care order.

Invalid Care Orders

Section 23 of the 1991 Act is designed to ensure that, where it subsequently transpires that a care order when originally made was invalid, the child the subject of the order can be kept in care pending the making of a new order authorising the care. Where the court finds that a care order is for any reason invalid, the court, of its own motion or on the application of any person, may refuse to order the delivery or return of the child to a parent or any other person, if it is of the opinion that this would not be in the best interests of the child.

Where the court refuses to order the delivery or return of the child, it may:

(a) make a care order as if it were the court to which the application for a care order had been made under section 18,

(b) make an order remitting the matter to a judge of the District Court in a district where the child resides or is for the time being, or was residing when the invalid care order was made or applied for,

(c) direct that a care order made under paragraph (a) be deemed to have been made by a judge of the District Court in a district specified by the court, or

(d) where it makes an order under paragraph (b), make a temporary order under paragraph (a) pending the making of an order by the court to which the matter or question has been remitted.

Conclusion

The State has a clearly defined role under the Constitution in protecting and controlling the family. However, the family is made up of individuals, who each have rights as members of that family. In the case of children who cannot be properly protected by the State while they remain within the family, Article 42.5 of the Constitution authorises their removal from the care and custody of their parents on a non-voluntary basis where there are "exceptional circumstances" for doing so. In setting out the minimum conditions that must exist before a court may make a care order, the Oireachtas has marked the boundary line between the different interests. A proper balance must be struck between the often conflicting rights of both children and parents. On the one side are the interests of parents in caring for their own child, a course which on the face of it is also in the interests of the child. On the other side, there will be circumstances in which the interests of the child may dictate a need for his care to be entrusted to others. The need to guard against precipitous intervention in the life of the family cannot be over emphasised.

CHAPTER 15

SUPERVISION ORDERS

Introduction

One of the innovative features of the 1991 Act is the reintroduction of an intermediate means of protecting a child from ill treatment, neglect or abuse. A supervision order is a form of compulsory intervention in the life of a child. By means of a supervision order, a health board is authorised to intervene in the life of a child in cases of suspected abuse, without having to remove the child from the family home. The supervision order enables a health board to supervise a family that is in some way or other inadequate to deal with children without supervision. A supervision order can be seen as a final attempt at improving a family situation before removing a child from the custody of his parents. The Report of the Kilkenny Incest Investigation 1993 described the introduction of supervision orders under the 1991 Act as offering "a method whereby a child may be protected in cases of suspected abuse without taking the traumatic and often damaging step of removing the child from the family home" (Chapter 11). This is in keeping with the principle enshrined in the 1991 Act of minimalist intervention by the State in the life of the child within the family unit.

The Grounds for Making a Supervision Order

Section 19 of the 1991 Act provides for the making of a supervision order, on the application of a health board, on grounds identical to those for making a care order. However, the standard of proof is not as stringent, in that the court may make a supervision order where it is "satisfied that there are reasonable grounds for believing" that the threshold conditions exist, whereas the court cannot make a care order unless it "is satisfied" that the threshold conditions do exist. Since the same threshold conditions apply to both orders, the court must decide which order is consistent with the child's welfare. Where the court makes a supervision order as opposed to a care order, it is in effect acknowledging that there is a risk that the child might suffer harm, albeit not serious enough to justify the making of a care order. For this reason, as part of providing for the child's welfare, on the authority of the judgment of McCracken J in *Eastern Health Board v McDonnell* 2000, the court could, on making a supervision order, give directions in relation to the care of the child the subject of the supervision order. Such directions would be designed mainly to facilitate the supervisor in carrying out the duty to visit the child and assist the parents.

There are a number of factors that might influence the court when deciding what type of order should be made in the context of protecting a child from abuse. Most importantly, the court must evaluate what future risks the child is likely to face. Where there is a risk of serious harm, such that the child needs to be removed from the family unit, a care order should be made. It should always be borne in mind that a supervision order affords only limited vigilance and, consequently, very little protection from a damaging environment. This is so, because under a supervision order the child is allowed to remain in the home and the parents retain parental responsibility. Even if the threshold criteria have been satisfied in a particular case, where adequate support from social services would avoid the risk of significant harm, the court could make a supervision order instead of a care order. In *Re G. (Children)* 2001, the mother had a moderate learning disability and needed the help and support of the local authority in caring for her children. The Court of Appeal upheld the decision of the trial judge that the best interests of the two children lay in being reunited with their mother with the help and support of the local authority.

Another important matter for the court to consider in deciding which type of order to make is the principle of proportionality, as expressed in the case law of the European Court of Human Rights (see *Gaskin v United Kingdom* 1989). This principle decrees that where a supervision order is proportionate as a response to the risk presented, it should be made to work. This can be done by requiring a health board to deliver the appropriate services to the family, and by requiring the parents of the child at risk to co-operate fully with the health board. A practical example of the principle of proportionality is the English case of *Re O. (Supervision Order)* 2001, where the Court of Appeal upheld the decision of the trial judge to make a supervision order. There was evidence before the court of a risk of significant harm to the child, attributable to the mother's mental health problems. The judge rejected the parents' argument that no order should be made, because of the risk of the parents' withdrawal from the regime of family support that had been put in place and the possibility that the mother's mental health might deteriorate. The judge also rejected the local authority's application for a care order, considering it to be important to the parents' self-esteem to retain parental responsibility for the child.

From the point of view of a health board concerned about the welfare of a child, the co-operation of parents will almost certainly be undermined where it moves for a care order as opposed to a supervision order. In *Re B. (A Minor) (Care or Supervision Order)* 1996, the English High Court, in making supervision orders in respect of three children aged eight, nine and eleven years respectively, acknowledged the fact that the making of care orders created the risk of the mother's co-operation being lost and the children's trust in the social services being damaged. However, in *Re D. (A Minor) (Care or*

Supervision Order) 1993, the court ignored the fact that the local authority feared that the making of a care order would undermine the co-operation that it was getting from the parents, holding that the protection of the child was the most important aspect of the case. These two cases are illustrative of the dilemma that is often presented to the court of choosing between a supervision order and a care order once the threshold criteria have been satisfied. At the end of the day, however, the litmus test is what order best secures the welfare of the child within the parameters of the Constitution and the 1991 Act.

Legal Effect of a Supervision Order

The legal effect of a supervision order is to authorise a health board to have the child visited in his home as often as it considers necessary for the purpose of satisfying itself as to the welfare of the child, and giving any necessary advice to parents or a person acting in loco parentis as to the care of the child. Unlike a care order, a supervision order does not confer parental responsibility for the child on the health board, and the parents retain exclusive parental responsibility. Essentially, the nature of a supervision order is to help and assist a child whose parents have full responsibility for its care and upbringing. As to the level of supervision required, the health board has almost complete discretion, in that there is no statutory level of monitoring specified in section 19 of the 1991 Act.

A parent or person acting *in loco parentis* who is not satisfied with the manner in which a health board is carrying out a supervision order may apply to the court for directions in relation to the supervision of the child. The court may give such directions as it considers appropriate and the health board must comply with any such directions. As a supervision order merely gives a health board the power to monitor a child within the home, it is important that the board should have the facility of applying to the court for directions as to the care of the child which might involve its temporary removal from the home. The court may give such directions as it thinks fit, which may require the parents of the child or a person acting *in loco parentis* to cause him to attend for medical or psychiatric examination, treatment or assessment at a hospital, clinic or other place specified by the court.

Relationship between Parent and Supervisor

For a supervision order to be effective in securing the welfare of a child, it is vital that there is a good working relationship between a parent or other guardian and the health board. It is of the essence of such an order that the board is capable of intervening in the life of the child. A typical example of the kind of difficulties faced by a health board in discharging its obligations under a supervision order is the English case of *Re D. (A Minor) and D. and A. (Minors)* 1997. In the course of child protection proceedings, the judge became so concerned about the well-being of a ten-year-old girl who was residing with her mother that she ordered a report under section 37 of the Children Act 1989. The mother had to be hospitalised from time to time because of debilitating illness when the girl and her two brothers (who resided with their father) were very young. As a result of the report, the local authority sought and obtained a supervision order. In dismissing the mother's appeal against the supervision order, the Court of Appeal remarked on the apparent devotion of the mother to her daughter, "a devotion that is so over-protective as to become stultifying, and that is the sadness and tragedy of the case". The girl suffered acutely from enuresis and encopresis, a condition that had beset her for many years. Because the mother rejected the advice and help that was being offered by the local authority, the continuing problems remained. As a result of the supervision order, the local authority was supposed to be capable of intervening. It was unable to do so because its relationship with the mother had broken down.

An unusual situation arose in the English case of *Re M. (A Minor)* 1998, in that a twelve-year-old boy the subject of a supervision order under which he resided with his mother applied to the local authority on three occasions during the currency of the order and asked to be taken back into care. He wanted to leave his mother and go to live with foster parents. The boy was born prematurely and had food and nutrition allergies. The mother herself had well-documented psychiatric problems. The court had originally made the supervision order having been satisfied that the mother had emotionally abused the boy and that the threshold criteria under section 31 of the Children Act 1989 had been met, a fact not challenged by the mother. As a result of the boy's persistent requests to be taken back into care, the local authority applied for and obtained an emergency protection order.

Obstruction of Supervisor

As the effectiveness of a supervision order is dependent on the supervising social worker having full access to the child for the purposes of supervision, the lack of co-operation by parents or the wilful obstruction of the supervisor will frustrate the whole process. For this reason, section 19(5) of the 1991 Act makes it an offence for any person to fail to comply with the terms of a supervision order or any directions given by the court under it. It is also an offence to prevent, impede or obstruct a person visiting a child on behalf of a health board. Any such offence is punishable on summary conviction by a fine not exceeding £500 and/or a term of imprisonment not exceeding six months. Of course, where there is any infringement of the terms of a supervision order, or directions given by the court under it, the health board can return to court and apply for a care order. Where a care order is made, the health board will be given the necessary powers to achieve its purpose.

Duration of Supervision Order

A supervision order remains in force for up to twelve months, or such shorter period as may be specified in the order and, in any event, shall cease to have effect when a child reaches the age of eighteen years. A supervision order automatically lapses where a care order is subsequently made in respect of a child. On or before the expiration of a supervision order, a further supervision order may be made on the application of the health board with effect from the expiration of the first mentioned order. However, there is no indication in section 19 of the 1991 Act as to what criteria must be satisfied before "a further supervision order may be made". This is in contrast to the position under section 18 of the 1991 Act, where the court must be satisfied that grounds for the making of a care order "continue to exist" before extending the operation of a care order. In the absence of any express statutory guidelines for extending a supervision order, there is nothing to suggest that different considerations would apply from the case of the extension of a care order. This is so, since the Supreme Court made it clear in *K.C. and A.C. v An Bord Uchtala* 1985 that the State cannot interfere in the authority of the family unless there are compelling reasons to do so, in that the parents must have failed and "continue to fail" to provide for the welfare of their children. Whether in the form of an extension of a care order or a supervision order, any court intervention in the authority of the family requires that there be a fresh consideration of that family's present circumstances.

Conclusion

While the desirable objective of minimalist intervention in the life of the family for the protection of children can in many cases be achieved without the need to take them into care, a cautionary note should be sounded about the overuse of supervision orders. If the principle of minimalist intervention is taken too far, there is a slight danger that a court, when faced with an application to take a child into care, may use a supervision order as a kind of compromise which is not too hurtful to the parent, even in cases where the welfare of the child really demands that he be taken into care. In deciding whether it should make a supervision order, the primary concern for the court is to consider the benefits of such an order for the child. In particular, the court should be slow to make a supervision order unless it is satisfied that the relationship between the health board and the parents is such as to enable the social worker assigned to the case to work effectively with the family.

CHAPTER 16

SPECIAL CARE ORDERS

Introduction

From time to time it may become necessary to detain children who have been adjudged to be out of control in secure residential units for their own protection and the protection of others. It should be borne in mind that the children in question have not been convicted of any wrongdoing and are being detained by order of the court for their own welfare. For this reason, detention in secure accommodation should be a last resort. This is borne out by Article 37 of the United Nations Convention on the Rights of the Child, which provides that the decision to deprive a child of his liberty "shall be used only as a measure of last resort and for the shortest appropriate period of time". In *D.G. v Eastern Health Board* 1998, Hamilton CJ said that the power to detain a child "should be exercised only in extreme and rare occasions, when the court is satisfied that it is required for a short period in the interests of the welfare of the child and there is, at the time, no other suitable facility".

Despite the comprehensive framework provided by the 1991 Act for dealing with children in need of care and protection, the Act did not permit any kind of civil containment or detention by a health board. Although the 1991 Act foisted a statutory function on health boards, whereby they were required to promote the welfare of children, they were not given the necessary statutory powers, funds or facilities to carry out these duties. Health boards did not even have a statutory entitlement to apply to a court for an order detaining a child. In order to fill the statutory vacuum that existed by reason of the failure of the legislature and executive, the courts had to intervene to ensure that the constitutional needs of children with acute behavioural problems were supplied. The High Court developed a jurisdiction to deprive a child of his liberty to provide safe, secure welfare in a child's residential centre. Indeed, because of the chronic shortage of secure accommodation for the care of troubled children, as documented in some of the cases discussed in this chapter, the ludicrous situation has arisen of children having to be detained in psychiatric institutions in the company of very disturbed adults and even in penal institutions.

The Inherent Jurisdiction of the High Court to Detain Children

This special jurisdiction of the High Court came about mainly as a result of young people and their families initiating judicial review proceedings claiming that the State had failed in its constitutional duty to them. In *F.N. v Minister for Education* 1995, the High Court held that where neither the parents nor the health board could deal with the very special needs of a child who was in urgent need of special treatment, attention and education, with an element of containment or detention necessary for the treatment to be effective, "there is a constitutional obligation on the State under Article 42.5 of the Constitution to cater for those needs in order to vindicate the constitutional rights of the child". In the course of his judgment, Geoghegan J cited the Supreme Court decision in *M.F. v Superintendent Ballymun Garda Station* 1990, where O'Flaherty J said that detention in those circumstances is justified for the purpose of "preserving the life and health of a child or young person and for the purpose of vindicating his constitutional rights. It is in no sense to be construed as meaning a deprivation of liberty or of any of his constitutional rights". In *T.D. v Minister for Education* 2001, the Supreme Court held that the High Court could not make a mandatory order compelling the executive to carry out its function of providing secure accommodation for the applicants, as the granting of such an order is inconsistent with the separation of powers principle. This principle requires the distribution of powers between the legislative, executive and judicial organs of Government mandated by the Constitution. It is of fundamental importance that each of the organs of Government should not only carry out the duties imposed on it by the Constitution, but should recognise that the Constitution also defines the boundaries within which they are confined in carrying out their functions.

The inherent jurisdiction of the High Court to detain children in secure accommodation does not extend to detention in a penal institution, in the absence of any other suitable facility. In *D.G. v Ireland* 2002, the European Court of Human Rights found Ireland to be in breach of Article 5 of the European Convention on Human Rights in detaining an out of control seventeen-year-old boy in St Patrick's Institution, which is a penal institution. Article 5 permits the detention of a minor by lawful order for the purposes of "educational supervision". This restriction on liberty is directed to the situation of those minors who are beyond normal parental control. In *Koniarska v United Kingdom* 2000, it was held that, in the context of detention of minors, the words "educational supervision" must not be equated rigidly with notions of classroom teaching. In the context of a young person in local authority care, "educational supervision must embrace many aspects of the exercise, by the local authority, of parental rights for the benefit and protection of the person concerned". Accordingly, educational supervision is much wider than normal parental control or academic lessons taught in the classroom. In the case of children with acute behavioural problems, the concept of educational supervision entails placing restrictions on the liberty of children with those problems for their own welfare, so that the underlying causes of the misbehaviour can be examined and addressed.

The Legislative Framework

The Children Act 2001, in amending the 1991 Act, has filled the legislative vacuum which necessitated the use of the inherent jurisdiction of the High Court to cater for the special needs of out of control non-offending children. The new legislative framework provides for the convening of family welfare conferences, which will enable health boards to intervene with other agencies at an early stage in relation to children who need special care and protection. A statutory duty is imposed on a health board to apply for a special care order or an interim special care order in relation to a child in its area who is in need of special care and protection, which he is unlikely to receive unless the court makes such an order. Health boards will have responsibility for ensuring the provision and operation of appropriate services and facilities for children who need to be detained in their own interests. Where a special care order is made, a health board will have power to detain the child the subject of the order. A child should only be detained in a special care unit as a last resort. For this reason, health boards are empowered to provide alternative arrangements or other accommodation for the child who is the subject of a special care order, as part of the programme for the care, education and treatment of the child.

Family Welfare Conference

The Family Welfare Conference is designed to maximise the use of the child's social and family support networks at a time of crisis in his life. There is now widespread acceptance of the practice of regularly involving families in making decisions about protecting and ensuring safety for their children. The principles underlying the use of the family welfare conference are that the child's interests are paramount and that, in so far as is possible, the child is best looked after within his own family. Section 23A of the 1991 Act requires a health board to arrange for the convening of a family welfare conference before applying for a special care order or interim special care order. This is designed to ensure that the important people in the child's life have explored other methods of meeting the child's particular needs, such as assisting the child within his own family or placing the child with foster carers or within the mainstream residential system. The power to detain a child in a secure unit should not be used simply because no other placement is available or because a child is likely to abscond from a residential centre. There is also the danger that unless vigilance is exercised at the family welfare conference stage, the shortage of mainstream residential placements will lead to inappropriate use of specialist units. At the same time, the use of secure accommodation with adequate therapeutic and educational facilities, if properly planned, can be a positive thing.

The circumstances in which a family welfare conference may be convened, and the functions and procedures of a conference, are contained in sections 7 to 15 of the 2001 Act. A conference can be convened either on a direction from the Children Court, where the court considers that a child before it on a criminal charge may be in need of special care or protection, or where it appears to a health board that a child in its area may require special care or protection which he is unlikely to receive unless a court makes a special care order in respect of him. Where a family welfare conference is to be convened, the health board must appoint a co-ordinator to convene and chair the conference. The conference may regulate its own procedures and shall be provided with administrative services by the health board. The proceedings of a family welfare conference are privileged, and no evidence shall be admissible in any court of any information, statement or admission disclosed or made in the course of the conference.

The persons entitled to attend a family welfare conference include the child, the parents or guardian of the child, any guardian *ad litem* appointed for the child, relatives of the child, where appropriate, and officers of the health board concerned. The term "relative", in relation to a child, means a brother, sister, uncle or aunt, or a spouse of the brother, sister, uncle or aunt, or a grandparent or step-parent, of the child. The co-ordinator, after consultation with the child and his parents, may allow any other persons who know the child or have a particular expertise in the matter to be discussed, and whose presence would benefit the conference, to attend. The co-ordinator has the power to exclude any person from participation or further participation in a family welfare conference if, before or during the conference, he is of the opinion that the presence or continued presence of that person is not in the best interests of the conference or the child.

It shall be the function of a family welfare conference to decide if a child in respect of whom the conference is being convened is in need of special care or protection. In reaching its decision, the conference will rely on the psychiatric and other professional evidence before it. The reported cases paint a picture of adolescents with disturbed personalities who are beyond control and who have proved stubbornly unresponsive to the protective or educational measures provided by mainstream placements. In *F.N. v Minister for Education*, above, the applicant had experienced behavioural problems when he was twelve years old. A psychiatric report showed that he suffered from hyperkinetic conduct disorder and required time in a secure unit for treatment. The psychiatric evidence in *P.S. v Eastern Health Board* 1994 indicated that the applicant, a fourteen-year-old boy, was seriously disturbed and had a history of drug abuse. *D.T. v Eastern Health Board* 1995 concerned a twelve-year-old girl with suicidal tendencies who was considered to be of such an unruly disposition that she needed to be cared for in some kind of suitable confinement. *D.H. (A Minor) v Ireland and Others* 2000 involved a sixteen-year-old girl, who was not psychiatrically ill, but was severely traumatised following neglect, rejection and sexual abuse as a young child. The evidence showed that she abused alcohol, sniffed lighter fuel and took drugs, engaged in prostitution and had suffered a miscarriage. She was violent, had frequent episodes of self-mutilation and had attempted to hang herself. She had set fire to herself and this had led to her detention at an adult psychiatric hospital with twenty-nine mentally ill adults.

Whether or not it decides that a child is in need of special care and protection, a family welfare conference may make recommendations to the health board relating to the care and protection of the child, including, where appropriate, a recommendation that the board should apply for a care order or a supervision order under the 1991 Act in respect of the child. Any recommendation made must have been agreed on unanimously, unless the disagreement of any person present is deemed by the co-ordinator to be unreasonable, in which case the co-ordinator can dispense with that person's agreement. Where a family welfare conference cannot reach agreement, even after disregarding any unreasonable disagreement by a member, the co-ordinator shall refer the matter to the health board for determination. The recommendations of a family welfare conference must be notified to the child in respect of whom the conference was convened, his parents or guardian, any guardian *ad litem* appointed for the child, any other person who attended the conference, the health board concerned and any other body or person at the co-ordinator's discretion. On receipt of the recommendations, the health board concerned may apply for a special care order, care order or supervision order under the 1991 Act, or may provide the necessary services or assistance to the child or his family.

Special Care Orders

The provisions of the Children Act 2001 that enable the court to make special care orders form part of the overall framework for the support and welfare of children who present particular difficulties and who, for their own protection and to ensure their continuing education, require that the accommodation in which they are looked after should be secure. A health board cannot detain a child by placing him in a special care unit without receiving the necessary authorisation from the court in the form of a special care order. Whereas, the making of a care order confers parental responsibility on the health board, enabling the board to control the movements of a child by placing various restrictions on his liberty, the placing of a child in secure accommodation does not represent the exercise of normal parental control.

The making of a special care order, which should really be a matter of last resort, is intended to reflect far wider restrictions on liberty than those which arise in a normal family situation. Indeed, the fact that a special care order is needed means that unless accommodation that is adequate for the purpose of restricting liberty is provided, there is likely to be a substantial risk to the health, safety, development or welfare of the child. This is so because there is a history and a continuing risk of the child absconding, with a likelihood of significant harm to himself and others. Accordingly, the child requires more supervision and attention than any normal parent could personally provide or be expected to provide, and in accommodation that is designed for the very purpose of restricting a child's freedom.

Section 23A of the 1991 Act imposes a statutory obligation on a health board to institute proceedings for a special care order or an interim special care order, as appropriate, in respect of a child in its area who appears to the board to be in need of special care or protection which he is unlikely to receive unless a court makes such an order. Before applying for such an order, the health board must arrange for the convening of a family welfare conference in respect of the child. The purpose of requiring a health board to seek the guidance of a family welfare conference in reaching a decision as to whether or not to apply for a special care order is to afford the conference an opportunity of considering the professional advice available to it. Having received the recommendation of the family welfare conference, the board can give effect to the recommendation by applying for a special care order, a care order or a supervision order, or provide the necessary services or assistance to the child and his family. In reaching its decision, the board must comply with the provisions of section 3 of the 1991 Act, which require it, having taken the other matters outlined in the section into account, to regard the welfare of the child as the first and paramount consideration. A parent may request a health board to apply for a special care order in respect of the child. If the board decides not to do so, it shall inform the parent in writing of the reasons for its decision.

The Grounds for Making a Special Care Order

The court can make a special care order under section 23B of the 1991 Act where it is satisfied, on the application of a health board, that:

(a) the behaviour of the child is such that it poses a real and substantial risk to his health, safety, development or welfare, and

(b) the child requires special care or protection which he is unlikely to receive unless the court makes such an order.

A special care order shall commit a child to the care of a health board and authorise the board to arrange for appropriate care, education and treatment for the child and for this purpose to detain the child in a special care unit (a special care unit operates to a high standard of security whereas a high support unit, while of similar design, operates to a lower standard of physical security). Section 23K of the 1991 Act obliges health boards to provide special care units (see Chapter 18). A health board shall notify a parent having custody of a child or a person acting in *loco parentis* of the placement of the child in a special care unit, unless the parent or person is missing or cannot be found (section 23E). When a child is detained in a special care unit, the health board may take such steps as are reasonably necessary to prevent the child from injuring himself or other persons in the unit, or from absconding from the unit. Where a special care order is in force, a health board may, as part of its programme for the care, education and treatment of the child, place the child in a children's residential centre, with foster parents or relatives, or give the child a temporary release. A special care order will remain in force for a period to be specified in the order of between six and twelve months, but it may be extended on the application of a health board, if the court is satisfied that the grounds for the making of such an order continue to exist. A special care order will cease to have effect when the person to whom it relates reaches eighteen years of age, unless the court orders otherwise in the interests of the person concerned.

A health board may apply to the court for the variation or discharge of a special care order if it appears to the board that the circumstances that led to the making of the order no longer exist. A special care order may be varied or discharged by the court of its own motion or on the application of any person (section 23F). In discharging a special care order the court may, of its own motion or on the application of a health board, make a supervision order in respect of the child. The court is also empowered to make a care order where it is satisfied that the child requires care and protection which he is unlikely to receive unless he remains in care, or where the return of the child to the custody of a parent or any other person would not be in the best interests of the child.

Interim Special Care Orders

The court may make an interim special care order where there is reasonable cause to believe that grounds exist for the making of a special care order and that it is necessary in the interests of the child that he be detained in a special care unit (section 23C). The application for an interim order can be made notwithstanding the fact that a family welfare conference is being arranged, or an application for a special care order is or has been made. The threshold applicable to an interim special care order is lower than that for a special care order, in that the court only has to be satisfied that "there is reasonable cause to believe", as opposed to being satisfied, that any of the grounds for the making of a special care order exist. An interim special care order shall authorise detention in a special care unit for up to twenty-eight days or, where the health board and parent having custody of the child or a person in *loco parentis* consent, for a period exceeding twenty-eight days. If the court is satisfied that the grounds for an interim care order continue to exist, it may extend any such period on the application of any of the parties. The court may also, with the consent of the parties, order an extension exceeding twenty-eight days. Normally, an application for an interim special care order or an extension thereof must be made on notice to a parent having custody of a child or a person acting in *loco parentis*. However, where the interests of justice or the welfare of the child so require, an application may be made *ex parte* without prior notice to a parent or other person.

Emergency Garda Síochána Intervention

Section 23D of the 1991 Act is an emergency provision, designed to facilitate intervention where out of control children come to the notice of An Garda Síochána. Where a garda has reasonable grounds for believing that the behaviour of a child is such that it poses a real and substantial risk to the child's health, safety, development or welfare, and the child is not receiving adequate care or protection, and it would not be sufficient for the protection of the child from such risk to await the making of an application for an interim special care order by a health board, the garda shall endeavour to deliver, or arrange for the child to be delivered, to the custody of the board. The health board must be informed of the circumstances in which the child came to the notice of the gardaí. Where it appears to the health board that the child requires special care or protection, the board shall apply for a special care order or an interim special care order. The section is clearly designed to cater for the situation where disturbed children constantly run away from open residential care centres and come to the notice of the gardaí because of their involvement in criminal activity or prostitution, or because they are homeless and associating with drug abusers and petty criminals. Section 23L enables a health board to seek the assistance of the gardaí to recover a child who absconds from a special care unit.

A good example of a situation that would justify emergency intervention is the case of *P.S. v Eastern Health Board*, above. A fourteen old boy had lived away from home for many years, during which time he had experienced many placements. His determined policy not to co-operate with those seeking to provide for his care and welfare led to his being expelled from a residential home, as a result of which he lived rough on the streets. He was accommodated in a hostel, but was expelled for violence and drug use. He returned to living rough on the streets, and on many nights he went to a garda station looking for somewhere to sleep. The gardaí contacted the health board, but there was no institution to take him in and he frequently had to stay in garda stations overnight.

Sections 23G to 23I apply the provisions of the 1991 Act governing appeals, invalid orders, jurisdiction and procedure to proceedings in relation to special care orders and interim special care orders. Section 23J provides for the application of the provisions of the 1991 Act dealing with access to children in care, reviews, aftercare and applications to the District Court for directions, to children committed to the care of a health board pursuant to a special care order or an interim special care order. Section 23M adds Part IVA to the parts of the 1991 Act to which section 4 (voluntary care) of that Act applies. Section 23N provides that a child on being found guilty of an offence may not be detained in a special care unit.

Conclusion

The putting in place of a comprehensive legislative framework for the special treatment of non-offending children who, because of acute behavioural difficulties, are deemed to be unruly or beyond control, coupled with the coming on stream of secure care units will go some way towards meeting the concerns expressed by the Committee on the Rights of the Child about Ireland's performance in complying with the United Nations Convention on the Rights of the Child. One of these concerns related to inadequate funding for alternative care provision, which necessitated frequent requests to the High Court to place children with special needs in residential facilities outside the State because of the lack of suitable facilities domestically (see concluding observations of the Committee dated 23 January 1998 – CRC/C/15/Add.85). On a more sombre note, the allocation by the State of adequate resources to provide modern, well-equipped, secure accommodation to meet the special needs of the very disturbed young people who require "educational supervision" will help to ensure that children who in the past had to be detained in unsuitable accommodation such as penal institutions and adult psychiatric hospitals for their welfare will no longer have to endure a similar plight (see *East Coast Area Health Board v O'Donovan* 2001).

CHAPTER 17

WARDS OF COURT

Introduction

Wardship is part of the High Court's ancient non-statutory (i.e. inherent) jurisdiction over children. This inherent jurisdiction can be invoked either by making the child a ward of court or by making an application to the High Court outside the wardship procedure. The wardship jurisdiction of the court is used to protect the interests of children where responsibility for the child rests with the court. The unique effect of wardship is that the court assumes the role of a parent in relation to the ward and no important step affecting the child can be taken without the court's consent. An application to bring a child into wardship can be made by a member of the child's family or by any person who satisfies the court that he has an interest in the child. In the past persons such as foster parents, teachers and members of the medical profession have successfully applied to make a child a ward of court. The circumstances in which a health board might wish to avail of the wardship procedure are considered below.

The inherent jurisdiction can be used to protect the interests of a child who has not been made a ward of court. It is generally used to settle a specific issue, very often a medical matter, and gives the court the ability to exceed the powers and overrule the decisions of parents. A very clear example of the inherent jurisdiction being invoked outside wardship occurred in the case of *North Western Health Board v H.W. and C.W.* 2001. The parents of a year-old child refused to consent to the PKU ('pin prick') test being carried out on the child. The test detects various disorders of the blood. The health board applied to the High Court for an order authorising it to carry out the test, as they claimed, to protect and vindicate the personal rights of the child under Article 40 of the Constitution. The court refused to make the order, on the basis that when it comes to decisions regarding their children's welfare, parents know best. While the decision of the parents in this case might be deemed ill-advised and against the weight of the medical evidence, it could not be regarded as such a default of their moral and constitutional duty as to warrant State intervention. On appeal, the Supreme Court upheld the decision of the trial judge (see also Chapter 6).

The Effect of Wardship

When a child is made a ward of court, the court takes control over all matters relating to the person and property of the child. In *Re A Ward of Court* 1995, the Supreme Court described the effect of wardship as vesting the court with jurisdiction over the ward's affairs. This jurisdiction is subject only to the provisions of the Constitution, and "there is no statute which in the slightest degree lessens the court's duty or frees it from the responsibility of exercising parental care". The court's duty includes giving directions with regard to the care, maintenance and well-being of the ward. Even where the court grants care and control of the child, in the sense that it delegates responsibility for his day-to-day upbringing, to an individual or body such as a health board, such individual or body "is subject to the directions of the court and all decisions with regard thereto as are made by the court". While routine decisions concerning the child can be made by the person or body with responsibility for the child, the court's prior consent will be required for such important decisions as the child receiving medical treatment or being adopted or being brought outside the jurisdiction.

In making any orders in wardship proceedings in relation to the custody, care or property of a child, the court makes the welfare of the child the first and paramount consideration. In *Re A Ward of Court*, the Supreme Court said that in the exercise of the wardship jurisdiction "the court's prime and paramount consideration must be the best interests of the ward". While the views of the ward's family should be heeded and given careful consideration, those views "cannot and should not prevail over the court's view of the ward's best interest". In deciding in any given case what is in the best interests of the ward, the court adopts the same attitude as would a responsible parent in the case of his own child. The court is not expected to adopt any higher or different standards than that which, viewed objectively, a reasonable and responsible parent would adopt. In describing the function of the judge in wardship proceedings involving a child as conducting an inquiry as to what, in all the circumstances, is in the best interests of the child, Denham J in *Re M.K., S.K. and W.K. (Infants)* 1999 said "the kernel of the jurisdiction is the welfare of the child".

Invocation of Wardship Jurisdiction

Private Law Matters

As the wardship jurisdiction is extremely flexible, in the sense that the court is not bound by strict statutory guidelines, it was availed of extensively in the past in private law matters. Custody disputes involving parents were resolved by making the child the subject of the dispute a ward of court, the court awarding custody to one parent, usually the mother, and access to the other parent. However, since the introduction of the Guardianship of Infants Act 1964, as amended, parents now rely almost exclusively on the procedures provided by the Act for resolving their disputes. In any event, parents should think twice before calling upon the scarce resources of the High Court, which can turn out to be a very expensive process. For this reason the inherent jurisdiction should be reserved for exceptional situations, where the element of continuing judicial control is thought to be necessary, or where questions relating to the child's upbringing and general welfare cannot be resolved under the statutory provisions.

Wardship is still of great practical importance in custody disputes between the parents of a child and third parties such as relatives and foster parents. As the 1964 Act only provides for the resolution of disputes between parents, extended family members, such as grandparents and uncles and aunts, and outsiders must avail of the wardship jurisdiction if they wish to gain custody of a child. In these cases, the court must balance the claims of parenthood against the welfare of the child, which is the first and paramount consideration. The court's approach to applications by outsiders was considered at length by the Supreme Court in the landmark decision in *K.C. and A.C. v An Bord Uchtala* 1985. In brief, the court decided that in view of the very special position of the family referred to in Articles 41 and 42 of the Constitution, there must be exceptional circumstances ('compelling reasons') before a child will be removed from the custody of parents and handed over to outsiders. Since the enactment of the Children Act 1997, there is no longer any need for grandparents or uncles or aunts to avail of wardship to obtain an order granting access to a child.

Pubic Law Matters

Prior to the implementation of the Child Care Act 1991, health boards tended to use the wardship jurisdiction as an alternative to the statutory scheme available under the now repealed Children Act 1908, in order to avoid its shortcomings. For example, in *Southern Health Board v C.H.* 1996, a father had placed his daughter in voluntary care following the death of his wife. Subsequently, the health board had the child made a ward of court in order to resist an application by the father to regain custody of her, as there were allegations that he had sexually abused her. The child had alleged that the father sexually abused her. In *Re M.K., S.K. and W.K. (Infants)* 1999, a health board used the wardship procedure to take three children into care, on the grounds that their father had sexually abused one of the children. Since the principal object of the 1991 Act, as amended, was to replace the outmoded procedures of the 1908 Act, and replace them with a comprehensive child protection mechanism, the wardship jurisdiction will only be availed of for those exceptional cases not specifically catered for in the legislation.

A novel use of the wardship jurisdiction to cater for a situation not specifically covered by child protection legislation occurred in the English case of *Re R.-J. (Minors)* 1998. The children the subject of the proceedings were in the interim care of foster parents whom the local authority considered to be eminently suitable to meet the long-term needs and welfare of the children. In the meantime, new regulations were introduced which made foster parents unsuitable to act as foster parents, in circumstances where a foster parent or any of his family had been cautioned by a constable for a specified offence. The foster father had in fact been cautioned in the past in respect of an assault occasioning actual bodily harm to a foster child, thereby barring him from fostering children. The local authority wished the children to remain with the foster parents. The Court of Appeal held that, in the peculiar circumstances of the case, the regulations should not prevent the judge deciding that the foster parents are suitable long-term carers, and making an order in the context of continuing wardship under which the children would remain in the long-term care of the foster parents.

Conclusion

There are very few occasions in which the wardship jurisdiction will have to be invoked in children's cases nowadays. In the majority of cases, the statutory scheme is perfectly adequate to meet the requirements of health boards and individual litigants. In cases where there is a need for continued supervision by the court or when a health board needs to supplement its statutory powers, it may still be necessary to invoke the inherent jurisdiction of the High Court. In cases involving the medical treatment of children, the emergency provisions of the 1991 Act are normally adequate to secure the welfare of a child. Where it is not appropriate to invoke the emergency provisions of the Act, or have the child warded, the inherent jurisdiction may be invoked to treat the child without the need to have him warded.

Part Four

CHILDREN IN THE CARE OF HEALTH BOARDS

CHAPTER 18

THE TREATMENT OF CHILDREN IN CARE

Introduction

The decision to remove a child from the custody of his parents and place him in the care of a health board is a serious interference with the child's right to respect for family life within the meaning of Article 8 of the European Convention on Human Rights. On the other hand, a failure to interfere where interference is called for may also amount to a violation of the child's Convention rights (see *Z. v United Kingdom* 2001). Where the State has to deprive a child of his family life by taking him into care, the 1991 Act imposes a positive obligation on the State to take reasonable and appropriate steps to fill the gap. Section 36 of the Act confers a very wide discretion on the health board in whose favour a care order has been made to make such arrangements as it thinks fit as to the most suitable placement for the child. The major objective of any placement, be it in residential care or with foster carers or relatives, is to obtain a good outcome for the child. A placement must depend on the facts of a particular case and the availability of resources at a given time. Ideally, a child should not be placed in residential care before other options are considered. Regardless of the type of placement, it is vital that the child's long-term future is considered and catered for in an effective care plan. As the child's circumstances change, many aspects of the care plan will need to be reviewed.

Foster Care

Foster care is the main form of alternative care provided by health boards for children in need of care and protection who cannot remain in their own homes. In *Gaskin v United Kingdom* 1989, the European Court of Human Rights held that family life within the meaning of Article 8 of the European Convention on Human Rights includes the relationship between a foster carer and a foster child. The majority of children in care now live with foster carers. Statistics available from the Department of Health and Children show that in 1998, 3,162 of the 3,984 children in care were in foster care. At the end of 1999, there were 3,289 children in foster care, an increase of 66 per cent compared with 1989. The provisions of the Children Act 2001, which permit the making of a special care order in respect of a child who appears to be in need of special care or protection, which he is unlikely to receive unless the court makes such an order, permit a health board to place the child on a temporary basis with foster carers.

The Report of the Working Group on Foster Care 2001, entitled "Foster Care: A Child-Centred Partnership", accepted that where a child requires care for long periods, he should, as a general rule, be cared for in another family. The main objective of foster care is to provide, in so far as is reasonably possible, a normal family environment with the love and support such an environment can provide. The Working Group expressed concern that the standards set out in the regulatory framework were not always adhered to, and formulated a number of general values and principles that should govern the provision of foster care. These should include the provision of high quality care in a family setting; priority for the needs of the child in determining foster placements; respect for ethnic origin, religion and language; continuity in the lives of children; a partnership approach; respect for foster carers and the provision of aftercare. As a result of the Report of the Working Group on Foster Care, the National Standards for Foster Care were issued by the Department of Health and Children in April 2003. These Standards will serve as a basis for consistently promoting quality of care in foster care services. It is against these Standards that the Social Services Inspectorate will form judgements about the quality of foster care services.

Regulation of Foster Care Placements

Section 39 of the 1991 Act requires the Minister to make regulations governing the placement of children in foster care, which may fix the conditions under which children may be placed with foster parents, prescribe the form of contract between the health board and foster parents, and provide for the supervision and visitation by the health board of children in foster care.

The relevant regulations are the Child Care (Placement of Children in Foster Care) Regulations 1995. Before placing a child with foster parents, a health board must investigate both the child's circumstances and his new home, to ensure that the foster parents are fit and proper persons to look after children, and that they are capable of meeting the child's needs. The assessment should include a medical examination, unless the health board is satisfied that it is unnecessary. This is intended to achieve the aim of 'matching' the child concerned to his new family as far as possible. The process of assessment and matching a child to his new family aims to minimise the risk of future breakdown in the placement. As regards the religious upbringing of a child in foster care, the wishes of the child's guardian should be respected as far as possible. In emergency placements, the Regulations provide that the assessment should be carried out as soon as it is practical to do so. The Working Group on Foster Care recommended that in the case of emergency placements, the assessment of the child's circumstances should commence within a week of the placement, and that, in general, children in need of emergency care, or who otherwise have serious difficulties, should be matched with more experienced foster carers.

Once a child has been placed with foster parents, the health board must supervise the placement and visit the child to ensure his continued welfare. The Regulations require that the child be visited by an authorised person as often as the health board considers necessary, but in any event, at intervals not exceeding three months during the first two years of the commencement of the placement, the first visit taking place within one month of that date, and thereafter at intervals not exceeding six months. The frequency of the visits set out in the Regulations should be regarded as the minimum requirement. The child's welfare may dictate more frequent visits. The supervision and visitation requirements, in addition to ensuring the child's welfare, will also benefit foster parents by enabling them to receive advice and practical help from the social worker supervising the placement. A note of every visit must be recorded in the case record relating to the child which the health board must maintain. Where his foster parents adopt a child, section 44 of the 1991 Act enables a health board to continue to contribute to the maintenance of the child as if he continued to be in foster care. Where a child is adopted, any care order in force in respect of him will cease to have effect.

Where possible, and provided that it is in the best interests of the child, a child should be placed with foster parents in his own community. The Working Group on Foster Care recommended that, in assessing the needs of the child, placement in the community should be considered a priority issue. This approach is intended to ensure that the child is enabled to maintain his friendships, remain in the same school and maintain contact with his family. Indeed, the need to consider placing the child in the community also arises in the context of the State's obligations under the European Convention on Human Rights to take practical measures to facilitate reunion with parents. In *Olsson v Sweden* 1988, the European Court of Human Rights held that the placement of three children of a family with different foster parents, at a considerable distance from each other and from their parents, amounted to a violation of the right to respect for family life under Article 8 of the Convention. Only where the special circumstances of a particular case make it desirable should a child be placed with foster carers outside the State. The Supreme Court held in *Western Health Board v K.M.* 2001 that, whilst a health board does not have authority to place a child with relatives or foster parents outside the State, the District Court does have such a power.

One of the issues identified by the Working Group on Foster Care as giving rise for concern is the very high proportion of children in care for two years or more. Because of the constitutional obstacles in the way of giving a legal status akin to guardianship to the foster parents of children in their long-term care, there is no way, short of adoption, that this can be achieved. Under the

Adoption Act 1988, the adoption of a marital child can only take place in exceptional circumstances, where the child has been in foster care with the proposed adopters for at least twelve months and the parents, for physical or moral reasons, have failed in their duty towards the child, and that such failure amounts to an abandonment of parental rights with respect to their child, and is likely to continue until the child reaches eighteen years of age. It is a matter of concern that some children remain in long-term foster care when adoption may be in their best interests. The Working Group received a number of submissions suggesting that there is a need to explore the possibility of open adoption arrangements for children in long-term care. An open adoption could allow a child to be adopted into a stable family environment, without the need to entirely relinquish his links with his natural parents and family. There are major constitutional issues involved, and maybe the time is right to consider revising Article 41 of the Constitution along the lines suggested by the Constitution Review Group in 1996 to give children rights as individuals rather than as members of a family unit, thereby facilitating the adoption of many of the children who are in long-term care.

Placement of Children with Relatives

Because of the acknowledged shortage of foster carers willing to take children into their homes and treat them as members of their families and the problems that have surfaced in the area of residential care, as highlighted in particular in the Overview Report of the Social Services Inspectorate discussed below, the placement of children with relatives is becoming more of a real option. The Minister is obliged by section 41 of the 1991 Act to make regulations governing the placement of children with relatives, which may fix the conditions under which children may be so placed, prescribe the form of contract between the health board and relatives, and provide for supervision and visitation by the health board. The relevant regulations are the Child Care (Placement of Children with Relatives) Regulations 1995. A relative is defined as including the spouse of a relative of the child and a person who has acted in *loco parentis*. Before placing a child with relatives, a health board must assess both the circumstances of the child and the suitability of the relatives. Once a placement has taken place, the health board must supervise it and arrange for the child to be visited by a social worker in accordance with the Regulations. The duties of relatives are prescribed. Generally, relatives are required to take all reasonable steps to promote the child's health, development and welfare. Specifically, relatives must permit visitation, maintain confidentiality, seek medical care for the child, co-operate in facilitating access by parents, notify a change of residence and arrange for the care of the child in their absence. The Report of the Working Group on Foster Care discussed above, with certain adjustments as appropriate, applies with equal effect to placements with relatives. Support for this view can be found in the fact that the Report exhibits the 1995 Regulations relating to both placement of children with foster carers and relatives as Appendices.

Residential Care

One of the ways in which a health board may fulfil its obligation under section 36 of the 1991 Act to provide care for a child is to place him in residential care. Residential care may be provided in a children's residential centre registered under the 1991 Act, in a residential home maintained by a health board or in a school or other suitable place of residence. In *East Coast Area Health Board v M.M.* 2002, the High Court, in reliance on the judgment of the Supreme Court in *Western Health Board v K.M.,* above, held that, whilst a health board does not have power to effect a residential placement outside the State, the District Court does have power to direct such a placement. Once it becomes necessary to provide a child with residential care, it is important that a range of alternative facilities is available, so that the child can receive help according to his needs. With this in mind, section 38 of the 1991 Act requires a health board to make arrangements with the registered proprietors of children's residential centres to ensure the provision of an adequate number of residential placements for children in its care. A health board may itself, with the approval of the Minister, provide and maintain a residential centre or other premises for the provision of residential care for children in its care.

A residential centre is defined in section 59 of the 1991 Act as any home or other institution, whether operated by a health board, a voluntary body or other person, which provides residential care for children in the care of a health board. Not included in the definition, however, are institutions that are under the control and management of the Minister or health boards, such as general medical hospitals, mental hospitals and schools that have been certified for the purposes of Part IV of the Children Act 1908. The Minister may make regulations under section 40 of the 1991 Act governing the placement of children in residential care. The Child Care (Placement of Children in Residential Care) Regulations 1995 set out the conditions under which children may be placed in residential care. The form of contract with persons providing residential care is prescribed, and provision is made for the supervision of children in residential care by health boards.

Despite the desirable objective of having a range of facilities available once a child has been assessed as in need of residential care, all too often in practice the reality is not so much a matter of choosing the most suitable place to fulfil a child's particular needs, but of finding a centre or other premises willing to take the child. According to a Report published by Focus Ireland in 1998, entitled "Out on Their Own: Young People Leaving Care in Ireland", there is a general lack of residential care facilities in health board areas, which at the time was particularly acute in the Eastern Health Board region. The lack of residential care placements is putting severe pressure on health board staff. Many young people are being driven into the homeless population, "as Community Care teams are unable to place young people who are assessed as needing residential care". According to the Report, the fact that many residential units were undergoing a transition, whereby control was being transferred from religious communities to State management, had compounded the problem. As the religious bodies withdraw from the provision of residential services, resulting in the closure of many of the large institutions, the State is under increased pressure to replace those services.

Registration of Children's Residential Centres

Section 60 of the 1991 Act provides that it shall not be lawful for any person to carry on a children's residential centre unless the centre is registered and the person is the registered proprietor thereof. Provision is made in section 61 of the Act for the registration by health boards of children's residential centres. Each health board must establish and maintain a register of any such centres in its area. The contents of the register are prescribed. The register shall be open for public inspection free of charge at all reasonable times. A health board may register or refuse to register any centre and may remove a centre from the register. Registration lasts for three years. The circumstances in which a health board may refuse registration or remove a centre from the register are set out. They include non-compliance by the centre with the Child Care (Standards in Children's Residential Centres) Regulations 1996, the unsuitability of the applicant for registration as a person convicted of an offence, failure to furnish information requested by the health board and the contravention of a condition imposed by the board. The refusal to register must be notified to the applicant. A health board may, on registration or thereafter, attach conditions to the operation of the centre, attach different conditions in the case of different centres and amend or revoke any condition. The form an application for registration of a centre must take is specified, as is the form an application for renewal of registration must take. It is an offence to contravene a condition attaching to a registration.

By virtue of section 63 of the 1991 Act, an appeal lies to the District Court against the decision of a health board to refuse to register a centre, to remove a centre from the register, to attach a condition to registration, or to amend or revoke a condition. An appeal must be brought within twenty-one days of the notification by the health board of its decision. The court may confirm the decision of the health board, or direct the board to register or restore registration of the centre, or direct the withdrawal of a condition or the amendment or revocation of a condition. The decision of the District Court on a question of fact is final.

Where the registered proprietor of a children's residential centre intends ceasing to carry on the centre, section 65 of the 1991 Act requires the proprietor to give six months' notice in writing to the health board for the area. A health board may accept shorter notice if it thinks fit. At the expiration of six months from the date of the notice (unless the notice is withdrawn or the period of registration has expired) the centre shall cease to be registered. Section 64 of the 1991 Act provides that a person found guilty on summary conviction of an offence under Part VIII of the Act, shall be liable to a fine not exceeding £1,000 or to imprisonment for up to twelve months.

Standards in Children's Residential Centres

The importance of monitoring compliance with operational standards laid down by legislation for children's residential centres is highlighted in a number of reports into the systematic abuse of children in children's homes both here and in the United Kingdom. The findings of abuse contained in the Report on the Inquiry into the Operation of Madonna House 1996, and the unlawful method of control used in children's homes in Staffordshire in England, as highlighted in the Report "The Pindown Experience and the Protection of Children" 1991, show that there is need for vigilance if children in residential care are to be spared the ordeal and resultant trauma of abuse. *Pindown* was an unlawful method of control used in children's homes which involved solitary confinement, the withdrawal of creature comforts of any kind and other forms of humiliating and degrading treatment. Article 3(3) of the United Nations Convention on the Rights of the Child requires State parties to ensure that the institutions, services and facilities responsible for the care or protection of children shall conform with the standards established by competent authorities, particularly in the areas of safety and health, in the number and suitability of their staff, as well as by competent supervision.

Section 63 of the 1991 Act requires the Minister to make regulations ensuring proper standards in children's residential centres, including adequate and suitable accommodation, food and care for children and the proper conduct of centres. The Child Care (Placement of Children in Residential Centres) Regulations 1995 oblige health boards to ensure that centres comply with the Regulations, and the Child Care (Standards in Children's Residential Centres) Regulations and the Guide to Good Practice in Children's Residential Centres 1996 impose specific obligations on the registered proprietor and person in charge of a centre. Where a person is convicted of an offence under section 63, the health board may within six months of the conviction, or the final determination of an appeal against conviction, obtain an order from the Circuit Court disqualifying that person for a specified period from carrying on, being in charge of, or concerned with the management of the centre to which the conviction relates.

The Regulations cover such matters as the maintenance, care and welfare of children. They also deal with staffing requirements, the design and maintenance of centres, the keeping of records and the inspection of premises in which centres are being carried on. New National Standards for Children's Residential Centres were issued by the Department of Health and Children in September 2001. The standards are based on the requirements of primary legislation and regulations, as well as findings from research and current knowledge about best practice in residential child care. The Overview Report of the Social Services Inspectorate, referred to below, was also relied on in framing the standards. The standards represent a good foundation for providing quality care and safeguarding the welfare of children in residential care. They deal with a wide range of issues, from children's rights to accommodation standards, and emphasise the need for care planning, the preparation of young people for leaving care and aftercare support. They will be applied to residential centres in both the voluntary and statutory sector.

Inspection of Children's Residential Centres

The authority for inspection of children's residential centres run by health boards is contained in section 69 of the 1991 Act. The Minister may have any service provided or premises maintained by a health board under the Act inspected by a person authorised by him in that behalf. For the purpose of conducting an inspection, the authorised person may enter any premises maintained by a health board under the Act and examine the state of management of the premises and the treatment of the children therein. The authorised person may also examine such records and interview such staff of the board as he thinks fit. The Irish Social Services Inspectorate (SSI), which is operationally independent from the Department of Health and Children, was established for the purpose of such inspection in 1999. Draft standards were adopted as the standards for children's residential centres run by the health boards. The main function of SSI is to support the child care services by promoting and ensuring the development of quality standards. It does this by monitoring the organisation, operation and management of child care services, and by evaluating the quality and responsiveness of services as experienced by both users and service providers. It is proposed to place SSI on a statutory footing in the near future.

As part of the inspection process, inspectors visit each residential centre over three days. The inspectors meet with management and staff, and separately with children, to explain the purpose of inspection. An inspection involves an examination of policies, records and individual case files. Interviews are conducted with management and staff and children themselves. Where possible, the inspectors listen to the views of parents. Practices in place at the centres are observed, and the premises are inspected to ascertain whether they provide suitable accommodation for the children. The performance of the centres is measured against the standards. Following inspection, reports are sent to the health boards concerned and the Department of Health and

Children. The Department seeks from the health boards concerned their initial response and an outline of their proposals for implementing the recommendations contained in the reports. The boards' responses are noted. Should there be concern about any particular centre, the inspectorate may carry out a follow-up inspection at an appropriate stage to determine whether there has been any improvement in the standard of care provided.

The remit of SSI does not extend to children's residential centres run by the voluntary sector. Under section 63 of the 1991 Act, the health boards carry out the inspection of those centres, and for this purpose some health boards have appointed their own inspectors. However, to ensure that the health boards are subject to some kind of monitoring in carrying out their statutory function, SSI receives copies of the health board inspection reports on voluntary sector centres. In its Overview Report issued in October 2000, SSI noted that a number of organisations operating centres in the voluntary sector are withdrawing from the provision of residential child care services. In many cases where this has occurred, the health boards have assumed responsibility for the running of those centres. Consequently, the number of children's residential centres subject to inspection by SSI is increasing. The annual report of SSI for 2002 shows that in October 2002, there were 176 residential centres, of which 102 were run by health boards, with the remainder being managed in the non-statutory sector.

The Overview Report also reveals that there was variation in the practice of the different centres, with some providing a very good standard of service. The inspectors found that there were high levels of staff turnover in some centres that did little to ensure that children in those centres were provided with the continuity of care they needed. Too many staff were employed on temporary contracts, and, in some centres, there were few staff with the relevant qualifications for child care work. In certain centres, insufficient attention was given to care planning by social workers who refer the children to the centres. This may lead to many children remaining in residential care longer than is necessary. The inspectorate identified the importance of involving parents and children in the development of plans which affect the children's lives. Inadequate support for young people leaving care is highlighted, with the result that too many of them are ending up with problems in the community. The Report states the need for closer monitoring by external managers, so that health boards are fully apprised of the extent to which residential care is being provided within the requirements of the Regulations. Health boards cannot rely on inspection alone to keep them informed of the quality of service being provided.

Secure Accommodation

Ideally, it should not be necessary to provide secure accommodation in a residential setting designed for the purpose of restricting the liberty of children in care. However, where a child is committed to the care of a health board on foot of a special care order, the board may detain the child in a special care unit. Restricting the liberty of children in care is a serious step, and it should be seen as a last resort only to take place where there is no other appropriate alternative placement. In *D.G. v Eastern Health Board* 1998, the Supreme Court held that where the restraint of liberty is necessary to secure the welfare of the child, the restraint to be imposed on the child "should be commensurate with his capacity to abscond". In the course of her dissenting judgment in *D.G.,* Denham J said that the function of a children's institution is education, correction and care. It relates to the capacity of the person, and it is not delivering a punishment. In identifying children with behavioural problems who are in trouble with the law as having additional needs, the National Children's Strategy provides that such children "will be supported in the least restrictive environment while having their needs addressed" (Chapter 5.2).

All the provisions of the 1991 Act governing the treatment of children in health board care, such as access, care planning, review of cases, aftercare and application to the District Court for directions, apply to children committed to the care of a health board pursuant to a special care order or an interim special care order. Section 23K of the 1991 Act enables health boards to provide special care units and make arrangements with voluntary bodies or other persons to provide secure care units on their behalf. The Minister's approval will be required for the provision of a secure care unit. The approval process will involve the unit being inspected by an authorised person. An approval will last for a period of three years. The Minister is authorised to make regulations governing the operation of special care units.

The Children Act 2001 (sections 225 to 244) provides for the establishment of a Special Residential Services Board, designed to ensure the efficient, effective and co-ordinated delivery of services to children placed in special care units. The Board will have a wide remit in relation to the co-ordination of such services, ensuring the appropriate use of them, liasing with the courts in relation to the level and nature of the services and advising the Minister for Health and Children in relation to any adjustments in the provision of accommodation or services for children who are out of control. The membership of the Board will be representative of all those professionals involved in the welfare of children. It will include three representatives of children detention schools, three of the Chief Executives of the health boards and five other members, including two experts in child care, two experts in special education and a probation and welfare officer. The Board is required to submit an annual report on the performance of its functions and other appropriate information to the Ministers for Health and Children and Education and Science. In the absence of any specific requirement in the legislation for health boards to do so, it is to be hoped that the annual report of the Special Residential Services Board will outline the number of children catered for in special care units per year, details of serious incidents occurring, staffing levels and the philosophy and methods of intervention. This should be complemented by a proper inspection system, with the publication of reports prepared by SSI.

Care Planning

The 1995 Regulations regulating the placement of children in care provide that a care plan must be drawn up for each child being placed. A court should hesitate to make a care order unless it is satisfied that a proper care plan has been devised for the child. Without an acceptable care plan the judicial role in making a care order cannot be fulfilled. The extent to which the court can become involved in the formulation and implementation of a care plan was considered in *Eastern Health Board v McDonnell* 2000 (see Chapter 14). In order to achieve the best possible outcome for the child entering care, great emphasis must be placed on positive long-term planning to ensure a particular placement is appropriate to the needs and general welfare of the child. Care planning should aim to promote the child's welfare in consultation with the child and his family, having regard to their wishes and feelings. A good care plan is crucial in providing a certain amount of stability and predictability for the vulnerable child in care. Unless proper attention is paid to care planning, a child may have to remain in care longer than is necessary. Ideally, a care plan should state what the placement hopes to achieve for the child. In addition, it should include details of what the placement hopes to do for the child and the arrangements that are in place as to contact with parents and other family members.

The Report of the Working Group on Foster Care emphasises the importance of care planning for a child being placed with foster carers or relatives. The Report emphasises that it is essential that the child, his parents and the various professionals involved in the child's life be consulted in the preparation of the care plan. It should address the issues of social skills, the disruption in the child's life, the difficulties the child may be experiencing in relationships and at school, and it should provide for the personal development of the child. The Working Group report expressed the view that the effectual operation of care plans is critical to the successful placement of children and that care plans are an essential part of the management and planning for a child's placement. A care plan should be drawn up regardless of whether a child is being placed in short, medium or long-term care. The care plan must, as a minimum, conform to the standards set out in the Regulations. It should clearly identify the particular needs of the child and the agreed supports to be provided for the child and his parents. A care plan should be maintained in writing and a copy of the plan should be provided for the child, where it is appropriate to his age or understanding, the child's parents and, in the case of a child in foster care, to the foster carers. In its annual report of 2002, SSI points out that planning for children was being taken more seriously, but that there was much room for improvement in the quality of plans and regularity of review.

Care Plan Reviews

Section 42 of the 1991 Act provides that the Minister may make regulations requiring the case of each child in the care of a health board to be reviewed. The regulations may provide for such matters as the manner in which each case is to be reviewed and the frequency of reviews. The regulations may also require a health board to consider whether it would be in the best interests of the child to be given into the custody of his parents. The purpose of review is to monitor how the child in care is doing and whether a particular milestone of the care plan has been achieved within a reasonable time of the date set at the hearing of the application for a care order. A review must consider whether the placement is the right one for the child and whether everything possible is being done to promote the child's welfare. The health board has power to make minor alterations to a care plan to cater for change. However, on the authority of *Eastern Health Board v McDonnell*, above, any fundamental change in the care plan requires the approval of the court. Where things have changed at home, a review must decide whether it is safe for the child to return home to the custody of his parents. Where the child is likely to leave care within the next two years, the help the child will need to cope with leaving care needs to be considered. The Working Group on Foster Care expressed its concern that if reviews are not carried out, there is a serious danger that the children will simply drift in care and that their care plans will become obsolete.

The 1995 Regulations provide that the case of each child in care shall be reviewed as often as is necessary, and at least every six months during the first two years of the child's placement. Reviews should be carried out at least annually after that. The first review must be carried out within two months of the placement. The Working Group on Foster Care recommended that statutory time-frames for review should be regarded as the absolute minimum, and that more frequent reviews should be carried out. A review meeting is held and is attended by the child and all those involved in the life of the child. In this regard, the health board must notify the child and his parents, foster carers, relatives and, in the case of residential care, the manager of a children's residential centre of the review meeting. They must be given an opportunity to be heard at the review meeting, and their views, where appropriate, must be taken into account. Any decision made as a result of a review meeting must be communicated to the child, where practicable, to foster carers, relatives and any other person whom the health board considers should be informed. In the case of residential care, the manager of the children's residential centre where the child is placed should also be informed of any review.

Aftercare

Many of the children who come into care will return to their families within a relatively short period. However, some children remain in care on a long-term basis and, in some cases, until they are eighteen. A large proportion of children who leave care do so because of placement breakdown. Findings by Focus Ireland published in its 1998 Report point to many children leaving care ending up in the homeless population. For this reason, it is important that the transition from care is planned and that children are supported after they leave care. Despite the desirability of providing aftercare support for children leaving care, the legislation is enabling only and does not oblige health boards to provide aftercare. Section 45 of the 1991 Act empowers health boards to provide aftercare support for children in their care. Where a child leaves care, a health board may provide assistance for the child until he reaches twenty-one years, provided the board is satisfied that he needs such care. Any such assistance may be continued beyond the age of twenty-one to enable a young person complete a course of education. The assistance may take the form of visiting the child and supporting him with education, training and accommodation requirements. The health board may contribute towards the cost of accommodation and pay the fees or costs involved in training.

Despite the importance of aftercare planning, SSI in its Overview Report 2000 found that only some residential centres were providing aftercare support for young people leaving their care. The Inspectorate concluded that, in general, aftercare planning is being left too late and in some cases it is not happening at all. Too often young people are leaving residential care in an unplanned way, which is not conducive to promoting their welfare. The National Standards for Children's Residential Centres 2001 state that a plan to prepare children for leaving care should be in place two years before their departure. The Report of the Working Group on Foster Care recommended that every health board have a clear written policy in relation to aftercare, and that every young person should have an aftercare plan as part of an overall care plan. The preparation of the aftercare plan should be undertaken at least two years before leaving care. The young person and foster carers should be fully involved in drawing up the plan.

Children Unlawfully Removed from Care

Where a child is removed from the custody of a health board or any person acting on behalf of the board without lawful authority, section 46 of the 1991 Act enables the board to seek the assistance of An Garda Síochána to recover the child. Where the court is satisfied by information on oath that a named person can produce the child, it may order such person to deliver up the child into the custody of a health board. Where the person having actual custody of the child, on being shown a copy of the order and having being required to hand over the child, refuses to do so, he is liable on conviction to a fine not exceeding £500 and/or imprisonment for up to six months. He may also be held to be in contempt of court. A person present in court when an order is made is deemed to have been shown a copy of the order. An application to hand over a child may be made *ex parte* and otherwise than at a public sitting of the court, where the urgency of the matter so requires. The court may issue a warrant authorising a member of An Garda Síochána, accompanied by other members of the force and such other persons as may be necessary, to enter any premises (if need be by force) to recover a child in respect of whom an order under this section has been made. A warrant may be issued elsewhere than at a public sitting of the court where the matter is urgent.

Conclusion

The whole purpose of legislating for the provision of alternative care by health boards is to ensure that a child's transition from family to care is as painless as possible. There can be little doubt that the separation of a child from family and familiar surroundings is a traumatic experience. Health boards should develop services to ensure that young children are not placed in care and that the number and length of placements is kept to the minimum. Where children are involuntarily admitted to the care of a health board following the making of a care order, it is envisaged that the child's stay in care will be for the shortest possible time and with a view to facilitating his return to the custody of his parents. Where a child must remain in care for an extended period, as a general rule he should be cared for by foster parents in a normal family environment. Where foster care is not suitable to the particular needs of the child, he will need to be placed in residential care. For this reason, a child's admission to care should be well planned and structured. It is vital that all children in care have quality care plans in order to obtain the best outcome for each child. This is particularly true in the case of children living in residential centres. It is necessary to constantly review the age, number and length of placements of children in residential centres. It is important to identify those children and young people who are extremely troubled for whom the residential provision is not suitable and whose needs are not being met. Those children need ongoing specialist psychological and support services in a suitable, secure environment.

Chapter 19

ACCESS TO CHILDREN IN CARE

Introduction

Child care professionals and the judiciary alike recognise the importance of ensuring that children in care maintain contact with their parents and extended family members. The Report of the Working Group on Foster Care 2001 states that "it is important for everyone to have a sense of their own identity and it is particularly the case for children in care". The Report refers to research that shows that the longer they are in care, contact between children and their families tends to diminish. For this reason, the Report states that it should be the child and family social worker's responsibility "to endeavour to maintain as much contact as is reasonably possible between the children and their own parents taking into account the child's safety" (Paragraph 3.23). Even in cases of severe abuse and neglect at the hands of parents or carers, provided the welfare of the child can be guaranteed, the benefits of contact are many and varied. Contact gives the child the security of knowing that, for all their shortcomings, his parents still love him. The child retains the necessary sense of family and personal identity. This, in turn, enables the child who is placed with foster carers or relatives to commit himself to the substitute family, in the knowledge that his parents approve this arrangement, thereby increasing the chances of the placement being successful.

Access as a Right of the Child

There has long been widespread acceptance in child welfare cases of the principle that access is the right of the child. In the English case of *M. v M.* 1973, the court held that access is a right of the child rather than a parental right and that access should only be denied where it is likely to be seriously injurious to the welfare of the child. This view of access found favour with Carroll J in *M.D. v G.D.* 1992, who held that section 11(1) of the Guardianship of Infants Act 1964 enables the court to make an access order allowing a child access to persons other than his natural parents, on the basis that "it is the right of the child with which the court is concerned, not the right of the adult". These judicial pronouncements as to access reflect very closely the requirement of Article 9(3) of the United Nations Convention on the Rights of the Child, which provides that "States Parties shall respect the right of the child who is separated from one or both parents to maintain personal relations and direct contact with both parents on a regular basis, except if it is contrary to the child's best interests".

The fact that contact or access is a right enjoyed by the child is clear from the case law of the European Court of Human Rights. In *Eriksson v Sweden* 1989, the court interpreted Article 8 of the European Convention on Human Rights (the right to respect for private and family life) as conferring on a child the right of automatic access to a parent or guardian, which should only be denied where the welfare of the child so required. In *Anderson v Sweden* 1992, the court identified the mutual enjoyment by parent and child of each other's company as constituting a fundamental element of family life under Article 8 of the Convention. The court held that there had been a violation of Article 8, in that the Swedish government had failed to show that the far-reaching and severe measures concerned, including prohibition on contact, were both necessary and aimed at reunification of mother and child. The measures were, therefore, disproportionate to the legitimate aims pursued and not necessary in a democratic society. Similarly, in *Johansen v Norway* 1996, the court held that the decision to deprive the applicant of her access and parental rights in respect of her daughter constituted a breach of Article 8. Such far-reaching measures could only be justified in exceptional circumstances, and could not be justified unless they were motivated by an overriding requirement pertaining to the child's best interests.

The importance of ensuring that children in care maintain contact with their families is reflected in section 37 of the Child Care Act 1991. A health board is obliged to facilitate reasonable access to a child in care for his parents, any person acting *in loco parentis* or any other person who, in the opinion of the board, has a bona fide interest in the child. Such access may include allowing the child to reside temporarily with any such person, including overnight stays. In most cases access takes the form of face-to-face contact. Sometimes, particularly in high-risk situations, less direct forms of contact are permitted, such as the exchange of letters and cards on birthdays and at Christmas. Any person who is dissatisfied with the arrangements made by a health board as to access may apply to the court, and the court may make such order as it thinks proper regarding access to the child by that person.

Access by Child to Members of Extended Family

As regards access by a child in care to members of his extended family, the European Commission of Human Rights held in *Boyle v United Kingdom* 1994 that "family life" within the meaning of Article 8 of the European Convention on Human Rights includes the ties between near relatives. Cohabitation is not a prerequisite for maintenance of family ties, but a factor to be taken into account. The Commission found that there was a significant bond between the applicant and his nephew to establish family ties. The decision of the local authority to refuse access to the applicant, with the exception of one visit to the child, amounted to an interference with his right to respect for family life. The decision to terminate access was made without giving the uncle any opportunity to present his views and without any forum or mechanism for him to present his requests for access. The interference was not necessary within the meaning of Article 8(2), as being "necessary in a democratic society in the interests of national security ... or for the protection of the rights and freedoms of others". A friendly settlement was later reached and the European Court of Human Rights struck the case off the list.

Access by blood relations to children in guardianship and custody matters is now regulated by section 11B of the Guardianship of Infants Act 1964 (as inserted by section 9 of the Children Act 1997). A person who is related to a child or parent of the child by blood may apply to the court for an order granting access to the child on such terms and conditions as the court may order. The prior leave of the court is a prerequisite to making an application for access. In deciding whether to grant leave to apply for an order granting access, the court must have regard to the applicant's connection with the child, the risk, if any, of the application disturbing the child's life to the extent that the child would be harmed by it and the wishes of the child's guardian. Clearly, in the light of the decision of the European Court of Human Rights in *Hokkenen v Finland* 1994, access should not be afforded to a blood relative against the wishes of a child who is mature enough for his views to be taken into account.

Order Refusing Access

Because of the statutory obligation imposed on a health board to allow parents and other persons with an interest in the child reasonable access, the board does not have the inherent power to refuse access. Indeed, where a child is in voluntary care, access can never be denied to a parent or person acting *in loco parentis*. However, on the application of a health board, the court may make an order refusing to allow a named person access to a child in care on foot of a care order, and it may vary or discharge that order on the application of any person (section 37(3)). In the *State (D. and D.) v G. and Midland Health Board* 1990, the Supreme Court held that proper access and communication between parents and the child may in some instances still be very necessary ingredients in the welfare of the child. Accordingly, it is only in "exceptional circumstances where it would be detrimental to the welfare of the child" that the court should withhold knowledge of the whereabouts of a child from parents to prevent access. In *M.F. v Superintendent Ballymun Garda Station* 1990, the Supreme Court held that unless there are exceptional circumstances justifying a different course, access and communication between parent and child should be maintained.

In *Elsholz v Germany* 2000, the European Court of Human Rights restated the principle enunciated in previous cases that in dealing with the issue of access, a fair balance must be struck between the interests of the child and those of the parent. While attaching particular importance to the best interests of the child, the parent must be involved in the decision-making process. The court held that, in refusing to allow the father introduce psychological expert evidence in order to evaluate the child's statements to the effect that he did not want contact with the father, the national authorities had violated the father's right to respect for family life under Article 8 and also his right to a fair hearing under Article 6 of the European Convention on Human Rights.

Access Subject to Conditions

Either on the occasion of making a care order or in a subsequent application by a person who is dissatisfied with the health board's arrangements as to access, the court may set out in detail the conditions under which access is to take place. For example, the court may stipulate the time, place, duration and frequency of the access. Access may be unsupervised or the court may stipulate that it is to be supervised by a named person or body. In child protection cases, access will be supervised by a health board social worker. Access may include the child being allowed to stay overnight with the non-custodial parent, and provision may be made for the child to have access over weekends or during holiday periods. In *Eastern Health Board v McDonnell* 2000, the District Court attached conditions to an order for access, by directing that access to the child shall be supervised by the board and conducted on the board's premises and that the second named respondent "have a regime of access which shall be so structured with a view to enabling him to enjoy overnight access at his home".

In England, the idea of 'indirect contact' between child and non-custodial parent has found favour with some judges, when considering applications for contact under the Children Act 1989. Obviously, in cases of serious abuse and exposure to domestic violence, the court will be aware of the dangers involved in allowing violent parents direct access to their children. In *Re G. (Domestic Violence: Direct Contact)* 2000, the child's father was convicted of the manslaughter of the mother. The child had witnessed their drunkenness and violent arguments. The child was placed with foster parents. The court refused the father's application to have direct contact, on the basis that he refused to acknowledge his violence or the adverse effect of that violence on the child. The father refused to accept that the child was suffering from nightmares and behaving in a disturbed way. The child was reluctant to see him, a fact that he also refused to accept. The court did permit indirect contact.

In *Re O. (Contact: Imposition of Conditions)* 1995, the Court of Appeal stated that in cases in which, for whatever reason, direct contact cannot for the time being be ordered, it is ordinarily highly desirable that there should be indirect contact so that the child grows up knowing of the love and interest of the absent parent with whom, in due course, direct contact should be established. This calls for a measure of restraint, common sense and unselfishness on the part of both parents. In *Re H. (Minors)* 1998, indirect contact took the form of cards and small presents being sent to two children by a father on certain occasions, including the occasion of a child's birthday and at Christmas. In echoing the principle that contact is a right of the child and not a parental right, the court stated that if contact were not a right of the child, it "would simply refuse this father any contact at all".

Enforcement of Right of Access

Whether in public or private law proceedings concerning the welfare of a child, the court has power to enforce orders for access, where it considers that it is in the best interests of the child to do so. The enforcement of access orders can be problematic. Where the parent having custody of a child is uncooperative in facilitating access or refuses to do so, the court could enforce the order for access by removing the child from that parent altogether. The court could also consider sending the custodial parent to prison for contempt of court in defying an access order. However, it is unlikely that a court would embark on such a course, as it could not possibly be in the best interests of a child to have a parent incarcerated. In *Glaser v United Kingdom* 2000, the European Court of Human Rights interpreted Article 8 of the European Convention of Human Rights (the right to respect for family life) as including the "right of a parent to have all measures taken with a view to his or her being reunited with the child, and an obligation for national authorities to take such measures". This applies not only to cases dealing with the compulsory taking of children into public care and the implementation of care measures, but also to cases where contact and residence disputes concerning children arise between parents and/or other members of the children's family (see *Olsson v Sweden (No.2)* 1992 and *Hokkanen v Finland* 1994).

Conclusion

The question of access is too important to be regarded as simply a matter of management within the sole control of a health board. Without more, parents and members of the child's extended family who wanted access would be wholly dependent upon the view of the case taken by the health board. It is for this reason that any person who is dissatisfied with the health board's arrangements as to access may invoke the assistance of the court in gaining access to a child in care. The power of the court to make an order as to access under section 37 of the 1991 Act is in keeping with the overall thrust of the Act that the court, in making a care order and entrusting a child into the custody of a health board, retains overall control of the child. In any dispute between the parents of a child and the health board, the court must recognise that access is the right of the child and should only be denied where the welfare of the child so requires.

PART FIVE

REFORM

CHAPTER 20

THE WAY AHEAD FOR CHILD CARE LAW

Introduction

The law does not stand still. It must constantly change if it is to stay abreast of changes and developments in society. Nowhere is the need for change so marked as in the area of family law and social policy. As Irish society in general becomes more open, as it is subjected to influences from abroad, the pace of change will accelerate. While our legislators may have been reluctant in the past to tackle controversial issues, they will no longer be able to resist the momentum for change being exerted domestically by well-organised voluntary bodies and pressure groups. Of course, the influence exerted by major international instruments such as the United Nations Convention on the Rights of the Child and the European Convention on Human Rights in the shaping of domestic policy has seen major legislative developments in recent years.

There has been a sea change in our attitude to adoption, which has seen a movement towards openness in the whole adoption process. The unfair discrimination that existed in the past towards people with disabilities will not be tolerated in future by a society that is becoming more aware of the need for social justice. Major developments in the area of disability, such as the Employment Equality Act 1998 and the Equality Act 2000, have helped to ensure that people with disabilities can participate more fully in the everyday life of the nation. To ensure that people with disabilities have equal opportunity in the area of education, the imminent publication of the Education for Persons with Special Educational Needs Bill will go some way towards eliminating discrimination in this area. Major advances have taken place in recent years in the capacity of medical science to intervene in the process of human reproduction. Techniques such as *in vitro* fertilisation (IVF), the freezing and storage of sperm and artificial insemination by donor are available in Ireland and have enabled many couples to conceive children despite impaired fertility. These are but some of the areas that will see major legislative developments in coming years. They are given some detailed consideration below.

Adoption

A thorough review of adoption law and practice is presently underway. In June 2003, the Department of Health and Children published a consultation document entitled "Adoption Legislation Consultation – Discussion Paper". The Minister for Children announced that he intended to have a wide-ranging consultation on adoption legislation covering the existing seven Adoption Acts, as well as proposed legislation on information rights for those affected by adoption and the ratification of the Hague Convention on Intercountry Adoption 1996. Interested individuals and organisations were invited to examine the issues set out in the consultation document and comment on them. Following the receipt of about three hundred submissions based on the consultation document, an oral consultation took place in October 2003. The main issues identified in the consultation document are considered below.

Access to Birth Information and Post-Adoption Contact

The main provisions of a proposed Adoption Information and Post-Adoption Contact Bill are considered in Chapter 10. The Adoption Board's response to the consultation document recommended the establishment of a restructured search and re-union service. The growth in demand for such a service is evident from figures quoted by the Board, which show that the number of enquiries for information increased from about a thousand in 1999 to about two and a half thousand in 2002. At present there is a two-year waiting list for requests for search and reunion. For a search and reunion service to be fully effective, rigorous retention requirements for all adoption records must be put in place. The Department is providing additional staff to enable the Board to establish a dedicated search and reunion service. The Board states that a rights-based rather than a welfare-based approach should underpin the legislative proposals. Since adoption involves "a hierarchy of legitimate interests", it is important that the needs of all parties should be addressed.

One of the most controversial issues emerging from the consultation process was the general opposition from interested groups to the suggestion that any attempt by an adopted person or a birth parent to make contact without the consent of the other party would attract a criminal sanction. Having read the submissions, the Minister expressed himself convinced that adoption legislation should be kept "outside the province of the criminal law". Whatever form future legislation will take, the Minister has given an assurance that there will be no criminal sanction for breaching a contact veto. In its submission, the Adoption Board is of the view that introducing specific legal sanctions (fines, etc.) on adopted people or birth or adoptive families is counter-productive and "introduces an unnecessary negativity into what is a very positive legislative initiative". As a possible solution, the Board proposes that those receiving information under the legislation should be required to sign an undertaking not to seek contact except through the arrangements provided for in the legislation. This is the sensible approach, as it is doubtful if a legal sanction of any kind would act as a sufficient deterrent to a party determined to make contact with another party in any event.

Rights of Non-Marital Father

The plight of the unmarried father has always sparked great debate. The unmarried father does not automatically acquire parental responsibility by the mere fact of paternity. It has been suggested that because the nature of unmarried relationships varies so much, it would be wrong to grant automatic parental responsibility to unmarried fathers, not least because some of them are not interested in possessing it. The rights of an unmarried father in relation to his child are considered in Chapter 7. In brief, the natural father of a non-marital child has no constitutional right to his child. The mother is the child's sole guardian under the Constitution and, as such, is automatically entitled to custody of the child. The father can become guardian of the child by agreement with the mother under section 4 of the Children Act 1997. In the absence of agreement, he may apply to the Circuit Court under section 12 of the Status of Children Act 1987 to be appointed guardian. The Adoption Act 1998 provides a procedure for consulting an unmarried father before his child is placed for adoption.

Clearly, the current approach fails to appreciate the reality of modern society, as more and more children are now being born to unmarried parents. Where a child is born to unmarried parents who are in a stable relationship, and the father has shown a degree of commitment to the child to the extent that a bond or attachment has been formed between them, it seems illogical to say that the father has no rights under the Constitution to his child. This "denies the relationship of parent and child and may, upon occasion, work a cruel injustice", per Barrington J in *W. O'R. v E.H.* 1996. As a possible method of conferring constitutional rights on unmarried fathers who are living in a stable relationship with the mother of the child, the Report of the Constitution Review Group 1996 recommended that all family rights, including those of unmarried mothers or fathers and children born of unmarried parents, should be placed in Article 41 of the Constitution. This would require a constitutional amendment, so that the family referred to in Article 41 was not confined to the family based on marriage. It should be left to the courts on a case-by-case basis to decide which type of family unit should constitute a family within the meaning of any such amended provision. While this could create uncertainty, it is essentially the approach of Article 8 of the European Convention on Human Rights which guarantees to every person respect for "family life", which has been interpreted by the European Court of Human Rights to include non-marital family life, where clear family ties exist between the mother and father (see *Keegan v Ireland* 1994).

The Government is currently conducting a review of family policy in Ireland. As part of the review, family fora were convened countrywide. The definition of the family, and the reality of the number of different family forms that now exist in Ireland, was one of the dominant themes at the fora. In an interview with the *Irish Independent* of the 12 January 2004, the Minister for Social and Family Affairs said that the State had to recognise the reality that there is now "a plethora of different types of families" and that if the Government took a restrictive view of the family "we'd be going nowhere". According to the Minister, the top priority for the Government with respect to family policy was encouraging proper care for children. The most important persons within the family are the children and how they are cared for. "If they can be adequately cared for in any family formation, then that should be acceptable". Despite this, she does not intend recommending any change in Article 41 of the Constitution.

Whether or not marriage should be the family structure, the family type does have a bearing on the well-being of its members. There can be little doubt that it is better for a child to be raised by both its parents. The Report of the Commission on the Family 1998, entitled "Strengthening Families for Life" states that "family well-being" is best achieved through stable joint parenting of children, wherever possible, irrespective of whether the parents are married to each other or living with each other. A study commissioned by the Department of Social and Family Affairs in 2003, entitled "Family Well-Being: What Makes a Difference", shows that lone parents reported lower levels of happiness than parents in other family forms. Significantly, in an interview with the *Sunday Tribune* of the 11 January 2004, Keane CJ makes a direct link between crime and fatherless families. He said that "the absence of the father is a very serious matter for society – it affects children very badly that there is no settled male figure in their lives".

Pending any constitutional change to the position of the unmarried father, which appears unlikely in the foreseeable future, the Adoption Board, in its response to the consultation document, agreed that it should have the power to attach conditions, where appropriate, to the making of an adoption order, to ensure that the birth father's relationship with his child will be recognised in law following an adoption order being made in favour of the mother and her husband. The Board is anxious that the issue of conditional adoption orders would be considered in a wider context than simply in connection with continued access by unmarried fathers. A similar recommendation was made by the Law Society's Law Reform Committee in its report, Adoption Law: the Case for Reform 2000.

Eligibility of Adoptive Parents

At present, only married couples or single or widowed people are eligible as prospective adopters (section 10 of the Adoption Act 1991). Unmarried couples are excluded from the adoption process. In the course of its Report, the Law Society describes this treatment of unmarried couples as clear discrimination. The Report also refers to what it describes as the "anomalous" situation that arises under the 1991 Act, which allows for single persons unrelated to the child, for one partner of a married but separated couple and for widowed people, to adopt, but excludes unmarried couples in stable cohabitation from eligibility. While an application could be made by one of the cohabiting couple, the other partner would not automatically acquire parental responsibility.

In its response to the consultation paper, the Adoption Board stated that it would support the removal of the statutory bar on unmarried couples adopting. The Board is of the view that the stability of the relationship and the capacity of both partners to meet the needs of the child should be the major determinants of suitability. For all couples, married and unmarried, their relationship should be established for a period of at least three years. In stepfamily adoptions, the Board suggests that the partner of the birth parent should, with the consent of the birth parents, be eligible to adopt without interfering with the child's legal relationship with the birth parent. As the law now stands, birth mothers have to make a joint application with their husbands to adopt their own children. They should be able to allow their husbands to adopt the children without the necessity of a joint application. Stepfamilies should be allowed the choice of shared guardianship or a full adoption order, if that is what fits their situation.

Guardianship as an Alternative to Adoption

Adoption is not always the appropriate form of care for some children who cannot return to their birth families. Adoption may not be suitable for children being cared for on a permanent basis by members of their wider birth families, such as grandparents or uncles and aunts. Some older children may not wish to be separated from their birth parents. For these children, there is no status which provides legal permanence, without a complete legal break with birth parents. In order to meet the needs of these children, the consultation paper invited submissions as to whether a special guardianship order should be introduced to provide permanence short of the legal separation involved in adoption. A legal guardianship order would give carers, such as foster parents, responsibility for taking decisions about the care and upbringing of the child, which are presently vested in the health board. While preserving the link between the child and his birth family, a permanent relationship between carer and child could be established. The Adoption Board, in its response to the consultation paper, stated that it would support the introduction of a special guardianship order, particularly for long-term foster children. The Board also stated that stepfamilies should be allowed the choice of shared guardianship or a full adoption order, if that is what fits their particular situation.

Adoption of Children of the Marriage

The adoption of marital children is now regulated by the Adoption Act 1988. As we have seen in Chapter 10, it is only in exceptional circumstances, amounting to an abandonment on the part of parents of all parental rights, that such children can be involuntarily adopted by order of the High Court. Adoption under the 1988 Act is non-consensual. In no circumstances can married parents waive their parental rights and give their child for adoption. The consultation paper points out that a small number of marital children remain in care and cannot be adopted because their parents are married. In its response to the consultation paper, the Adoption Board states that it is mindful of the constitutional restraints which apply in the context of the adoption of marital children. It is of the view, however, that consideration must be given to placing the right of a child "to have its welfare and best interests assured on at least an equal constitutional footing with the rights of the marital family". Married parents should be able to make the decision to have their child adopted without having to satisfy a requirement of an inability or failure to care for the child. But adoption in such circumstances would only be with the consent of both parents, or at least with the consent of the caring parent, with the other parent not having displayed an ability or desire to care for the child. For example, in *Western Health Board v An Bord Uchtala* 1996, the separated father played no part whatever in the upbringing of his child. Of course, there are serious constitutional issues involved, and in view of the attitude of the present Government to any change in Article 41 of the Constitution, it is unlikely that the Board's suggestions will be implemented in the foreseeable future.

Ongoing Contact between Child and Birth Family

Existing adoption legislation allows only for closed adoption, where all contact between a birth parent and an adopted child is terminated. An adoption order cannot be made conditional on contact being maintained between birth parent and child. The idea that there could be no contact following the making of an adoption order has its origins in an era when the social climate prevailing stigmatised women who gave birth to children outside marriage. Unmarried mothers were forced by pressure of events to part with their children. A veil of secrecy descended over the whole adoption process, as this was thought to be in the best interests of mother and child. As mentioned in Chapter 10, there has been a noticeable openness in adoption practices in recent times and such practices are clearly to be encouraged where possible. Open adoption allows ongoing contact between birth parent and child. The level of contact will differ, depending on the circumstances of a particular case. As in the case of access by parents to children in care, contact may take the form of supervised or unsupervised contact. In some cases, indirect contact, in the form of an exchange of letters and photographs on certain occasions such as birthdays and at Christmas, may be permitted, where it is not in the best interests of the child to sanction direct contact. Of course, closed adoptions will always be required in circumstances where it is clearly in the best interests of the child that the relationship between birth parent and child be completely severed.

Education and Disability

Prior to the landmark decision in *O'Donoghue v Minister Health* 1996, which declared beyond doubt that people with disabilities have a constitutional right to free primary education under Article 42 of the Constitution, there was a widely held misconception that such people were uneducable. The notion that persons with disabilities were incapable through education of developing their full potential as human beings smacked of invidious discrimination towards such persons and was clearly contrary to the guarantee of equality enshrined in Article 40 of the Constitution. In delivering the judgment of the High Court, O'Hanlon J made reference to expert testimony in a number of cases that came before the courts in the United States, which indicated that a person with an intellectual disability was capable of benefiting from a programme of education and training at any time in his life. The State's constitutional obligation to provide for the education of persons with disabilities was confirmed in *Sinnott v Minister for Education* 2001. However, in that case the Supreme Court stated that the obligation of the State was age-related and ceased when a person reached eighteen years of age. It is significant that when the *Sinnott* case was before the High Court, Barr J described the failure of the State to provide for the applicant's education as an "indictment of the State and cogently illustrates that it has failed to participate actively and meaningfully in the provision of appropriate services for him and those like him over the years".

Both of these hugely significant judgments clearly illustrate that the courts have the power and, in certain circumstances, a duty to intervene in circumstances where constitutional rights have been violated, or to protect constitutional rights. In ensuring that constitutional rights are available to all citizens, regardless of physical or mental capacity, the State clearly has a duty to expend funds and provide resources in ensuring equality of opportunity for all. In *Goldberg v Kelly* 1969, cited with approval by O'Hanlon J in the *O'Donoghue* case, the US Supreme Court said that "constitutional rights must be afforded citizens despite the greater expense involved". Whereas the failure of the State to provide a publicly supported education for children with an intellectual disability cannot be supported by the claim that there are insufficient funds, the courts generally cannot intervene, by means of a mandatory order, to compel the State to carry out its constitutional duty. Such an intervention would be inconsistent with the doctrine of the separation of powers (see *T.D. v Minister for Education* 2001). However, Denham J made it clear in the

Sinnott case that she would not exclude the possibility of a mandatory order against the State "in the rare and exceptional case where it may be necessary in the circumstances to protect constitutional rights". The question of a mandatory order in that case did not arise, as the applicant was an adult at the time of the hearing.

There is general acceptance, even at Government level, that in the past our education system focused primarily on the majority of children who do not have special needs. While resources were provided for those with disabilities, sufficient attention was not given to special education. Lack of resources, poor planning and a disconnection in the provision of services all combined to act to the detriment of the child with special educational needs. In an effort to ensure that children with disabilities are not at risk of being marginalised and suffering disadvantage because of their special educational needs, the Minister for Education introduced the Education for Persons with Special Educational Needs Bill 2003. The publication of the Bill resulted in many concerns being expressed by the various voluntary agencies working in the area of disabilities that it had not gone far enough. The opposition parties in the Oireachtas were critical of certain provisions, in the main those voiced by the voluntary agencies, and proposed numerous amendments to cure what they perceived to be shortcomings in the proposed legislation. As a result of considerable discussion and consultation, the Minister has indicated his willingness to introduce a number of significant amendments. These amendments are designed to strengthen the role of parents in the provision of enhanced services for disabled children, by providing them with further rights of appeal. Voluntary groups representing disabled people will have an official input on education policy and services through their inclusion on statutory bodies established under the legislation.

The purpose of the Bill is to make detailed provision through which the education of children who have special educational needs because of disabilities can be guaranteed as a right enforceable in law. On the face of it, the Bill appears to take a rights-based approach to the education of children with disabilities. In this regard, section 12 of the Bill imposes a statutory duty on the Minister for Education and Science and the Minister for Health and Children to make resources available to schools for the provision of adequate and appropriate education for children with special educational needs. However, in carrying out their functions, the Ministers must have the consent of the Minister for Finance. This provision effectively dilutes the rights-based approach to the provision of education which the voluntary agencies working with children with disabilities had called for and expected. The old resource-constrained approach seems to have won out. The proponents of the rights-based approach argue that a rights-based perspective denies that people with disabilities are problems. They have the right to have resources made available to them so that they have access to and participate meaningfully in education and training. Of course, one is mindful of the argument put forward by the

Government that making resources available, whether it is to special education or any other publicly funded service, has to take place in the overall context of public spending and revenue. This line of argument focuses on the equitable treatment of all children, including those with special needs, in resource allocation decisions, without allocating resources unreasonably to any particular category of child. One can only hope that this cautious and minimalist approach in legislation designed to provide equal access to education for children with disabilities will not lead to another stream of parents going before the courts to get education for their children.

The main provisions of the Bill are:

(a) to make further provision for the education of persons with disabilities,

(b) to provide that persons with disabilities will have the same right as everyone else to avail of and benefit from appropriate education,

(c) to help children with disabilities to leave school with the skills necessary to participate, to the level of their capacity, in an inclusive way in the social and economic activities of society and to lead independent lives,

(d) to provide for consultation with parents of children with disabilities to ensure that they have a central role in all important decisions in relation to the education of their children,

(e) to establish the National Council for Special Education. The function of the Council is to disseminate information on best practice for the education of children with special educational needs, their entitlements and the planning and co-ordination of the provision of special education and integration in conjunction with schools and health boards. The Minister appointed the first Council in October 2003 on a non-statutory basis,

(f) to confer certain functions on health boards in relation to the education of children with disabilities,

(g) to establish an independent appeals system, including mediation, when needs are not met.

A "child" is defined for the purposes of the legislation as a person not more than eighteen years of age. Section 14 of the Bill makes provision for the planning of a person's education, while that person is still a child, after the age of eighteen and for the continuation of education beyond eighteen in some circumstances. This provision is in line with the expressed intention of the Government, in the wake of the decision of the Supreme Court in the *Sinnott* case, to provide primary education for people with disabilities beyond the age of eighteen, even though there is no right to such education that can be enforced by a disabled person. A "child with special educational needs" is defined as a child who has an educational disability. This latter term is defined as a restriction in the capacity of the child to participate in, and benefit from, education on account of an enduring physical, sensory, mental health or intellectual impairment. There were certain concerns expressed by interested bodies that this definition of educational disability was narrower than the definition of the term in the Education Act 1998, in that it did not include attention deficit disorder and dyslexia. Dyslexia is not a physical, sensory or mental health or intellectual impairment. It is a specific learning disability, independent of intellectual or physical ability. It is not an intellectual impairment. The Minister for Education and Science has agreed to amend the proposed legislation to include both conditions in the definition

The Bill establishes the principle of inclusive education for as many as possible. Where this very desirable aspiration cannot be achieved, children with special educational needs can be taught in special classes and join other students at other times. In particular cases, a child can be educated in a special school. This integrated approach must achieve balance, in that it must not impact negatively on other children (section 2). A school must make all practicable efforts to assist a child not benefiting from the regular education programme. Where those efforts fail, the school must consult with the parents and arrange to have the child assessed within three months. The school should draw up a plan for the child where his needs are relatively uncomplicated (section 3).

The National Council for Special Education will set guidelines to assist schools in making assessments. Where a child is attending school, the primary responsibility for assessment falls on the Council. Health boards must arrange for assessments in the case of pre-school children. Parents can ask for assessments to be carried out. Assessments are to be holistic and take a whole-child approach, and must comply with standards laid down by the Minister for Health and Children (section 4). Persons with appropriate expertise must carry out assessments. Parental consent is necessary before an assessment can take place. Where parents refuse assessment, a dispute as to what is in the child's best interests will be decided by the Circuit Court (section 5). Following on from an assessment, the Council or health board, as the case may be, must provide the child with the services identified in the education plan or assessment, which are necessary to enable the child to participate in and benefit from education (section 6).

In the case of children whose needs are more complex, the Council must undertake a more formal planning process. A special educational needs organiser will convene a team of people, which must include the child's parents and may also involve the child, school principal and a psychologist. While the plan focuses on educational needs, it must also have regard to any other needs identified in the child's assessment and must be consistent with those needs (section 7). The matters to be dealt with in an education plan include the nature and degree of the child's skills and talents; the degree of educational disability; the child's special educational needs; the services to be provided for him; and the outcomes or goals which the child is to achieve over a specified period not exceeding twelve months (section 8). Educational plans must be reviewed at regular intervals (section 10).

Acknowledging that parents lie at the heart of the assessment and planning process, the Bill provides an accessible and efficient appeals mechanism. Parents have the right to appeal to an independent appeals board against any statement or description of their child's special educational needs, or any other statement or description appearing in the education plan, which they consider incorrect or inadequate to meet the child's special educational needs. They may also appeal where they believe that there has been a failure to implement an education plan. Where parents wish to pursue a less formal approach to a review of decisions, the appeals board must ensure that the parties to an appeal are assisted to reach agreement. On hearing an appeal, the appeals board may give directions to the Council or school which it must implement, or it may dismiss the appeal (section 11).

If the new order for persons with disabilities having equal access to education envisaged by the Bill is to become a reality, there must be general acceptance of the fact that every child is educable. The Commission on the Status of People with Disabilities in its report, *A Strategy for Equality* 1996, stated that the State has a responsibility "to provide sufficient resources to ensure that pre-school children, children of school-going age and adults with disabilities have an education appropriate to their needs in the best possible environment". If the State is serious about achieving this very desirable goal, adequate resources must be provided, even in times of budgetary constraints. In conclusion, if the State wishes to embrace all the children of the nation equally, it might do well to have regard to General Assembly Resolution: *The United Nations Standard Rules on the Equalisation of Opportunities for People with Disabilities*, 1993, Rule 25 (adopted unanimously by the General Assembly, including Ireland) which provides as follows:

> The principle of equal rights implies that the needs of each and every individual are of equal importance and must be made the basis for the planning of societies and that all resources must be employed in such a way as to ensure that every individual has equal opportunity to participation.

Human Assisted Reproduction

The ability of science to intervene in, control or even alter the natural process of the creation of human life poses fundamental ethical questions for the medical profession, for governments and for society as a whole. Recourse to human assisted reproduction has already transformed the lives of many couples, whether they conceive or not with such treatment. *In vitro* fertilisation (IVF) involves isolating ova and sperm from the prospective parents and allowing fertilisation to occur in controlled laboratory conditions. Hence, the derivation of the term "test tube" babies to describe babies born by means of the technique. The practice in such countries as the United Kingdom is to fertilise ten to twelve ova, of which usually only three are implanted. The rest are frozen for future use. If they are not required at a later date by the couple undergoing the treatment, they are destroyed or used for research. It is the destruction of surplus embryos or using them for research that gives rise to concern, especially amongst those persons who argue that the protection afforded to the "unborn" by Article 40.3.3 of the Constitution encompasses *in vitro* embryos. Article 40.3.3 provides:

> The State acknowledges the right to life of the unborn, and with due regard to the equal right to life of the mother, guarantees in its laws to respect, and as far as practicable by its laws to defend and vindicate that right.

The issue of human assisted reproduction raises fundamental ethical, legal and constitutional considerations. It is generally accepted that there can be no serious objection to the therapeutic application of *in vitro* fertilisation within the ethical guidelines of the Medical Council. The guidelines are:

(a) the creation of new forms of life for experimental purposes or any deliberate intentional destruction of human life already formed is professional misconduct,

(b) if the intention is the creation of embryos for experimental purposes, it would be professional misconduct,

(c) any fertilised ovum must be used for normal implantation and must not be deliberately destroyed.

In essence, the ethical position of the Medical Council seems to be that *in vitro* fertilisation is a clinical technique used for the treatment of human infertility, and in no circumstances should it be used to produce or store human embryos for research purposes. There is no objection to the preservation of sperm or ova to be used subsequently on behalf of those from whom they were originally taken. Many countries have legislated to set down the parameters within which such interventions can take place, while recognising that scientific development can often outpace the legislative controls. In Ireland, however, national regulation in the area of human assisted reproduction is governed by Medical Council guidelines. These guidelines apply only to registered medical practitioners and would be ineffective in the case of any service operated by other persons. With a view to establishing a statutory regulatory framework, in February 2000 the Minister for Health and Children announced that the Government had approved the setting up of the Commission on Human Assisted Reproduction.

The terms of reference of the Commission are "to prepare a report on the possible approaches to the regulation of all aspects of human reproduction and the social, ethical and legal factors to be taken into account in determining public policy in the area". In announcing the setting up of the Commission, the Minister said that he was conscious of the "growing public concern" that such complex and controversial procedures are being practised in Ireland "in the absence of any legislative controls". The Commission would provide the medical, ethical and legal expertise necessary for a detailed examination of the possible approaches to legislation. The publication of the Commission's report would provide the basis for informed public debate before the finalisation of any policy proposals. The Commission held a public conference on the 6 February 2003, at which a variety of experts in philosophical, medical and legal issues expressed their views on the way forward. The publication of the Commission's report is imminent.

The constitutional implications for the regulation of human assisted reproduction are huge. The central issue at stake is the status of the child embryo, and the protection to be given to him. What is the status of embryos under the Constitution? At what point does genetic material become an "unborn", so as to be protected by Article 40.3.3? As we have seen, there may be as many as ten or more fertilised eggs. What is the legal status of a fertilised egg left over after a transfer resulting in pregnancy? Before designing the regulatory system, it will be necessary to define at what point in time an embryo attracts constitutional rights guaranteed to unborn life under Article 40.3.3. At the time of the Eighth Amendment to the Constitution in 1983, there appears to have been no attempt to define the precise moment in time at which the life of the unborn begins. The Amendment was directed at the protection of individuals yet unborn, but identifiable as having the capacity to be born. A legal status is not conferred on an unimplanted fertilised ovum under the Constitution. Should legislation definitively declare that, for the purpose of regulating human assisted reproduction, a woman is not to be treated as carrying a child until the embryo has become implanted? Or is "unborn" life to be regarded as beginning at fertilisation or from the moment of conception? There are many difficult issues to be clarified before legislation eventually reaches the statute book. Whatever the difficulties involved, the regulation of *in vitro* fertilisation is now a matter of some urgency.

In Britain, IVF treatment is regulated by the Human Fertility and Embryology Act 1990, and the general principles of the Act have been followed in most other European Union countries, with the notable exception of Germany, which has more restrictive legislation. In Germany, the Embryo Protection Act 1990 prohibits the fertilisation of an ovum for any purpose other than bringing about a pregnancy, the fertilisation of more ova than can be transferred to a woman and the *in vitro* development of an embryo for any purpose other than to transfer it to a woman. In the United States of America, there is no federal regulation, and the market determines what services can and do operate. The main purpose of the British Act is to regulate the provision of certain types of infertility treatment, and to make provision about those who in certain circumstances are to be treated as parents of a child. The use of donated gametes, whether sperm or eggs, the creation of embryos outside the body and the storage of gametes or embryos can only be carried out by centres licensed by the Human Fertilisation and Embryology Authority set up under the Act. The most important function of the Authority is to regulate treatments permitted under the Act by means of licences granted to clinics. The treatments which the clinics can offer, and the terms on which they can offer them, are carefully regulated. The two main principles to be found in the British Act are the welfare of the child who may be born as a result of the treatment and the requirement of consent to treatment.

Several conditions must be contained in every treatment licence. A woman shall not be provided with treatment services unless account has been taken of the welfare of any child who may be born as a result of the treatment (including the need of that child for a father) and of any other child who may be affected by the birth (section 13(3)). The Act provides that "proper counselling about the implications of taking the proposed steps" involved in the treatment be given to the prospective parents (section 13(6)). Detailed guidance about the assessment of the child's welfare, and the counselling to be offered to those seeking treatment, is given in the Code of Practice issued under the Act. Clinics are required to take all reasonable steps to ascertain who would be legally responsible for any child born as a result of the proposed procedure and who it is intended will be bringing up the child. If donated gametes are to be used, extra factors are to be taken into account, including any possibility known to the clinic of a dispute about the legal fatherhood of the child. It is a condition of every licence that the provisions of Schedule 3 of the Act shall be complied with. The Schedule deals with the consents to be given to the use or storage of gametes or embryos by the people who supplied those gametes or the gametes which created those embryos. An embryo must not be used for any purpose unless there is an effective consent by each gamete provider to the use of the embryo for that purpose. Consents shall be in writing and remain effective unless they are withdrawn by notice to the person keeping the gametes or embryos. In *Evans v Amicus Healthcare Ltd and Others* 2003, the Family Division of the High Court of England and Wales held that Schedule 3 gives to each party to IVF treatment "an unconditional right" to vary or withdraw a consent to treatment and to the continued storage of any embryos, at any time up to the point at which the embryos are "used" in the treatment, i.e. until the moment the embryos are transferred into the woman.

The British Act also makes provision for those who, in certain circumstances, are to be treated as the parents of a child. The fact that strangers may donate the sperm or embryo being used in the treatment of a couple means that a child born as a result of the treatment may not be genetically related to its "parents". To cater for this situation, the Act provides that where a married woman is carrying or has carried a child as a result of placing in her an embryo sperm or eggs, she is the mother of the child (section 27). As far as the male is concerned, the rule is that the genetic father, i.e. the donor of the sperm, is the legal father. However, there are two exceptions to this rule. Firstly, where a married woman is carrying a child, notwithstanding that the sperm was not donated by her husband, and the husband has consented to the wife's treatment, he and no other person will be treated as father of the child (section 28(2)). Secondly, if donated sperm is used in the course of licensed treatment provided for a woman and man together, then the man is treated as the father of the child (section 28(3)). The latter provision was designed to cater for persons co-habiting outside marriage.

However, a cautionary note needs to be struck before deciding to model a regulatory framework for this country on the British model. This is so for a number of reasons, not least the fact that Britain is not subject to fixed constitutional provisions similar to Article 40.3.3 (the right to life of the unborn) and Article 41 (family rights) of the Constitution. It is significant that in the *Evans* case, above, the court held that under English law a foetus does not have the right to life under Article 2 of the European Convention on Human Rights and concluded that it must follow that an embryo cannot have rights under Article 2. This will have to be taken into account in the drafting of Irish legislation. What will be the status of a child born by means of IVF treatment to an unmarried couple? In the present constitutional order, the child and its parents cannot be regarded as a "family" within the meaning of Article 41. In the absence of constitutional amendment, the parents and child will be confined to the limited legal recognition that Irish law currently affords to non-marital families.

Adoption Ireland: The Adopted People's Association, an organisation representing the interests of adopted people, contends that egg and sperm donation put children in the exact same situation as the children of closed adoptions. This is at a time when the general consensus appears to be that closed adoptions should only occur in exceptional circumstances, and then only in the best interests of the child. Like the children who were the subject of closed adoptions in the past, children born as a result of egg and sperm donation will have problems with loss of identity and not knowing their origins. This in turn can give rise to complications when urgent medical treatment is needed. Does this mean that we should ban the anonymous donation of eggs and sperm to clinics? What about such issues as embryo sex screening, which would allow parents to choose the sex of a child? Current guidelines in Britain restrict embryo sex screening to where there is a medical condition that is gender based, even though this entails the destruction of the embryos of the opposite gender. In conclusion, on a more sombre note, how do we ensure that a situation, such as that which was the subject of proceedings in *Leeds Teaching Hospital NHS Trust v A. and Others* 2003, does not occur in Ireland in the future? In that case, a black man, whose sperm was mistakenly used to fertilise the eggs of a white woman, was declared father of mixed-race twins, even though the woman and her husband have been given parental responsibility for the twins. One can only be confident that the Commission will get it right and recommend a regulatory framework that will cater for all eventualities within the strictures imposed by the Constitution.

GLOSSARY OF TERMS

Ab initio* – from the beginning

Ad litem* – for the purpose of legal proceedings, e.g. guardian *ad litem*

Adduce – to bring forward, as in evidence

Admissibility of evidence – evidence which can be produced in court

Adversarial – involving opponents, such as plaintiff and defendant in legal proceedings

Affidavit – a sworn written statement

Affirmation – solemnly promising to tell the truth when giving evidence

Appellant – the party who is appealing a decision of a court

Case law – law that is based on the results of previous court cases

Certiorari* – an order by the High Court that a case decided in a lower court or tribunal should be reviewed

Chambers – a judge's private rooms within the court building where a child can be interviewed in private

Charge – formally accuse someone of committing a crime

Common law – the body of law based on judicial decisions, as distinct from statute law

Competency of witness – a witness is competent unless, in the opinion of the judge, he is prevented by extreme youth, disease of the mind or other similar cause from giving evidence

Contemporaneous – at the same time

Contempt of court – wilful disobedience of a court order

Corroboration – confirmation by further evidence

Court of first instance – the court before which an action is first tried, as distinct from an appeal court

Cross-examine – to question a witness for the other side

Domicile – the country where your permanent home is, even if you reside elsewhere

Due process – the right of an accused to a fair trial

Equity – the principles of equity are based on fairness

Ex parte* – court application made without notice to the other party to the proceedings

Habeas corpus* – a procedure to have a person brought before the High Court to inquire into the lawfulness of that person's detention

Hearsay – evidence given in court of something said to the witness by another person

In camera* – a hearing in a court from which the public is excluded

Injunction – an order of the court that forbids a party from acting unlawfully or that compels a person to perform a legal obligation

In loco parentis* – in the place of a parent

Inter alia* – among other things

Judicial precedent – the practice of lower courts following the decisions of higher courts

Jurisdiction – the power of a court to deal with particular matters

Leading questions – questions which suggest to the witness the answer desired or which embody the answer

Litigant – a person who is involved in a legal action

Litigation – taking legal action through the courts

Mandamus* – an order of the High Court commanding an individual, organisation, administrative tribunal or court to perform a certain action, usually to correct an earlier action or failure to fulfil some duty

Natural justice – the requirement that fair procedures be applied whenever a person is charged with wrongdoing before a court or tribunal, for example the right to be tried by an impartial judge and the right to be heard in one's own defence

Petition – formal written application to a court for a court order

Pleadings – written claims delivered by one party to another setting out the facts supporting his position

Prima facie* – on the face of it

Proceedings – the name given to the events which occur when an action is heard

Prohibition – an order of the High Court preventing a body or person from exercising a function it does not legally possess

Respondent – the name given to the person against whom a petition or appeal is brought

Testify – give evidence

Testimony – the evidence a witness gives in court

Tort – a civil wrong, as opposed to a crime, for which the usual remedy is an action for damages

Ultra vires* – beyond the powers of

Ward of Court – a person, such as a minor or person of unsound mind, who is protected by the High Court

Writ – a summons or order from a court of law

Note: The terms marked * are of Latin origin.

REFERENCES AND FURTHER READING

Butler-Sloss, L.J., *Report of the Inquiry into Child Abuse in Cleveland in 1987*, London: HMSO, 1988.

Casey, J., *Constitutional Law in Ireland*, Dublin: Round Hall Sweet and Maxwell, 3rd edition, 2000.

Clynes, M., "United Kingdom Embryo Research Model is Not the Way", Dublin: *The Irish Times*, 7 March 2003.

Colbert, M.J., "Legal Uncertainty over Status of Foetus Needs Urgent Clarification", Dublin: *The Irish Times* 5 December 2003.

Dent, H. and Flin, R., *Children as Witnesses*, New York: Wiley, 1992.

Department of Health and Children, *A Guide to What Works in Family Support Services for Vulnerable Children*, Dublin: Stationery Office, 2000.

Department of Health and Children, *Adoption Legislation Consultation – Discussion Paper (G. Shannon)*, Dublin: The Stationery Office, 2003.

Department of Health and Children, *Children First – National Guidelines for the Protection and Welfare of Children*, Dublin: The Stationery Office, 1999.

Department of Health and Children, Commission on Human Assisted Reproduction, Public Conference 6 February 2003, Conference Documents, Dublin: Stationery Office 2003.

Department of Health and Children, Discussion Document on Mandatory Reporting, *Putting Children First*, Dublin: Stationery Office, 1996.

Department of Health and Children, *Our Duty to Care: The Principles of Good Practice for the Protection of Children and Young People,* Dublin: Stationery Office, 2002.

Department of Health and Children, Overview Report of Social Services Inspectorate, Dublin: Stationery Office, 2000.

Department of Health and Children, Report of Social Services Inspectorate, Dublin: Stationery Office, 2002.

Department of Health and Children, *Report on the Inquiry into the Operation of Madonna House,* Dublin: Stationery Office, 1996.

Department of Health and Children, Report on Working Group on Foster Care, *Foster Care: A Child Centred Partnership*, Dublin, Stationery Office, 2001.

Department of Health and Children, *The National Children's Strategy, Our*

Children – Their Lives, Dublin: The Stationery Office, 2000.

Department of Health and Children, *Youth Homeless Strategy*, Dublin: The Stationery Office, 2001.

Department of Social, Community and Family Affairs, *Family Well Being: What Works with Families,* Shannon, Co Clare: The Ceifin Centre, 2003.

Department of Social, Community and Family Affairs, Report of the Commission on the Family, *Strengthening Families for Life*, Dublin: Stationery Office, 1998.

Eastern Health Board, Report of the Forum on Youth Homelessness, Dublin: Eastern Health Board, 2000.

Ferguson, H. and Kenny, P., *On Behalf of the Child*, Dublin: A&A Farmer, 1995.

Focus Ireland Report, *Out On Their Own: Young People Leaving Care in Ireland*, Dublin: Focus Ireland, 1998.

Home Office, *Memorandum of Good Practice on Video Recorded Interviews,* London: Stationery Office, 1992.

Kilkelly, U., *The Child and the European Convention on Human Rights*, Dartmouth: Ashgate, 1999.

Law Reform Commission, *Report on Child Sexual Abuse*, Dublin: Law Reform Commission, 1990.

Law Society, Report of Law Reform Committee, *Adoption Law: the Case for Reform,* Dublin: Incorporated Law Society, 2000.

Levy, A. and Kahan, B., *ThePindown Experience and the Protection of Children: Report of Staffordshire Child Care Inquiry*, Staffordshire: Staffordshire County Council, 1991.

Martin, F., *The Politics of Children's Rights*, Cork: Cork University Press, 2000.

McGuinness, C., *Report of the Kilkenny Incest Investigation*, Dublin: Stationery Office, 1993.

National Literacy Agency, *A Plain Guide to Legal Terms*, Dublin: National Literacy Agency, 2003.

Northern Area Health Board, *Report of the Forum of Youth Homelessness*, Dublin: Northern Area Health Board, 2000.

Quill, E., *Torts in Ireland*, Dublin: Gill and MacMillan, 1999.

Report of Constitution Review Group, Dublin: Stationery Office, 1996.

Shannon, G., *Family Law Practitioner: Children and the Law*, Dublin: Round Hall Sweet & Maxwell, 2001.

Shatter, A., *Family Law*, Dublin: Butterworth, 4th edition, 1997.

United Nations Committee on the Rights of the Child, *Concluding Observations: Ireland*, UN Committee on the Rights of the Child, Seventh Session, January 1998 (UN Doc CRC/C/15 Add. 85).

Ward, P., *The Child Care Act 1991 (Annotated Legislation)*, Dublin: Round Hall Sweet & Maxwell, 1997.

INDEX